PARANOID

PARANOID

EXPLORING SUSPICION FROM
THE DUBIOUS TO THE DELUSIONAL
(No, this book is not about you)

DAVID J. LAPORTE

Prometheus Books

59 John Glenn Drive
Amherst, New York 14228

Published 2015 by Prometheus Books

Cover illustration © Daniel Allan / Media Bakery
Cover design by Jacqueline Nasso Cooke

Inquiries should be addressed to

Prometheus Books
59 John Glenn Drive
Amherst, New York 14228
VOICE: 716–691–0133
FAX: 716–691–0137
WWW.PROMETHEUSBOOKS.COM

19 18 17 16 15   5 4 3 2 1

Library of Congress Cataloging-in-Publication Data

LaPorte, David J., 1954-
    Paranoid : exploring suspicion from the dubious to the delusional / by David J. LaPorte.
        pages cm
    Includes bibliographical references and index.
    ISBN 978-1-63388-068-9 (paperback) — ISBN 978-1-63388-069-6 (e-book)
    1. Paranoia. 2. Delusions. I. Title.

RC520.L35 2015
616.89'7—dc23

                                                                    2015011832

Printed in the United States of America

To my family: Megan, Kelly, Kyle, and Robin

SUSPICIONS amongst thoughts are like bats amongst birds, they ever fly by twilight. Certainly they are to be repressed, or at least well guarded: for they cloud the mind; they leese [lose] friends; and they check with business, whereby business cannot go on currently and constantly. They dispose kings to tyranny, husbands to jealousy, wise men to irresolution and melancholy. They are defects, not in the heart, but in the brain.

—Sir Francis Bacon, *The Essayes or Counsels,*
Civil and Moral (1625)

CONTENTS

FOREWORD BY
DR. WILLIAM T. CARPENTER, JR.

Suspiciousness is ubiquitous, evolutionary, and essential for individual and group safety. When valid it is precious. It is part of life for all of us. But when suspiciousness is *excessive* and *unfounded*—when it mutates into paranoia—it creates problems for the individual, his or her social group, and those involved in workplace and leisure activities. It sometimes leads to harm or violence when none is warranted. Now, Professor David LaPorte offers us a fascinating look into this mindset—one that can affect us in every area of our daily lives.

Paranoia is often thought to indicate the presence of a mental illness, but this is most often not the case. Paranoid ideation is common, may undermine the quality of life for the person or for others, and may lead to decisions that are damaging to relationships or to the person's well-being. Distress to self and conflict with others may be a basis for seeking counseling from a friend or spiritual adviser or a mental health professional. This may be very beneficial in helping the person minimize adverse effects even if the paranoid ideation remains.

This book provocatively raises the possibility that suspiciousness and paranoia may be on the rise. Ultimately, scientific inquiry will answer this question, but modern communication technology provides extensive access to paranoid thinking and provides unprecedented invasion into privacy and personal space. There seems to be more cause for suspicion than previously. Dr. LaPorte's survey of societal invasion by those seeking financial, political, or social advantage is indeed sobering.

The surge in gun violence in our society is, in part, a reflection of paranoia with or without mental illness. The shooting of Gabrielle Giffords in Tucson by a mentally ill man who harbored delusional beliefs about the popular congresswoman is an example, but the mentally ill are not responsible for the extraordinary gun violence in the United States. Mentally ill persons shoot other people at about the same rate as the general population. They are not responsible for our present epidemic of violence. Such acts do shine a spotlight on those with psychotic illnesses, and from a mental illness perspective, it underscores the need for those with violent paranoid delusions to remain in treatment. Most acts of violence by those in this category are performed before diagnosis and treatment or during periods when treatment is refused.

Paranoid delusions are often a symptom of mental illness. My interest is that of a physician-scientist involved in the care and study of persons with schizophrenia. In this context it is important to distinguish paranoia as a disease symptom from paranoia representing the full range of human experience. This task is often not difficult because the excessive suspiciousness will be in the context of other compelling signs of mental illness. The person may have disorganized thinking and behavior; experience hallucinations; have abnormal body movement and posture; and have impairments in motivation, impulse control, and emotional experience. There may also be grandiose false beliefs, rapid-fire speech, excessive energy, paranoid beliefs that he or she is being interfered with by others, or that they have superior IQs and ideas too brilliant for others to understand. Here paranoid ideation may be an aspect of a manic episode in a person with bipolar illness.

Professor LaPorte nicely articulates that just as a suspicious nature is common in the population, paranoia is common in many mental disorders without necessarily being a pathological manifestation of the illness. We are most confident that the paranoia is pathological when one is delusional—harboring ideas that are clearly false, such as the belief that others are stealing one's thoughts directly from the brain. In this instance, the person firmly holds onto the false belief despite compelling evidence that it is not valid. Contrast this with the beliefs Professor LaPorte describes as shared, but false, among members of a militia group. For a pathological interpretation, the paranoid delusions must also be a source of distress, disability, and/or dysfunction. The common view that a person's paranoid ideas are "crazy" is quite different from a judgment of mental illness made by a clinician. The latter is based on a range and pattern of pathological signs and symptoms, which may include paranoid thinking or a paranoid delusion as a symptom manifestation.

More complicated is a person with a single paranoid delusion where irrefutable proof is not available and the idea is plausible, even if the probability is near zero. This is more readily seen as mental illness if the idea is bizarre, such as "unknown mystical forces sending covert messages to my boss." Change that to coworkers conspiring against the person, and it seems plausible, even though there may be no evidence to support the belief.

Perhaps most common of these single-theme false but fixed beliefs are delusions of jealousy. When does excessive and unjustified suspicion of spousal infidelity cross the line and become a delusional disorder? The criteria are easy to understand: firmly held false beliefs without insight that are the basis for distress, disability, or dysfunction. But just when is the line crossed when the same belief is not so firmly held or is less disruptive?

These and other questions will arise as one explores the phenomenon of paranoia in Professor LaPorte's intriguing and highly informative book. It is a good read and will help the reader develop a perspective on a very common and troublesome phenomena in human society.

William T. Carpenter, MD
Professor of Psychiatry and Pharmacology,
University of Maryland School of Medicine
Member, National Academy of Sciences
Editor in chief, *Schizophrenia Bulletin*
Expert witness, *State of Pennsylvania v. John du Pont* and
United States v. John Hinckley, Jr.

PREFACE

Why are you reading this preface? I never read prefaces. At least I didn't until I started writing this book and realized this is where the author's reason for writing the book in the first place is traditionally stated.

The origins of this book go back many years. I noted that a common element in many sensational crimes, such as the murder of Dave Schultz by the millionaire John du Pont, is the fact that the perpetrator was, at some level, paranoid. So prevalent were these types of crimes that one night while dining with friends I commented that someone should write a book about paranoia since few existed. Sufficient amounts of wine had been consumed, so my friends, who also happen to be colleagues, suggested that I write such a book. I demurred, figuring that it was such a hot topic that certainly someone was already busily at work on just such a book. Well, I continued to dine with this same group of friends, made up of neuroscientists, a pharmacologist, a psychiatrist, and well-read others, and I continued to comment about paranoia. Finally, enough bottles of wine were emptied and enough years had passed with no book being written, so one friend finally got fed up with me and told me in clear terms to "write the damn book." What you hold in your hands is the product of that order.

Now, why write a book on paranoia and all its aspects? Well, the short (preface) answer is that paranoia and its manifestations are all around us. It takes many forms, and it would be a rare individual whose life has not in some way been touched by paranoia. The excessively jealous boyfriend, the cranky neighbor, your grandmother suffering from dementia who believes you are stealing her money: each share aspects of paranoia. Moreover, we have all experienced that feeling that someone "has it in for us," or that the intentions of others toward us are malevolent in some way. That feeling we commonly label as paranoia.

So in a sense, we all have experienced, to greater or lesser degrees, the same feelings and fears as someone we might identify as suffering from clinical paranoia. We are not so far apart from "them." But is there danger we could become one of them? The more you know about paranoia, the better you will understand yourself and the people who populate your life, for better or worse.

Finally, I should note that the case examples used in this book are taken from news reports on famous, or infamous, personages; news stories on the less-than-famous; clinical cases I have personally witnessed—many from forensic settings; and cases provided by colleagues interviewed for this book. The examples involving lesser-known people—although a matter of public record in many cases—are all sufficiently disguised to protect the rights of the individual yet retain the flavor and character of the clinical picture being conveyed.

ACKNOWLEDGMENTS

I am deeply indebted to a number of individuals who I have encountered throughout my professional life. First are those who served as mentors and left their professional mark on me. Their names are well known within their respective fields, and in listing them I run the risk of name-dropping. However, my contact with each was of sufficient length and substantive nature to merit my genuine gratitude and a public thank you. In order of encounter: Drs. Thomas McLellan, Arthur Alterman, Albert Stunkard, Kelly Brownell, Manfred Meier, James Mitchell, and William Carpenter Jr.

I have been fortunate to be associated with one of the premier research institutions in the world, the Maryland Psychiatric Research Center. Colleagues I've had the pleasure of working with and learning from include Drs. Gunvant Thaker, Brian Kirkpatrick, Robert Buchanan, and Carol Tamminga.

In my home department here at Indiana University of Pennsylvania, Drs. Don Robertson and Krys Kaniasty deserves many thanks.

A special group of friends and colleagues are particularly deserving of note: Drs. Adrienne Lahti, Rosy Roberts, and the late Dr. Bob Lahti.

Finally and perhaps most importantly, thanks to my family, who suffered through years of this book.

Introduction

WHY YOU NEED (REALLY NEED) TO READ THIS BOOK

The Virginia Tech massacre, the Oklahoma City bombing, the Washington Navy Yard carnage, anthrax mail murders—what do they have in common besides death? Each act was perpetrated by individuals who displayed classic signs of paranoia.[1]

This book describes exactly what paranoia is, how and why it manifests, and the forms it takes, including stalking, pathological jealousy, and even—on a larger scale—perhaps militia movements. The book will also reveal why many "normal" individuals experience feelings of paranoia and the seemingly increasing phenomenon of drastic action taken by people acting on their paranoid beliefs.

It is proposed that life in our post-9/11 world is a fertile environment for paranoia to develop, thanks to its numerous threats to our individual security (computer hackers, omnipresent security cameras, government monitoring, and terrorism). I believe this proposal is accurate. And the deadly violence perpetrated by individuals such as Seung-Hui Cho (Virginia Tech), Timothy McVeigh (Oklahoma City bombing), Jared Loughner (Tucson, Arizona, shooting), and most recently, Aaron Alexis (Washington Navy Yard) is a chilling testament to the effects of that paranoia.

The massacres of young children at Sandy Hook Elementary School in Connecticut raised more than a debate about gun control; it fanned the discussion about mental illness and violence. Everyone wants to know why some mentally ill persons turn to violence and what can be done to prevent such acts from recurring. Further, recent revelations regarding the National Security Agency

(NSA) surveillance programs have decreased our trust in the government and has reminded us that we are living in a new, often unsafe world.

This book addresses issues of violent behavior but encompasses many other aspects of paranoia that are even more common than mass murders. For example, millions of baby boomers will be developing dementia over the next several decades, and paranoia is a common feature of that malady.

We read about acts like the hostage taking of a five-year-old boy off a school bus and the murders of LA police officers perpetrated by individuals who appeared to be paranoid—both in consecutive months. Is this problem getting worse? Perhaps, yet noteworthy paranoia-related violence is rare and may be getting worse, while paranoia-related violence at lower levels is probably not all that rare; in fact, it has been ongoing and are more frequent than most people are aware.

In the pages that follow, a full picture of paranoia will be developed and discussed in its many manifestations and degrees.

Chapter 1

MEET PARANOIA

T he content of the 911 call was not remarkable for a large metropolitan area. A man reported that someone had been killed in a drug-related shooting. What the operator found unusual was his calm, matter-of-fact manner.

When the police arrived at the scene that afternoon, they, too, were struck by the serious but strangely composed demeanor of the middle-aged man who answered the door. He escorted them to an upstairs bathroom where the body of a young woman lay slumped next to the tub, and provided details of what had happened and why.

Without any discernible change in expression, the man explained that the woman, who had been renting a room in his large Victorian home, had recently fallen in with what he called "the wrong crowd." According to the homeowner, she and her drug-dealer friends had been planning to murder him, so he had simply killed her first.

When an officer asked what led him to conclude that his life was at risk, the self-confessed killer provided a litany of "facts." For instance, he had overheard the muffled, one-sided telephone conversations in which the woman was surely plotting his death. She had also received suspicious letters cleverly disguised to look like ordinary advertisements for magazines or credit cards. "But what proof was there that your life was in imminent danger?" the incredulous policeman asked. Smiling slightly for the first time he motioned for the officers to follow him into the young woman's bedroom. There he showed them a hairbrush lying on the dresser.

"You see the position?" he asked. "It is usually placed with the handle pointing toward the front. Today, the handle was pointed *away*!" Seeing the quizzical looks on the officers' faces, he provided further explanation. "They positioned it that way last night to signal her that today would be the day."

He then offered the rest of his so-called proof: the garage door across the street had opened and closed twice that morning, indicating that the plan was in motion. Then there was the green minivan that had cruised slowly down the street.

Once the signs had become clear to him, the man retrieved the gun he kept between his mattress and box spring and calmly went to the woman's bathroom and shot her point-blank.

The police could perceive no hint that the man was putting them on. As bizarre as his story and explanations sounded, his delivery was utterly flat and straightforward, as if he were describing a mundane, everyday occurrence such as taking out the trash.

Finally one of the officers asked the obvious question. "If you thought your life was in danger, why didn't you just call the police?" A hint of a knowing smile crossed the man's face again as he replied, "The drug dealers have infiltrated the police department. I couldn't trust that anyone there would protect me."

An elderly woman believes that thieves enter her room every night to steal her possessions. A student, who had borrowed notes from a classmate for a lecture he missed, thinks that some of the pages have been removed purposely so he will fail the upcoming exam. A woman who recently emigrated from Afghanistan is certain that people are continually laughing at her and talking behind her back. A member of the Tea Party describes burying guns vertically in his backyard so they will be less easy to sense with metal detectors.

You may not be familiar with those particular cases, but what about these? Timothy McVeigh, a young Gulf War veteran, tells a friend that the army has implanted a computer chip in his buttock in order to keep track of his movements (no pun intended). Ted Kaczynski, a brilliant mathematician, conducts an eighteen-year vendetta against mere acquaintances and people he's never even met because he thinks he is being controlled and harmed by modern technology. John du Pont, a reclusive multimillionaire, has razor wire installed inside the walls of his mansion to prevent people he suspects are tunneling under his estate from reaching his living quarters. While we're at it, let's not forget Seung-Hui Cho or Jared Loughner, mentioned above.

What all these individuals have in common is paranoia: the topic of this book. Each of them is unduly suspicious about the intent and actions of others and feels that someone has it in for them.

As should be obvious from even the brief descriptions presented above, each of these people exhibited paranoia in somewhat different ways and, perhaps, for different reasons. The object of this book is to describe the many facets of paranoia, to provide explanations for how it comes about, and to address the potentially serious consequences of paranoid feelings and beliefs. To illustrate this information, I am including actual case examples I have personally seen, as well as cases provided by trusted colleagues (no paranoia here).

A primary assumption of this book is that most of us have experienced the feeling we commonly label *paranoia* at least once in our lives, and most of us have also known someone who was paranoid. In some of these cases, we may have had a legitimate reason to distrust the motives and intentions of others, but many of us will still question our assumptions before passing judgment. We often seek verification of our suspicions, sometimes by asking others whether their perceptions of a given situation are similar (*Am I paranoid, or is Ray always smirking when I say something during meetings?*). If the answer is yes, then we may conclude that our feelings of suspicion were justified because they were confirmed by another, possibly more objective, person.

Clinical paranoia isn't simply a mistrust of others until or unless they are proven wrong; it is the extreme end on a trust continuum. Unfortunately, individuals who suffer from clinical paranoia feel that their conclusions are justified and will often point to confirming evidence *that seems quite real to them although utterly erroneous to the rest of us.* Therein lies part of the difference between what most of us may refer to as paranoia and the extreme versions that mental health professionals are trained to identify.

As this book will describe, responses to and consequences of paranoia can range from healthy situational adaptation to seemingly inexplicable and tragic violence as the case examples presented above demonstrate.

In this electronic age there is, arguably, good reason to feel paranoid. Indeed, if the cell phone conversations of the heir to the throne of England can be monitored relatively easily, what hope do us common folk have of maintaining our privacy? Thankfully, most people's lives are not considered interesting enough to warrant that kind of intrusion . . . although the NSA may beg to differ.

The government has been monitoring our phone calls, e-mails, text messages, and web browsing. It can also tap into ATM systems around the country and know when and where we are withdrawing money and how much. Already unmanned drones are circling our skies; not to drop missiles but to engage in a variety of other purposes, one of which might be to monitor our activities.

Computer hackers have been able to break into sophisticated government and corporate computer systems, seemingly at will; never mind our less protected personal ones. Handheld recorders and cell phone cameras are now capturing much of our behavior on video, which can be shared immediately with the rest of the world. At any moment, something we do could "go viral" and be viewed by millions.

We are now able to place computer chips under the skin of our pets to protect against loss, so that all anyone has to do is pass Fido under a scanner—much like we do a box of cereal at the supermarket—and all the relevant information about the owner will pop up on a computer monitor. If they can do that to pets, what about us? Revelations about our government's past experiments with drugs on unsuspecting and nonvoluntary subjects certainly raise concerns in even the most trusting and naive of us. And these are just the things we know. What super-secret technology really exists that we don't know about?

One of the points made in this book is that this era, with all its sophisticated technology, is not responsible for paranoid disorders. People have likely suffered from paranoia since early in the history of human development. Whether all this electronic sophistication, with its ability to violate our privacy in novel ways, is increasing the number of people experiencing paranoia is a reasonable question. Might it be elevating the paranoia levels of all of us? Well, the answers are to be found in the following pages.

PARANOIA'S OPPOSITE: TRUST

A reasonable antonym for paranoia is trust. Because I focus on the former in this book, it is important to at least mention its opposite. Trust is essentially the expectation that you will receive from another person an expected outcome, usually a positive one. If you feel that you can rely on that person's word or promise, then you are willing to put yourself at risk. Trust develops based on past experiences and interactions with others. It produces a sense of predictability and dependability.

Yet not all our interactions with others result in that reliable outcome. So how is it that we all don't become paranoid as a result? Well, the notion of faith enters the picture. We're not guaranteed a certain outcome, but most of us have some degree of faith in the behaviors of others. The amount varies understandably from person to person and from situation to situation. The person selling a "genuine Rolex" on the street corner for $50 is probably not going to be trusted by most of us. On the other hand, most of us do trust that when we walk into an expensive jewelry store, the $5,000 Rolex in the display case is the genuine item. Again, we have faith that it is. The rest of the book will focus on why some of us do not have that trust and faith.

A BIT OF BACKGROUND

The position of paranoia in psychology is much like that of depression. *Depression* is a word that has leaked into our common language and is now synonymous with sadness (*Mari looks depressed today.*). At the same time it is also a major psychiatric disorder and a prominent feature of a variety of clinical disorders, such as bipolar disorder. Further, depressive features are also commonly found in a variety of other psychiatric disturbances. The majority of individuals suffering from bulimia nervosa or panic attacks, for instance, have depression.

Similarly, *paranoia* and *paranoid* are terms that have crept into our everyday vocabularies. They refer to someone who feels excessively suspicious, typically with little or no reason to feel so, and who has a firm belief in the malevolent intentions of others. It, too, takes the form of major mental illnesses such as paranoid schizophrenia and delusional disorder. Paranoid symptoms are also commonly found in other disorders such as alcoholism or Alzheimer's, even though they are not the essential or defining feature of them.

Paranoia shares another similarity with depression, as both terms are used clinically to define an essential feature of a disorder: prominent suspiciousness in the case of paranoia; a sad feeling state in depression. Yet in both paranoia and depression there are a number of clinical characteristics that actually comprise the *syndrome* of depression or paranoia. In the case of depression, sad mood is at the heart of the disorder. But typically depressed individuals will also commonly lose their appetite, have problems sleeping, have trouble making decisions, experience low energy, and lose their sex drive, among other things.

Excessive suspiciousness is at the heart of paranoia, yet characteristic features also include hostility, rigidity, and lack of trust.

A final commonality is that both depression and paranoia are *dimensional* in nature. We all experience *degrees* of paranoia or depression. Actually, it is probably more accurate to say that we all experience degrees of *suspiciousness* or *sadness*. For some— those featured in this book—the experience is rather severe and stable. Such is also the case for depression. Thus it is important to establish that paranoia is a pathological clinical state. Suspiciousness may not necessarily be abnormal. This theme will be developed more below.

THE PROBLEM WITH PARANOIA

One of the major differences between depression and paranoia is that volumes have been written about depression. Whole journals are devoted to the study of it. In contrast, the literature on paranoia is scant. There are four primary reasons for this disparity.

First, there is, presumably, a higher rate of depression in our society. This is a debatable point. Depression can easily be isolated from the many disorders and conditions in which it is found. For example, someone with cancer can easily be identified as suffering from depression. Hence the rate of "pure" depression and depression embedded within other disorders is relatively easy to determine. Moreover, its treatment is usually independent of the treatment of the other disorder it may be associated with. So the depressed cancer patient can receive chemotherapy *and* be treated separately for depression.

Not so with paranoia. Paranoid individuals don't tend to show up complaining of paranoia like depressed patients do of their condition. Moreover, the paranoia is frequently so embedded within the disorder it is associated with— alcoholism, for example—that it does not get diagnosed or counted. So we treat the alcoholism but not the paranoia per se.

Second, the ultimate consequence of depression is perceived to be more

serious than any of paranoia: successful suicide. However, as the opening anec-
dote demonstrates, paranoia can lead to very serious and deadly consequences.

Third, little cross-talk exists between clinical researchers interested in
paranoia. I attend conferences on Alzheimer's and usually find a talk or two
related to paranoia in patients with Alzheimer's. A conference on schizophrenia
will yield a great deal more discussion on paranoia within schizophrenia and
even an occasional talk focusing just on paranoia.

But I have never encountered a conference devoted solely to paranoia,
where researchers congregate and discuss such simple, and to date, unanswered
questions, such as whether the presentation of paranoia is the same in other disorders. Do Alzheimer's paranoid patients tend to focus on family stealing from
them because they fail to remember where they put or spent their money? Why
do some paranoid individuals focus on government malfeasance, while others
worry about their neighbors? What percentage of alcoholics, people with traumatic brain injuries, hypothyroidism, posttraumatic stress disorder, and so on
have paranoia? There are dozens more of these basic questions, all with little
data to address them. Similar questions about depression are easily answered.

The final reason so little has been published about paranoia is the nature
of conducting research into mental illnesses; more specifically, studying actual
people with the disorders.

FINDING PARANOID INDIVIDUALS

There is an inherent problem in the study of individuals with paranoia. If we want
to study depression, for example, we would hang around in the waiting rooms of
psychiatrists, psychologists, members of the clergy, psychiatric hospitals, general
practitioners, and other places where depressed individuals will show up. Advertisements in local newspapers or TV commercials, often asking the reader/viewer
if they "are suffering from depression" or "feeling afraid for no reason" are used
and work well. Based on these and other sampling methods, we could gather data
on a representative group of depressed individuals. Studying this group would
yield results that would be generalizable to other depressed individuals.

Now imagine the same situation with paranoid individuals. First, they don't tend to come in asking for help or treatment. Unlike people with depression, or phobias, or sexual dysfunction, persons with paranoia don't necessarily think there is anything wrong with them. Thus there is little intrinsic motivation for them to seek help. From their perspective, it's the person out to get them (*you*) who has the problem, not them.

So going places where people with emotional/psychological problems seek help will not result in a large catch of paranoid individuals. Further, if patients in general are asked about paranoid issues, the truly paranoid are likely to deny such problems.

I recently interviewed a patient on the medical floor of a hospital—literally on the floor, as she was too paranoid to be interviewed in her room. I asked directly if she was concerned about staff and if she felt safe. She denied any suspiciousness, but while I was talking to her she entered her room, snooping around for the nurses she was convinced were in the closet or bathroom spying on her.

But imagine for a moment that we were able to identify a group of paranoid individuals. Let's say, for the sake of making a point, that all militia groups are comprised of paranoid members. No data exists to support such a generalization, so this is for illustrative purposes only. (The militia movement will be discussed later in the book.) Now imagine that at the monthly meeting of the local militia faction I knock on the door and ask to be admitted. I introduce myself as a university professor of psychology interested in learning more about the psychological functioning of members of the militia. Further, I inform this group of paranoid individuals that I'd like to ask them some questions about their emotional/personal lives. As I'm sure you can envision, there is no reason to believe that any of them would be lining up to participate in my study. Lining up to escort me off my feet and out the door, probably yes.

Then there is the standard disclaimer made to research subjects: "Any data collected will be reported in group form only, without reference to or identification of the individual participants." Those with paranoia don't trust people in general, let alone someone who is going to gather potentially revealing information about them. It is unlikely that they would trust anyone's assurance of confidentiality.

Thus, our knowledge about paranoia is very limited compared to most other mental disorders. As the many case examples used in this book suggest, some portion of these individuals are found in prison settings as a result of crimes committed. In most cases the crime was the result of their paranoia. However, we don't know how representative these cases are of the entire population of paranoid individuals. It is likely that most people with paranoia don't violate the law.

The bottom line is that it is inherently difficult finding and studying people with paranoia in a systematic and scientific manner. This is not the case with most psychological disorders.

JAMES TILLY MATTHEWS

One of the most fascinating cases of paranoia, and one of the first to be well documented, involves the unfortunate Englishman James Tilly Matthews. In the late eighteenth century he developed a *fixed*, or unchangeable, delusion involving an "air loom," which he believed to operate in silence beneath the streets of London, influencing his thoughts.

The loom operated via pneumatic chemistry—air or gases—recently discovered at the time. Gases were mysterious phenomena as they were undetectable yet had profound effects. Gases and magnetic waves, which, thanks to the Viennese physician-cum-hypnotist Anton Mesmer, were believed to flow through our bodies. They were the eighteenth-century equivalent of today's x-rays and radio waves, and they became the stuff of paranoid delusions along with the textile machines of the age. Put together with a loom, gases and magnetic waves sent messages and exerted control over one's mind and constituted one of the first "influencing machines."

The machine was an elegant contraption and was eventually brought to life, to an extent, by Matthews's own detailed drawing (below). It was powered by a bizarre combination of gases that were described by the physician in charge of Matthews, John Haslam, as containing "seminal fluid, male and female—Effluvia of copper—ditto of sulphur—effluvia of dogs—stinking human breath—stench of the sesspool—gaz from the anus of the horse—human gaz—gaz of the horse's greasy heels."[1] And this is the short list!

According to Matthews, the gases were stored in barrels that had been magnetized and were then fed into the loom. From there they were channeled out. The loom was operated much like a pipe organ with various levers and stops employed to mix the gases. Then some sort of magnetic rays were emitted that caused a variety of influences on the person they were directed toward, "attacking the human body and mind, whether to actuate or render inactive; to make ideas or to steal others; to bewilder or to deceive."[2]

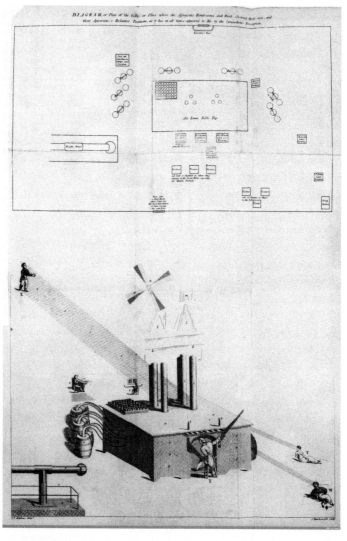

James Tilly Matthews's "Assassins Air-Loom Machine," 1810. From *Illustrations of Madness*, by John Haslam. *From Wellcome Library, London.*

Matthews gave these effects peculiar names like kiteing, lobster-cracking, and brain-sayings. These types of descriptions are entirely consistent with what is seen today in patients with psychosis. Today we use the clinical terms: *thought insertion/withdrawal* (thoughts being inserted or taken out of one's mind), *thought blocking* (when one entirely forgets what he was saying), and *inappropriate affect* (responding to a situation with the wrong emotion; for example, laughing at the news of someone's death).

These magnetic rays, like today's x-rays and radio waves, were capable of penetrating walls but were most effective when closer to the source. The victims of these nefarious deeds were selected, then duped into conversation and made to inhale pressurized magnetic fluid released from a bottle. This "impregnated" them, thereby rendering them susceptible to future magnetic manipulation.

Matthews believed that most government officials were so affected (which today would certainly provide a convenient explanation for the failings of Congress). This process of *event-working* was accomplished via "pneumatic chemistry and pneumatic magnetism."

His delusions are eerily similar to those of today's paranoid patients who believe that computer chips have been placed in their brains. Matthews believed that a magnet had been implanted in his brain by "political chemists" to influence his thoughts.

The seven members of the "loom gang" required to work the contraption—"pneumaticians"—were a rogues' gallery of characters with colorful names and detailed descriptions, including Bill the King; Sir Archy, who some in the gang believed to be a woman in male clothing; Charlotte, who was French but who communicated her thoughts telepathically in English; and Glove Woman, who didn't speak but possessed "a considerable quantity of fine downy hair" on her chin and upper lip.

What makes Matthews's story even more interesting are his assertions that he was a spy sent to France. He claimed to have met with various government officials who largely denied knowledge of him or his actions. Historical records, extensively reviewed in Mike Jay's book *The Air Loom Gang*, suggest that he may indeed have been a spy, just as he claimed. Or perhaps his espionage, like the air loom lurking beneath London, was just another delusion. Sadly, he was considered to be enough of a political inconvenience and nuisance to be imprisoned in London's famed Bethlem Royal Hospital (nicknamed Bedlam), a lunatic asylum, until his death.[3]

Although Matthews held onto his delusion until the bitter end, not all paranoid individuals do so. Jay describes the case of one of France's most prestigious psychiatrists, Philippe Pinel, who admitted a clockmaker to his hospital. This patient believed that he had been beheaded during the Revolution only to have the verdict reversed and his head reattached. Unfortunately, it was the wrong head among the basket of heads.

The poor clockmaker then became obsessed with building a perpetual motion machine. Like Matthews, he produced drawings and was quite obsessed with the construction of the machine. The resourceful Pinel, rather than confronting the delusional pursuit head-on as is commonly done even today, aided and abetted the clockmaker until he actually created a working machine. Falling short of perpetuity, it functioned for a few days then expired, as did the patient's delusion. He returned to his normal life as a clockmaker without further diversion.[4]

THE FEW OR THE MANY?

Obviously individuals labeled as having a paranoid *disorder* will eventually be characterized by paranoid experiences. Yet research indicates that many of us, perhaps 15 to 30 percent, will *regularly* experience suspiciousness/paranoid thoughts.[5] For most, this will take low-level forms (*Someone has it in for me*; *People are talking about me behind my back*). We cannot rule out the possibility that, when a person reports the feeling that someone is out to get them, there really *isn't* somebody out to get them. Nicole Hill believed, and told neighbors, that her ex-husband, Bradley Stone, would someday kill her. She was not paranoid; she was right. Stone killed her and five members of her family in 2014.

Alarmingly, about 8 to 10 percent of us have actual persecutory *delusions*. In other words, paranoia that is manifestly bizarre or extreme (*The government is stealing my brain and replacing it with computers*). The rate of paranoia among those admitted to a hospital for any psychological problems is on the order of 40 percent.[6]

So a fair number of us have paranoid experiences. For some of us, our suspicions may be justified; for others, perhaps not. But how many people have what professionals might identify as clinical levels of paranoia? Well, for reasons given previously, that's not an easy question to answer. The available evidence would suggest that it is rather common.

One way of determining how many people experience paranoia is to canvass a particular geographic area. For instance, select a neighborhood and simply ask anybody willing to answer your questions if they are paranoid. Keep in mind that *real* paranoid persons are likely to decline to answer such questions.

When such a survey was conducted in east Baltimore in the early 1990s it was found that about 10 percent of people had some form of paranoid beliefs.[7] That is not to say that 10 percent of people in east Baltimore have a paranoid *disorder*. I lived there for a number of years and can guarantee you that, for every ten people I met, I did not find that there was one paranoid person among each group.

The results do suggest that paranoid thinking and beliefs are fairly common. A similar study in Great Britain found that around 19 percent of people interviewed reported feeling, at some point, that people were against them. Close to 2 percent of those surveyed felt that others were actually plotting to do them serious harm. Although 2 percent of the population doesn't seem like much, it is quite a lot of people.[8]

A whopping 42 percent of college students in one survey reported that at least once a week others were circulating negative comments about them. Further, 27 percent felt people were deliberately trying to irritate them, 19 percent were being observed/followed, and 5 percent were being conspired against. Accompanying those symptoms were depressed mood, anxiety, and lowered self-esteem.[9]

In New York City one thousand adults were interviewed, and almost 11 percent believed that others were following or spying on them. Nearly 7 percent thought that others were trying to poison them or were plotting against them. Almost 5 percent felt that others were experimenting on them or secretly testing them in some way.[10] Think about those numbers for a minute. Walk down any busy street in New York City and realize that one out of ten people you pass feel that someone (perhaps you) is spying on or following them.

Another way doctors and researchers can determine the rates of paranoia is to ask people who visit their primary care physician. That is exactly what

Dr. Hélène Verdoux did in France. She found that fully 25 percent of general medical patients, with no psychiatric history, felt that they were being persecuted in some way. Ten percent felt they were being conspired against, 16 percent worried about their partner's fidelity, and 18 percent felt that others were looking at them in a strange way.[11]

Yet a third method to circumvent the usual problems of finding and studying paranoid individuals is with an online (anonymous) survey.[12] A British survey of this sort found that on a weekly basis almost 50 percent of Brits felt that they were being looked at critically by friends or strangers. Over 40 percent believed that negative comments were being circulated about them. Twenty percent felt they were being observed or followed (ironically, this statistic is probably fairly accurate, given the large number of surveillance cameras in England). Roughly 30 percent reported that people were hostile toward them, were saying bad things behind their back, were deliberately trying to irritate them, and were laughing at them. And about 10 percent felt people were trying to upset them; had bad intentions toward them; had it in for them; would harm them if given the chance; and were threatened by others. At the extreme end of the paranoia spectrum, 5 percent of individuals felt there was a conspiracy against them. Again, these were not rare or isolated feelings but beliefs that individuals experienced on a *weekly* basis.

The level of conviction given to these beliefs as well as the level of distress engendered by them were both quite high. Individuals who acknowledge paranoia are less happy, more anxious, and have poorer social functioning than those who don't. They are also more likely to be thinking about suicide and have more medical problems. Again, these are for the most part not individuals with actual paranoid disorders.[13]

In Switzerland, between 4 to 9 percent of individuals interviewed endorsed some form of paranoid thinking, such as feeling most people can't be trusted. The same individuals were interviewed regularly over the next twenty years. The number endorsing paranoid thinking remained much the same.[14]

One of the surprising findings about paranoia is how many children report such experiences. In a British study of nine- to twelve-year-olds, fully 33 percent of boys and 24 percent of girls reported feeling spied upon.[15]

A study out of Australia found that 1.3 percent of people in the community had extreme (psychotic) levels of paranoia. Interestingly, an individual was much more likely to be paranoid if he was a non-English-speaking immigrant. Additionally, living in an urban setting, trauma, and drug use all increased one's chances of suffering psychotic-like symptoms, paranoia included. We'll return to this subject when we discuss the causes of paranoia. Fortunately, for most (75 to 90 percent), these experiences are transitory.

ELEVATOR MAN

I was on my way to the Probation and Parole Office in the local courthouse for a meeting about an individual I was to evaluate. It was a warm and humid day, and rather than walking the stairs, I decided to ride the elevator to the third floor, where the offices were located.

As I walked toward the elevator the door began to close, and it was clear that no burst of speed would be enough to get me in on this particular flight up. Much to my surprise the door opened after about five seconds, and I walked in to find a diminutive male in his early forties wearing a leather motorcycle jacket with the sleeves removed, revealing well-muscled and well-tattooed arms. Long hair and earrings completed the picture. "Damn elevators don't work right . . . nothing works right, and then they want to raise my taxes. Well, they'd better fix the goddamn elevators. I wonder where my tax money is going. They are all just stealing from me. And they got my house bugged too. What are all of them doing in their offices all day?"

It was a short ride to the third floor, but the guy managed to fill every second of air time with his tirade. I found it less than coincidental that we both ended up at the same office, Probation and Parole, although for different reasons, I imagine.

EVERYDAY PARANOIA

The discussion above reveals that many of us regularly experience paranoid thoughts and distress associated with those thoughts. There is likely some variability depending on which country the data were collected in, and perhaps anthropologists or sociologists can shed light on the factors that make a citizen of one country more likely to feel paranoid than another. People living in the former Soviet Union or the former German Democratic Republic probably had understandably high levels of paranoia.

However, we are not yet talking about the paranoid *disorders*. The paranoid individuals described above are you and me, so to speak. We must keep in mind that the statistics quoted above are conservative. No matter how you attempt to collect information on paranoia: anonymous Internet survey, interviews in primary care settings, interviews on the street, paranoid individuals are more likely to refuse to participate. As will be discussed later, these high rates of paranoia in the general population may be the result of a variety of factors and may be the harbinger of increased rates of actual paranoid disorders.

RICHARD SHAVER

James Tilly Matthews's magnetic-pneumatic loom is one of the first examples of what became known as "influencing machines." Fast-forward a century or so and we have Richard Shaver.

Shaver was variously an artist, meat cutter, art teacher, assembly line laborer, and author, of sorts. In 1934, at the age of twenty-seven, he began demonstrating paranoid behavior, claiming that people were watching and following him. He was probably ill for quite a while before this, as he acknowledged always having heard voices.

He was admitted to the state mental institution in Ypsilanti, Michigan, where he believed the physicians were trying to poison him. Other patients were calling him a communist and a homosexual.

In the early 1940s he submitted long treatises to the pulp magazine *Amazing Stories* regarding the existence of an extensive underground world. Not only were these published, but the readership increased, and many individuals wrote to document their personal encounters with this nether world and its denizens.

According to Shaver, over a million years ago a race he called the *Titans*, or the *Elder Gods*, came to Earth from outer space. They colonized the planet, creating extensive civilizations on land and under the seas. Unfortunately a change in the winds, in this case solar winds, brought unwanted radiation to Earth and threatened the survival of the Titans.

Most decided to flee Earth in spaceships and sought more hospitable planets to colonize. A portion chose to remain and, using gigantic machines, hollowed out the earth. They created a vast subterranean world where they could reside, safe from the effects of radiation. Shaver noted that there were various access points to enter this underground world, one of which can even be seen on an old Disney nature program about the life of coyotes!

Alas, the race of Titans began to deteriorate as the cumulative effects of genetic mutations reduced their lifespan and intelligence. Those who did survive turned into a mendacious lot Shaver called the *deros*, short for *detrimental robot*.

A description of one dero he had the displeasure of encountering painted a graphic picture of these underground miscreants: "Its body was enormously fat and bloated, with yellowish-gray, bristly skin covered in seeping sores and lumpy tumors. The face resembled a burn victim with the skin hanging in great, fat folds across the forehead, cheeks, and chin. The hands were strong and hairy, ending in long sharp and filthy fingernails."[16]

Replete with warts on his penis, the only thing this dero lacked was bad breath and poor table manners. According to Shaver, the deros use various ray machines to plague us terrestrials with car and plane accidents, create war and pestilence, cause us to stub our toes, and generally make our lives as miserable as an IRS audit. The rays could alter our sense of time because of its hypnotic properties, cause pain and itching, and even heal illness and prolong life. The latter properties of these rays were only used to keep torture victims alive even longer, in order to prolong their agony and the dero's perverse pleasure. They were even used, Shaver avowed, to take over Lee Harvey Oswald's mind, causing him to assassinate President John F. Kennedy.

Shaver believed that he and the editor of *Amazing Stories* were being followed by the FBI and CIA using the paranoid's classic black cars or vans. This caused him to muse, "I often wondered if the US Government knew the truth about the deros, or were possibly in cahoots with them. That wouldn't surprise me considering the types of people who get involved in politics. As far as I am concerned, there isn't much difference between most politicians and the dero."

All indications are that Shaver believed what he wrote. At the end of his life, on his way to Hollywood to consult on a movie about the underground world, a bowel obstruction forced him to enter the hospital for surgery. He predicted that the deros would not permit such a movie to be made and that he would never leave the hospital alive. He was right, if perhaps for the wrong reason. He died before ever leaving the hospital.

Chapter 2

INSIDE THE MIND
OF PARANOIA

I am assuming that up to this point the reader has a general sense of what paranoia is all about. But paranoia and paranoid disorders are multifaceted in nature.

It will be important to keep in mind that paranoia occupies the extreme end of a continuum. We can perhaps call the continuum in question *suspiciousness*. In that sense it reflects a normal and healthy human psychological experience, much like anger, love, happiness, and so on. At the low end of the continuum is naïveté, while paranoia sits at the other end. Each end is abnormal/pathological. In the middle are varying degrees of healthy trust or suspiciousness. So by definition paranoia and paranoid disorders are pathological states. They represent an extreme of a normal, adaptive emotion.

VENT MAN

The interview/therapy rooms at the university where I teach are fully wired for sight and sound. Amid the paintings depicting pretty forest and mountain scenes, video cameras protrude noticeably from the corners of the room. A video monitor is suspended on the wall, and a small but powerful microphone hangs just above head level in the middle of the room. These are essential tools in the supervision and training of neophyte clinicians, and they are a paranoiac's nightmare.

The young man who was the focus of the assessment was informed, as all clients are, that he would be videotaped during the interview. Being paranoid, the man requested that the equipment be turned off while he was in the room. He insisted on being shown the monitoring room where the microphone and cameras were turned on and off. Not quite satisfied that they would remain off, he asked that a plastic bag be placed over the camera lens.

Throughout the interview he evinced the characteristic demeanor of a paranoid individual: edgy defensiveness and heightened suspiciousness. As one hour turned into two and almost three, he became somewhat more relaxed. While the evaluation started wrapping up his faced tensed and flushed. "Is there something wrong?" the graduate student-clinician asked. "No, nothing; I'm just angry at myself for not having seen that air duct up there," pointing to an eight-by-five-inch grate near the ceiling. "You could have easily hidden a microphone or video camera up there."

SUSPICIOUSNESS

The most salient symptom of paranoia is excessive, undue, or unreasonable *suspiciousness*. Paranoid people are typically mistrustful of others and harbor a view that others have malicious or evil intentions. Or, put another way, they feel that others are persecuting them.

The level of suspiciousness can be as simple as thinking that others are talking behind their back, or as extreme as the truly delusional belief that someone is malevolently trying to harm them, often in bizarre ways, for example, by beaming x-rays into their head or stealing their thoughts.[1] The "someone" can be their neighbor, family members, or organizations. The government, the FBI, the CIA, and other such groups are frequently blamed in this regard. Others are seen as trying to harm, humiliate, discredit, blackmail, or even kill them. They are being talked about, laughed at, vilified, disrespected, threatened, followed, stared at, harassed, oppressed, observed, wronged, plotted against, disparaged, and discussed by others, known and unknown.

Now, if you imagine that some organization such as the Mafia or CIA is after you, there is a high probability that sophisticated monitoring devices are involved. Needless to say, paranoid individuals tend to be preoccupied with such devices. In the nineteenth century hydraulic instruments, gasses, and animal magnetism were the focus of their concern. Today, microwaves, x-rays, microphones, cameras, computers, radio waves, and computer chips figure prominently in their delusions. I saw a patient with the withdrawal syndrome from alcohol, the so-called DT's, who claimed she saw very thin wires connected to listening devices throughout her house. Placed there by her husband and his lover to spy on her, the wires were of a special quality such that they disintegrated when a person's body heat approached them. She spent what must have been a bizarre afternoon chasing these dissolving wires throughout the house.

Another paranoid individual believed that the neighbors were using their satellite dish to monitor his thoughts and eavesdrop on him electronically. His solution was to dig up the telephone and electric cables underneath their house and cut the lines with an ax.

HOW DO PARANOID INDIVIDUALS THINK?

Ultimately it is distorted thoughts that generate and reinforce the paranoid person's suspiciousness. The reasoning behind their suspiciousness is highly specious. They are capable of making tremendous inferential leaps based solely on insignificant or, at best, ambiguous details. Whoever coined the term "mountains out of molehills" must have had paranoid individuals in mind. Gray is not in the paranoid person's cognitive palette—things are black or white. Yet no amount of evidence can displace their beliefs; in part because they largely ignore contradictory evidence or alternative explanations.

The force of logic is impotent when faced with evidence that someone who is paranoid is able to assemble. For nothing is "innocent," happens by chance, or appears as it seems. A shrug, a wave of the hand, or a cough can all have meaning. As a result, inordinate attention is paid to small, petty details. Minor events or innocuous things in the environment can be twisted to fit the paranoid individual's belief system.

Someone who fails to flush the toilet in a public restroom did so just to annoy and antagonize them. Being jostled or bumped in a crowd feels like they are being intentionally run into. The curtains drawn over at the neighbors' house are an indication that someone is spying on them. A comment made by a coworker about how much road salt and grime has built up on their car is a jab at how lazy and unclean they are. You can't underestimate how good paranoid people are at finding the hidden meaning in just about everything. And invariably, that hidden meaning is directed toward them and has a negative connotation. Even compliments, like "I love your new jacket," can be interpreted as a subtle insult implying that their previous jacket was trash and they have no taste.

You can't trust what you see, so you need to interpret and see behind the surface presentations of situations, so the paranoid person believes. This often results in what Dr. William Carpenter, director of the Maryland Psychiatric Research Center in Baltimore, and an expert in psychotic disorders, refers to as *sudden clarification*. Others have used different terms, but the notion is the same. The paranoid individual experiences an event they immediately recognize for "what it really is." It is a signal of immediate danger or the last piece of a puzzle indicating who the tormentor is or where the attack will come from. It is an overheard comment, an unsuspecting wink from another, a song on the radio, a line in a book, or a million other possible things. To the paranoid individual the smallest word or gesture has meaning and makes crystal clear something they had only a sense of before. As we shall see later in regard to violence, this seemingly insignificant event is often the final straw that precipitates the violence.

Paranoid individuals are thin-skinned and hypersensitive, which causes them to interpret events as being directed or referenced toward them. They hear a song with sexual content and believe it is an attempt by the artist to comment on their personal behavior and publicly humiliate them via the airwaves. Nothing is mundane or ordinary. Everything is somehow related to and has meaning for them. When the paranoid person becomes delusional, their ideas are airtight, rigidly held, logically consistent, and unshakeable.

The paranoid person typically has limited or nonexistent insight into his condition and disordered way of thinking. At best he retains some insight that results in a kind of internal debate over the reality and validity of his perceptions. Once convinced of his stance, however, there is no further vacillation, and all energies are turned toward the enemy. Yet the issues are far from resolved. The paranoid person will tend to dwell on them in a perseverative, spinning-your-wheels-in-the-mud manner. Such ruminative thinking does not result in any kind of new solution or perspective but rather in increased anger and resolution to take action. Such actions are justified by the special circumstances the paranoid person finds himself in—being put upon or attacked.

It is more than a bit ironic that paranoid individuals are distrustful of almost everything, yet accept as veridical any innuendo or interpretation that is negatively related to them.

DUCT TAPE AND BUBBLE WRAP

The mechanism was obvious to Jim: they were poisoning him through the heating system in his house. The solution was easy but inconvenient; all he had to do was turn off the heat. The problem with that, of course, was the cold, but a little Bubble Wrap and a roll of duct tape fixed that problem: he simply wrapped himself up with both until he resembled the Michelin Man. Bathing, however, represented a bit of a problem, and Jim became quite aromatic by the time he was admitted to the hospital for his paranoia.

GETTING ALONG WITH OTHERS

In most normal interpersonal relationships a basic level of trust is necessary. Absent that trust, people remain somewhat guarded, at best. Obviously, paranoid individuals don't trust others and so are not willing to open up and reveal anything about themselves. As far as they are concerned, anything you learn *about* them, you will use *against* them.

Rather than looking for ways to deepen a relationship, with a mutual sharing of information and feelings, they are guarded, too busy looking for signs of threats. Attempts to penetrate the palpable wall that surrounds paranoid individuals will be met with defensiveness and, not uncommonly, hostility. The motives and intentions of others is a primary concern in all situations. Certain topics are more likely to elicit reactions than others, although these topics are rarely advertised. One prominent theme, however, is the fidelity of anyone they are in a relationship with. So-called pathological jealousy is viewed as a paranoid characteristic, albeit a special one meriting an in-depth discussion later.

For the rest of us, dealing with a paranoid individual's hypersensitivity is like walking on eggshells—an endeavor we soon tire of and simply avoid as much as possible. The rigidity of their thinking, impervious as it is to reason, makes them frustrating to us. Their edgy defensiveness renders them prickly and hard to develop tender feelings toward.

The world is perceived by the paranoid person as a dangerous place where a "dog-eat-dog" mentality prevails. As such you must be constantly on your guard and *hypervigilant* lest someone sneak behind your back and stab you there. Even if it is dog-eat-dog out there, for some reason their dog gets eaten more. *They* are the ones being persecuted. Evidence for that is all around—evidence that exists only in their mind.

Paranoid persons need to be mobilized at all times since they never know when the attack is going to come. It is like being on orange alert 24/7 with frequent red alerts thrown in. Empathy and concern for the welfare of others are emotions they have little time for, inasmuch as they would take valuable energies from home-land defense. They don't expect you to cut them a break—quite the opposite; they expect you to harm them—so don't expect one from them. Warm and fuzzy are not terms that come to mind when thinking about the paranoid individual.

Like the rest of us, but probably no more so than the rest of us, they occa-sionally are the butt of a joke, insult, or slight. And like the rest of us, they feel hurt when that happens. How they differ from the rest of us is that a slight/insult/joke hurts *more* and *they don't forgive or forget it*. They are capable of bearing grudges for years and acting on those cold-dish grudges even years later. Not uncommonly, they take the litigious route. In this regard, a not insignificant number of complaints filed with police emanate from paranoid individuals.

Needless to say, if you lived in the type of world in which the paranoid person does, as described above, you'd be a less-than-pleasant individual. Para-noid people tend to have an edgy defensiveness about them. Irritable, queru-lous, and quarrelsome, many have the lovely disposition of a wolverine with boils. This prevents most people from developing much sympathy toward them. In fact, quite the opposite tends to develop. You can often tell if you are dealing with someone who is paranoid if, after a few minutes of talking with them, you find yourself angry and annoyed at them. (Paranoid individuals are not unique in eliciting this reaction; people respond this way to sufferers of a variety of psychological disorders.) Yet it must be remembered that a common reaction to the feeling that someone is out to harm you, or that at any moment some ill fate awaits you, is fear/anxiety.

Keeping in mind that there are degrees to which someone experiences paranoia, their interpersonal relationships can range from nonexistent to guarded. Some can be aloof and quiet as they "take it all in" and avoid revealing information. Others are chronically argumentative and complaining.

Their cold, humorless manner is not something most of us seek in a companion. Tolerating someone with this disorder will entail suffering their frequent biting sarcasm, stubbornness, outbursts of hostility, and questions of fidelity and loyalty. Their behavior is often met not with patience but with reciprocal hostility. A vicious cycle is then created in which their initial fears about someone are confirmed by their obvious hostility toward them, to which they react with an equal or greater measure of hostility. This, in turn, increases the other person's hostility, which, predictably, increases theirs, and the cycle escalates. The paranoid person lacks insight into her contribution to this process.

Putting aside for the moment the question "What possessed you to ever get involved in a romantic or marital relationship with such an individual in the first place?" don't expect warm and tender feelings. Instead, expect your sexual faithfulness to be questioned. Your clothing will be inspected for the stray hairs of your lover. The smell of your paramour's perfume or cologne will be sniffed out. Were it not painful and upsetting, it would be almost comical to see these bloodhound sleuths burying their noses in your clothing to find the scent.

However, this process is more likely to go on out of earshot, or noseshot, as the case might be, given their devious and secretive nature. One way of ensuring that you don't betray them with your secret lover is to control you and the relationship. Your cell phone will be checked to see who you are calling. The credit cards and bank accounts are in their name. Your allowance will provide for the amount of gas you need to get to work and back, but not the side trips to your lover's. Expect them to know how long it takes you to get to work/the store/the cleaners and back again. Any deviations from this allotted time will be "evidence" of your tryst. And again, a vicious cycle begins: if you are constantly being accused of being unfaithful and cannot counter the "proof" against you, then you have nothing to lose by actually having an affair as you have already been found guilty in their eyes anyway. Once revealed, the paranoid individual's initial concerns over your trustworthiness, or lack thereof, are confirmed.

Given the above scenario, it is not surprising that these individuals often find themselves alone. Part of them is quite comfortable with this because having no trust in others forces them to become self-sufficient and self-reliant. Autonomous, they don't need anyone, so when they are betrayed, they don't risk having all their eggs in somebody else's basket.

KIM

Kim has been in therapy with me for quite a while now. Although her initial reason for seeking treatment was depression, which she did have, it took about a minute to note how strange and paranoid she was acting.

Her movements are stilted and awkward, as if she had just been given her body and is still trying to figure out just how to make the thing work properly. Eye contact is rarely made, and she often sits in session with her eyes closed. Her strange, tangential asides and allusions to esoteric topics are punctuated by a short, strange laugh.

Her story is a sad one. Teased as a child because she "always did things the proper way," she was subsequently home-schooled. It is easy to imagine how cruel other children must have been to her, given her peculiar manner. The lack of contact with peers during her childhood and adolescent years only served to make her more uncomfortable and less socially facile. Certain that others were making fun of her, she had pervasive paranoia, and the first year of therapy was spent simply building a trusting therapeutic relationship.

THE EMOTIONS OF A PARANOID PERSON

Paranoid individuals suffer more slings and arrows than the rest of us. The constant threat of harm certainly generates a fair amount of chronic fear, as noted above. Yet because of the paranoiac's secretive nature, that emotion may not be prominent or even detectable. Instead, they express anger over being targeted for harm, humiliation, and so on. It must be remembered that their fears (and anger) are backed up by considerable "evidence" they have systematically gathered.

Because nothing is as it seems and there is hidden meaning everywhere, jokes do not live in the paranoid person's world. Humor relies on double entendre, odd ways of looking at situations, incongruous combinations, and so forth. Not infrequently, someone is a butt of a joke. Paranoid individuals are far too rigid, read far too much into everything that is said, and are far too sensitive to be able to possess a sense of humor. Imagine walking down the aisle of an airplane while trying to locate your seat. In shuffling by seat 24F the occupant quips, "Is that a box-cutter in your pocket, or are you just happy to see me?" Well, few Americans would find the humor in that statement. Substituting the word "cell phone" or "iPod" for box-cutter might elicit at least a weak smile for a lame joke. The point is that the joke is a little too close to home, striking a raw nerve for most Americans. Well, paranoid individuals are nothing but raw nerves.

Based on everything said above, the overall emotional state of a person who is paranoid is a negative one. It is fueled not only by the ongoing (mis)interpretations of events, but also by the legacy of grudges they carry with them from past ills. If you lived in the world in which paranoid individuals do, you, too, would become cynical, given the state of the world.

HI HO, HI HO: PARANOID INDIVIDUALS AT WORK

Because people with paranoia—unlike those with some other psychological disorders—function within what is considered a normal range regarding intellect and thinking processes, such as memory, problem-solving, and the like, they are prevalent in the workforce and perhaps in your workplace. Alas, they do not play well with others. Quick to criticize, they are not open to being criticized themselves. Even constructive criticism is construed as attacks on their character, competence, or integrity. At times you may feel that they have been placed there just to make your life at work miserable. If it is any consolation, they feel the same way about you.

How paranoid individuals function in the workplace likely depends on the degree of paranoia they experience. A delusional paranoid person who is constantly going on about how the CIA is putting drugs into the water system to turn us into zombies isn't going to last long in most jobs. Some aspects of a paranoid's makeup may be beneficial, however, for example in jobs that require a skeptical attitude or a cold, unsympathetic demeanor. But rarely does the whole package of a paranoid individual's personality make them an ideal employee or good coworker.

BISWANATH "BIZZY" HALDER

The denizens of Case Western Reserve University's computer lab were well acquainted with Biswanath Halder, a sixty-two-year-old India-born male who earned an MBA from the institution. By all accounts he appears to fit the profile of someone with a paranoid disorder.

After living and studying in Europe, he arrived in the United States and eventually became a citizen. Unfortunately, he did not meet with economic success in the land of opportunity and blamed the various companies who failed to hire him of racial prejudice. He filed numerous lawsuits alleging discrimination to the point that his attorney apparently quit, citing the many suits and changes in Halder's mental state as the cause. Not to be deterred, Halder began acting as his own attorney with the predictable outcome of dismissal of all his lawsuits.

By all accounts he was an eccentric, prickly loner, who not only lacked friends but had no contact with family. He complained to neighbors about trivial matters, such as leaving the washing machine lid open in the laundry room. Rarely was he thankful for kindnesses shown him, and he was so unpleasant that students started a Halder-Sucks.org website. At least one student apparently took his pique even further and erased files on Halder's personal computer related to a business he was starting. Halder claimed that the university failed to take action, and so he took matters, as well as a semiautomatic gun, into his own hands. A shooting rampage left one dead and two wounded. Claiming a conspiracy against him, which included his attorneys, Halder was found guilty of his crimes and sentenced to life without parole.[2]

OTHER SIDES OF PARANOIA

Trust and loyalty are important issues in relationships for most of us, but they are particularly significant for paranoid individuals. Coworkers, friends, associates and even family members are not exempt from distrust although they generally are trusted.

Constantly on guard for threats to their integrity, they harbor grudges against those who have impugned their character. Perceived slights or insults are met with swift anger. And such slights are common given their hypersensitivity and tendency to use twisted logic in reaching their conclusions. They are able to use logical reasoning to solve problems in other domains, so the problem is not that they are illogical. When it comes to certain interpersonal situations, however, their ability to draw conclusions appears to use a twisted form of logic. If given a task that requires problem-solving or skills of drawing conclusions, for example, they are able to complete such tasks adequately. The moment the task moves closer to home and can possibly be related to them personally in some way, errors in their thinking increase.

These individuals have a pervasive tendency to misconstrue benign events as indications of the hostility and ill will of others. Any sign of sincerity by others is seen as a smoke screen designed to hide their true intentions. Hidden meanings are found everywhere. A twisted logic somehow leads the paranoid individual to conclusions about the intention or meaning of what is being said or done. They are intense listeners, for they never know what is "really" being said or implied, and so they must listen carefully lest an important piece of information or slip of the tongue get by them. Their listening is tuned to the nuances and double meanings embedded within the other person's speech. One personality theorist likened it to that of a sound technician who, rather than listening to the beauty of music, is attuned to the fidelity, relative balance, and more technical aspects of the music.[3] The forest is clearly lost for the trees.

At the same time there is a sense of grandiosity about these individuals. Confident that they are right and others have it wrong, they tend to have an air of moral superiority. Slights against them are interpreted as being malicious and intentional and are often met with swift retaliation, frequently in the form of lawsuits or complaints to the police, supervisors, or others in charge. In this regard hostility is one of the key features, along with suspiciousness, that defines the disorder. This hostility is constantly stoked by the nefarious deeds of others, and since that is occurring all the time—in the eyes of the paranoid person—the hostility is more or less constant.

The nature of paranoia results in a simplistic, black-and-white view of the world. Rarely, of course, is the world black or white. Like it or not, we all inhabit a world of varying degrees of gray, a maddening and intolerable situation for paranoid individuals. Obviously, most ambiguity is to be found in interpersonal dynamics. What did that nod or wink really mean? Why did they say that? What do they really want? These are tough questions for all of us, made tougher by the individual set of circumstances in which they arise. The stress engendered by these and other situations the paranoid individual finds herself in can result in significant increases in distress.

Someone with paranoia is like a good crime novel detective. Always alert to peculiarities in the environment, they look for frequently occurring events, or events that don't occur frequently enough. Each event becomes evidence for the mal-intent of others. In a rich environment, there are countless events or situations that are somehow out of the ordinary. Most of us take that information in, maybe lifting an eyebrow but little more unless of course it is astoundingly out of the ordinary. Such events are pieces of the puzzle for people who are paranoid. Each new piece, no matter how oddly shaped it might appear to the rest of us, is made to fit in the puzzle. The picture that emerges only goes to support the paranoid individual's preexisting belief. "I knew they were trying to take my ideas at work and not give me the credit. The fact that my boss is driving a new car is proof that he is benefiting at my expense." Not infrequently these pieces of evidence— scraps of paper, cryptic notes—are saved for use in future legal battles.

AM I PARANOID?

It is not unreasonable to assume that some might be reading this book to see if some of their thoughts or behaviors might be considered paranoid. Additionally, some readers may have succumbed to a version of "medical student syndrome," so named for young, healthy medical students who come to feel that they are suffering from the various illnesses they are studying. I should note that a similar phenomenon occurs for those studying psychological disorders. Over the years so many students taking my Abnormal Psychology class come to believe that they have some (or all) of the conditions we are studying in class that I eventually put a warning of sorts in my syllabus alerting them to this effect.

So for those of you concerned about possibly being paranoid, answer the following questions, which are modeled after questions taken from standard interviews used to determine paranoia in patients being seen by a clinician.

- Do you often find hidden insults or threats in the things people say to you?
- Do you find yourself not telling other people a lot about yourself because you fear they will use that information against you?
- When in social situations do you worry that you are being rejected or criticized by others?
- Do you find it hard to open up to people, including people you are close to?
- Do you feel at times other people are deliberately trying to harm you or your interests?
- Do you often feel that you are being observed, watched, or stared at when you are around other people?
- Do you find yourself spending a fair amount of time wondering if you can trust friends or those you work with?
- Do you avoid getting to know other people unless you feel for certain they will like you?
- Do you sometimes feel that a group of individuals is plotting to cause you serious harm or injury?
- Do you often feel that you have to be on guard to prevent others from abusing, exploiting, or harming you?
- Do you often feel that others are against you?
- Do you sometimes feel that your thoughts are being controlled or interfered with by someone else or by some force?
- Do you often feel that people you see talking in public are talking about you?[4]

Most people will probably answer yes to at least one or two of these questions. It is natural to experience some of these feelings at various times. But most paranoid persons will answer yes to most if not all questions and experience these thoughts and feelings frequently. There is no set number of affirmative answers that determines clinical paranoia, however, so if you are concerned then it would be advisable to consult a mental health professional or your primary care physician.

Chapter 3

KINDS OF PARANOIA

N ow, at this point a bit of a confession is in order. Technically, the term *paranoia* has always included under its rubric a number of different types of conditions, all of which have delusions as the organizing theme. Some of these, such as *persecutory delusions* and *delusional jealousy*, concern us in our discussion of paranoia. However, to be thorough the other types of paranoid disorders at least need to be acknowledged, if for no other reason than they are often quite bizarre. Some of these disorders include the delusional belief that one changes into a wolf or wild beast at times (*lycanthropy*), or that one is infested by insects or worms (*parasitosis*), or that the many people around one are in fact only a single individual who changes his disguise (*Fregoli syndrome*), or that a friend or family member has been replaced by an imposter (*Capgras syndrome*).[1]

Often there are elements of paranoia, in the manner that we have been describing it, found in these variants. For example, those with Capgras syndrome typically suspect a conspiracy involving replacing family members with identical doubles. In Fregoli syndrome the person who alters their appearance is often felt to be persecuting the individual who suffers from the syndrome. For reasons that will become clearer later, I will continue to use the term *paranoid* in its more narrow meaning: undue suspiciousness, including jealousy.

DELUSIONS

Previously a thumbnail definition of delusions was presented with a promise to return to the issue later. Now is later, and it behooves us to discuss the nature of delusions in a bit more detail.

When John du Pont was finally extracted from his mansion after killing

Olympic wrestler Dave Schultz he believed he was the Dalai Lama, among other deities.[2]

We all recognize such a belief as delusional, yet what aspects of that belief make it a delusion? Many people in the United States and around the world believe that centuries ago a woman was impregnated by a god, without the benefit of sexual intercourse, only to give birth to a human/deity who walked on water, transformed water into wine, and defied death. Is this any less "delusional" than John Dalai Lama du Pont?

Extremely religious individuals hold steadfastly to beliefs that under the cold light of science and logic are patently absurd. Similarly, the delusionally paranoid individual also holds steadfastly to beliefs that do not pass the reality test. The point being made here is that the ability to adhere to beliefs based on questionable evidence, such as ancient scripture or misinterpreted events, is something that many if not most of us are capable of. The real question is why the beliefs of one concern a deity while the other concern plots against them.

Typically delusions include several elements: First, the belief is held onto with extreme conviction and absolute subjective certainty. Second, the delusion is unassailable by evidence to the contrary or by counterargument. Finally, the content is typically held to be impossible. Few would argue against these being elements of a delusion, yet further clarification is necessary. Excluded are beliefs that, while fantastic or highly implausible, are held by a large number of individuals, as occurs in most organized religions.

So, a more complete and accurate definition of a delusion would include the following elements: the belief is abnormal and not shared by others of a similar cultural or social background. In fact, most people would consider it to be incredible based on the available evidence. The delusion reflects disturbances in judgment to the extent that reality is distorted. Although many delusional individuals have an absolute conviction in their belief, some do not.

Largely unmodifiable by experience and unamenable to alteration by reason, these delusions are held to be self-evidently true, typically with great personal significance to the individual, as opposed to issues involving politics, science, and other objective topics. So, much as some of us might like to, we really don't identify those who do not believe in global warming as being delusional despite the overwhelming evidence to the contrary. Like any issue of personal significance, a particular delusion is thought of and talked about frequently, typically resulting in distress, disruptions in interpersonal relationships, and the ability to work or study. Finally, unlike the obsessional thinking that accompanies obsessive-compulsive disorder (*My hands are covered with germs*), delusional thoughts are not viewed as alien intrusions into ongoing thinking that need to be resisted.[3] In other words, delusional thinking is interweaved into the fabric of our thoughts, so such thinking is not identified as abnormal. Someone with an obsession about turning off the lights knows that such recurring thoughts are abnormal, exaggerated, and forced into her mind. Not so with delusional thoughts.

It is important to note that research has indicated that delusions are not distinctly different from "normal" thought but reflect *degrees* of abnormal thinking. It turns out that most of us walk around with some pretty wild ideas in our heads. Gallup polls reveal that 30 percent of us believe in ghosts, one in five believe in witches, and most of us believe in ESP.[4] Lots of us believe we have perhaps been abducted by aliens. One wacky idea does not a delusion make. Most of us figure out along the way that when our beliefs are contrary to the majority's opinion, we keep it to ourselves. This internal monitoring and sense of restraint in expressing our views is typically lost in most delusional individuals. How preoccupied we are with a belief, how strong the belief is, how well articulated (*systematized*) the belief is are all dimensions that vary in degree. So to label someone as delusional or suffering from delusional disorder, many but not all of the above features need to be found. No one criterion is necessary or sufficient.

Well, in what specific ways then is delusional thinking abnormal? One way is how two unrelated events somehow become related. The fact that the mail carrier only put the mail flag halfway down on your mailbox does not mean that it is a sign there is letter bomb aimed at doing you in.[5] Paranoid individuals have a tendency to quickly arrive at conclusions, especially in circumstances that are ambiguous, and to be overconfident that the conclusions drawn in those circumstances are accurate. Further, past regular occurrences are ignored in favor of current experiences. The fact may be that the mail flag is frequently only halfway down. Those prior multiple events are not brought into the equation when an interpretation of the current half-flag situation is taking place.

One of the more important findings to emerge from research on delusions is that the vast majority, close to 90 percent of people with delusions, act on them in some way.[6] In the case of paranoid delusions, that act is frequently one of violence. This is probably related to another statistic: close to 90 percent of individuals with delusions believe their delusion to be completely true. Unlike normal thoughts about a topic; for example, which team one thinks is going to win a particular game, people with delusions are *absolutely 100 percent convinced about the topic at hand*. One can believe that a team will win, but usually there is an absence of certainty about it.

This chapter focuses on delusions involving paranoia, such as persecutory delusions or delusions of jealousy, which are persistent enough to be labeled as a delusional disorder. However, paranoid delusions in and of themselves are quite common in a variety of medical conditions (see Appendix 2), suggesting no common cause per se. As complex mental phenomena, they reflect an interplay of biological factors, personality traits, emotions, perceptions, and judgments.

PHILIPPE PINEL AND THE TAILOR

The general wisdom regarding delusions is that their sufferers often hold onto them despite strenuous efforts by others to uproot them. Even with modern, powerful antipsychotic medications, many people remain delusional for numbers of years. So it is heartening to revisit one of the major pioneers in psychiatry, Philippe Pinel. He is credited, along with many reformers in the United Kingdom and the United States, with removing the shackles from the insane (as they were known at the time) in France and treating them with dignity and respect. This humane treatment worked wonders in many cases, although the paranoid disorders may have been a bit more of a challenge.

Fortunately Pinel appeared to be up to that challenge as evidenced by the case of a tailor who became convinced that the revolutionaries doubted his patriotism and that certain death awaited him. This was no minor issue, as the revolutionaries in the post-revolution period were as bloody and savage as the regime they had just overthrown. Preoccupied with this fear, he could not be reasoned out of it and was eventually hospitalized in the famous lunatic asylum of Bicêtre. Pinel was able to obtain a small sum of money for the tailor to resume his trade repairing the patients' clothing. This restored the gentleman to better health, although only temporarily.

Undaunted, Pinel enlisted the aid of three physicians who impersonated "delegates from the legislative body" and concocted a sham "trial" for the paranoid tailor. "The principal part was assigned to the eldest and gravest of them [the physicians], whose appearance and manner were most calculated to command attention and respect." Dressed in black robes they listened to the accused plead his case. Gravely and solemnly they deliberated and delivered the verdict: "We have found the said Citizen____ a truly loyal patriot, and, pronouncing his acquittal, we forbid further proceedings against him." The result was that the tailor's paranoia and melancholia lifted, and he became a productive citizen again. Alas, the story has an unhappy ending, as someone apparently told the tailor of the ruse, and his paranoia returned, prompting Pinel to consider him "absolutely incurable."

DELUSIONAL PARANOIA

When people experience delusional paranoia their delusions are often ingenious and elaborate. Unlike what is seen in the paranoid schizophrenia, the delusions are of a plausible nature, so at some level they make sense on the surface, even if most of the evidence does not support the conclusion. For example, it is possible for someone to break into your house to steal your possessions; it happens all the time. It is also possible for helicopters to follow someone around in order to monitor their movements, even if this is unlikely or the belief is based on flimsy or no evidence. In contrast, we would all agree that space aliens removing your brain and replacing it with a computer chip is in the realm of the fantastic. The latter delusion would more typically be found in someone suffering from paranoid schizophrenia.

Many people with delusional paranoia are not manifestly strange or even easy to pick out. In most other aspects of life they are pretty much like you and me . . . well, at least me; I don't know much about you. It is only when you stumble across their delusion that they depart from normality. That said, sometimes their paranoid delusions cause them to engage in behaviors that are odd but grossly consistent with the nature of their delusions.

An individual with this condition accepts her persecutory delusions as patently true. They become central to her life and exert influence in many aspects of her existence. Attempts by others to contradict, argue with, or challenge the paranoid individual's assumptions result in a predictably hostile reaction.

Although paranoid individuals become irritable and querulous when challenged—and sometimes violent—a more common reaction is litigiousness, a common enough variation that some have identified it as a subtype: *litigious paranoia*. This is not an official diagnosis in the United States, but it is in Germany and Scandinavia and thus has important legal implications, since, from a legal standpoint, we treat people who suffer from a mental illness differently. These individuals feel that they have been wronged or that their reputations have been impugned. Fortunately for us, they do not seek vengeance via violence. Unfortunately for court personnel, they seek legal redress.

JOINED AT THE HIP

Randy and Deb, married for thirty years, lived in a remote rural area and were in their fifties when they first came to the attention of mental health professionals. Prior to that they were well known to utility and government officials based on their numerous complaints over the years.

The complaints revolved around the subterranean noises and vibrations that were making their home a living nightmare. They claimed that the problems began after a natural gas company drilled a well nearby. It was after that drilling that the strange sounds began.

Described as ranging from a "grumbling" sound to occasional loud banging noises, the commotion was of sufficient severity to wake them while sleeping. More ominously, they were also being "zapped" by bolts of electricity emanating from electrical outlets. These zaps of electricity were causing both of them to suffer seizures and lose their hair. Were that not bad enough, they had recently begun to experience these zaps when in public buildings, as if the power surges were now following them around, like in a bad sci-fi movie.

Their home had been examined by the water company; the electric company; the Environmental Protection Agency; and sundry other local, state, and federal officials. All found no evidence to support their claims. Receiving no satisfaction from these efforts they took matters into their own hands: they dug a trench around their home and built a concrete underground moat to stop the problem. This failed, and their growing sense of desperation and despair eventually resulted in their hospitalization for treatment of depression, with a secondary diagnosis of folie à deux ("madness of two"; essentially contagious paranoia such that one person develops it, and another "catches" it).

It is interesting to note that the events above occurred in the heart of the Marcellus gas fields in the eastern United States, where hydraulic fracturing (aka *fracking*) was used to free up the deep gas reserves. One of the consequences of this drilling technique has been small earthquakes. Perhaps there is more to this case than initially meets the eye.

WHAT CAUSES IT?

It appears that a variety of neurologic and other conditions can result in delusions. In a sense delusions can be viewed much like a fever: nonspecific in the sense that they can be caused by a variety of maladies. It will be argued later that there is something special about paranoia that makes it more likely to emerge within the context of these various maladies.

If we were to liken the social and logical reasoning skills of a paranoid individual to the software of a computer, everything would look as it should. People with delusional disorder know that it is appropriate to say "hello" when meeting someone else, and what to do if someone extends their hand for a handshake. Further, if you asked them to solve a problem using a logical sequence of steps, they would be able to do so.

Perhaps, then, there is something amiss with the data entered into those software programs. From this standpoint there are a variety of conditions that can cause delusions, ranging from medication side effects to hearing loss to blows to the head, all of which result in scrambled reality due to alterations in normal brain functioning.

Confused, abnormal data are then fed into the brain's software, which is desperately trying to make sense of it all. The emergence of paranoia reflects an evolutionary default mode. If you can't make good sense of what is going on around you, especially in the social realm, you had better be cautious. If fact, you had better be more than cautious. Assume that others are out to get you and act accordingly. That way you survive and live to pass on your genes. This evolutionary default mode serves to structure the interpretation of experiences, the result of which is a paranoid delusion.

PARANOIA AND THE LEGAL SYSTEM

As I alluded to previously, many paranoid individuals take matters into their own hands, the result of which is often violence. We will return to this in a later chapter. However, most individuals with paranoia resort to legal means to seek redress for the perceived wrongs done to them. Given their tendency to harbor grudges against those who cross them, when they do become litigious it is with a true passion. Bordering on a moral crusade, they seek redress for all that they have had to suffer.

Many become obsessed, devoting considerable amounts of time and energy to the fruitless endeavor. Letters of complaint distributed to a wide array of individuals and institutions is a common tactic. Writing from his position as manager of the police complaints division in Australia, Ian Freckelton describes these missives as being "pages long with the writing densely packed, covering almost all of the page and eschewing margins or spaces between paragraphs. There is . . . liberal use of capitalization . . . multiple exclamation marks . . . different colored inks for emphasis . . . and a particular affinity with the star and asterisk key."[7]

Now, the ethics code of the legal profession requires that attorneys do the bidding of their clients, although conscientious lawyers will certainly attempt to talk their clients out of the large numbers of frivolous suits they may file. Invariably, the paranoid client comes to believe that he is not being adequately represented or, worse yet, that the attorney has become part of the conspiracy against him. The attorney is sacked, frequently with bills outstanding, and the paranoid individual takes the reins and defends himself. One can easily anticipate the outcome of this move. Yet there is something admirable about the tenacity of the paranoid person, misdirected as it may be. Frequent judgments against him or dismissals do naught to dim his ardor.

SUSAN POLK

On October 13, 2002, Dr. Felix Polk, a holocaust survivor and psychologist, was murdered in his California home. Suspicion immediately fell on his wife, Susan Polk, and she was arrested and sent to trial.

Initially denying any knowledge of her husband's death, as the evidence mounted she eventually claimed self-defense. The trial of Susan Polk developed into an O. J. Simpson-esque theater. Filled with bizarre elements—her husband was her ex-therapist who had sex with her when she was his client at age sixteen—she defended herself. That fact alone is generally not an indication of good mental health, however as the trial proceeded significant elements of paranoia permeated the picture.

She decided to defend herself after firing four attorneys. The first was let go for refusing to turn information over to her, and she described him as "not a trustworthy source." She fired her unpaid assistant during the trial as well for failing to get a witness to testify for free. While cross-examining her own son, who was testifying against her, she was described as being "delusional" by him. Her open admission in court of paranormal abilities to foresee the future, including the events of 9/11, did little to deflect this accusation. Not surprising, one of her "expert witnesses" was a psychic. More surprising was that the judge allowed this "expert" to testify.

Susan alleged that over the course of her marriage she suffered abuse at the hands of her husband, claiming that his death was the result of self-defense after *he* attacked *her* with a knife. Prior to his father's death her son had called 911 fearing for his life, and the son testified that Susan often made death threats toward his father. Her retort to this: he was setting up his alibi by calling 911, knowing that he would soon kill her. The prosecution (and son) suggested that the only thing she suffered from were perhaps delusions of persecution.

She accused her husband of being a member of the Israeli intelligence agency Mossad, having money in offshore accounts in the Cayman Islands, poisoning their dog, poisoning her, having plans to overthrow the US government, and possessing foreknowledge of the terrorist attack on 9/11.

Her behavior during the trial did little to counter the general picture of someone with questionable mental health. Demanding, disruptive, and argumentative with the judge, prosecuting attorney, and her son/witness, she was in constant danger of losing her right to defend herself. The judge admonished her on numerous occasions regarding baseless accusations of misconduct on the part of the prosecutor and for arguing with the judge over every ruling. A single line of questioning from the prosecution would elicit a string of objections: "hearsay," "testifying from the podium," "speculation," "compound question," "cumulative," all overruled leading her to "object that you [the judge] are aligning yourself with the prosecution." She told the jury that "I am not going to pretend that this DA isn't out to frame me for murder and this judge's rulings are not biased, when I believe they are."

Her numerous "for the record" allegations of misconduct and malicious prosecution on the part of the prosecuting attorney, complaints that "he has a lot of resentment and animosity toward me," along with demands for his removal finally caused the attorney to slam the table with his fist in exasperation and refer to her as "obstreperous and obstructionistic." Later he put an even finer point on it by reading from the psychiatric diagnostic manual, accusing her of having a persecutory delusional disorder.

She accused him of making faces at her in the courtroom, taking "potshots" at her, and goading her. She argued with the judge, the prosecuting attorney, the court deputies, and even the court stenographer. Both the judge and the prosecutor were admonished for their "tricky, nefarious, and devious actions."

She demanded that the overhead projector be moved because it blocked her view of two jurors who were allegedly talking with each other during the trial. Demands for a mistrial based on judicial misconduct were numerous. Among her allegations: the police poured water over her dead husband's head to make the dried blood appear fresh; there was a campaign of judicial misconduct directed toward her with the judge and prosecuting attorney in a conspiracy against her; she was not getting a fair trial in part because she had previously accused another judge of taking a bribe and police misconduct in a case involving her son; a prosecution witness was said to be part of a conspiracy to loot her of the money from her deceased husband's estate; the investigating police had "staged the crime scene," in part, by going into her bedroom, taking one of her shoes, and stamping it around the head of the victim, thereby leaving her shoeprint at the scene; and finally that her life was in danger while being held in jail between court appearances. Allegedly someone had tipped her off that her life was in danger. "I'm going to be accused of some misdeed ["doing something to an officer"] as a pretense for disciplining me," in the form of a beating.

Eventually Polk's antics began to register on the faces of the jurors. According to one court reporter, "Several jurors have started openly showing their feelings for the defendant. Eye-rolling, quick glances to one another, and barely concealed smirks increased during Polk's many confrontations with the witness and the prosecutor."[8]

One of the more interesting aspects of this bizarre case is that two of Susan's three sons testified against her. They claimed that she believed that school officials were out to get her other son, aided by her husband, and that she would look through the newspaper to find secret codes used by the Mossad to communicate with her husband. They referred to her on the stand as "delusional," "crazy," and "cuckoo for Cocoa Puffs."

The third son appeared to be as paranoid as his mother, believing that there was a conspiracy to steal her money, that the prosecutor was "smiling" at him, and that the court lied and manipulated evidence. (As they say, the apple doesn't fall far from the tree.) The bemused jury, after much eye-rolling and a few days of deliberation, rejected her claims and found her guilty of second-degree murder. In the post-deliberations interviews with the jurors the word "delusional" was used in reference to Susan Polk, probably appropriately so.[9]

PARANOID IN EXTREME: PARANOID SCHIZOPHRENIA

Schizophrenia is one of the saddest of all human afflictions. Striking in the prime years of late adolescence and early adulthood, it robs the individual of important human qualities such as the ability to think clearly, experience normal emotions, form attachments to others, and follow a life plan. It stops the development of personality and often torments the individual with critical auditory hallucinations. Equally tormenting, and more to the point of this book, are the individuals' beliefs in nefarious plots against them involving everyone: you, their neighbor, the government, and even aliens from other planets.

BATHROOM SAMPLES

I had been seeing Jarad for about a year, monitoring him for exacerbations of chronic schizophrenia. His insight into delusions had always been fair, but he believes them nonetheless, as all delusional individuals do. He would often terminate sessions prematurely as he answered the call of nature. He eschewed the use of my bathroom as he believed that his urine and feces were somehow captured in the drainage system after being flushed down the toilet and sent to be analyzed. He had cleverly rearranged the plumbing in his residence to preclude this from happening. I didn't inquire as to the nature of those plumbing alterations.

My experience in teaching an undergraduate abnormal psychology course suggests to me that few conditions possess an aura of fear to the degree that *paranoid schizophrenia* does. Certainly a major contributor to this aura is the violence that can result from paranoid delusions, which is not uncommon and is often extreme. This is likely due to the bizarre nature of the delusions underlying the paranoia and subsequent violence.

VOODOO HEX

Baltimore police arrested Douglas Clark and charged him with the bizarre beheading of an elderly gypsy fortune teller, Sister Myra. He had initially sought her assistance after a Jamaican reportedly placed a hex on him, called the "roots." This voodoo curse apparently resulted in the loss of his spine and an inability to die. Unfortunately, he realized that Sister Myra was a demon who had to be killed. Long suffering from the paranoid form of schizophrenia he was committed to a forensic psychiatric institution.[10]

As the name implies, paranoid schizophrenia is characterized by delusions and hallucinations of a persecutory nature. Sufferers believe in the malintent of others, that they are being selectively persecuted. The major difference in the paranoid delusions found in paranoid schizophrenia versus those found in delusional disorder is in how that malintent and persecution is delivered, so to speak, by others. Rather than just spying on them, others read their minds or use sophisticated devices to beam information in. Their plots are more elaborate and bizarre, as, for example, the case of James Tilly Matthews (pp. 27–30) demonstrated.

PARANOIA AND THE *OXFORD ENGLISH DICTIONARY*

The decades-long development of the *Oxford English Dictionary* is a remarkable tale, well told by Simon Winchester in his book *The Professor and the Madman.*[11] Rather than rely on his staff, James Murray, the professor from the book's title and the man in charge of the project, opened up the compiling of the dictionary to learned persons from throughout the world, asking them to submit words. Not just words, but their definitions and earliest-known written use in the English language. Only the most erudite contributed. One of the foremost among them was Dr. William Minor, a Yale-educated physician who served as a surgeon during the Civil War—the "madman" of the title.

Submitting thousands of words and accompanying documentation, an arduous undertaking, he was eventually recognized for his contributions in the acknowledgment section when the dictionary was finally finished. And all of that painstaking work was done while he was an inmate at the Broadmoor Asylum for the Criminally Insane in Crowthorne, Berkshire, England. The events that resulted in Dr. Minor's incarceration make an interesting read.

There was nothing exceptional in Minor's early life that hints at the paranoia to come. It was the events of the bloody American Civil War that began the descent into paranoia, although whether such events *caused* that paranoia is unknown. One event in particular stands out: the branding of a young deserter from Ireland. The young Dr. Minor was required to press the hot iron onto the cheek of the twenty-year-old, leaving him writhing and screaming in pain and forever branded. Reportedly the young man vowed to tell all in Ireland of the doctor's misdeed so that someone would eventually exact revenge.

Soon after Dr. Minor branded the young lad signs of paranoia emerged. He began carrying a pistol, even when not in uniform. He believed that his fellow soldiers were looking at and talking about him. Lethal blows with a good friend almost came to pass, as he believed the man to be plotting against him. He was diagnosed as delusional and sent to what is now St. Elizabeth's, a Washington, DC, psychiatric institution, for eighteen months. Determined to be "incurable" he was given a service-related disability discharge from the military.

He eventually settled in London where he presented himself to the police, complaining that members of the Fenian Brotherhood, a violent Irish nationalist organization, were breaking into his room at night, hiding in the rafters, and trying to poison him. One night George Merrett, a young brewery worker on his way to work, heard someone yelling at him. Turning, he saw Dr. Minor running after him, screaming in anger. Fearing for his life Merrett began running but was quickly killed by a bullet through his neck. He left behind a wife and seven children. The constables arriving on the scene found Minor with the proverbial smoking gun still in hand. He acknowledged shooting the man ("You do not suppose I would be so cowardly as to shoot a *woman*," he allegedly retorted) but claimed he had shot the wrong man. The one he was after was the one who had broken into his room.

While awaiting trial he was observed to waken, accuse the jailors of molesting him in the night, spit repeatedly to remove the poison in his mouth, and then begin the search for those hidden under his bed. At his trial, Minor described how the Irish would enter his room at night to "violate" him. Such nocturnal torments were not new, as his brother reported that at home in Connecticut, Minor believed that persons hiding in the attic would descend each night to torment him and attempt to kill him with poison-coated metal biscuits. On the night of the crime, Minor saw someone next to his bed, grabbed his pistol, and gave chase, firing at the would-be assassin.

Acquitted for reasons of insanity, Minor was transferred to the Broadmoor Asylum, where his paranoia deepened, developed greater elaboration, and became more entrenched over the next thirty years of his confinement.

The rafters above now contained young boys who chloroformed him at night so that indecent acts could be performed. Acting as any paranoid individual would, he "barricades the door of his room with furniture, and connects the handle of the door with the furniture using a piece of string, so that he will awaken if anyone tries to enter the bedroom."[12] He requested to be weighed each morning to document the additional weight he had gained overnight as a result of the poison poured down his gullet through a funnel. Nightly he was "operated on"; had electric current passed through his body; and was placed in a wagon to be taken around the countryside and beyond—Constantinople being the farthest location—where he performed lewd acts with small girls, in public, at the tormentors' insistence.

The tormentors stole his possessions, tampered with his wine, beat him, and spirited him away at night in the newest invention of the age: the airplane. At the same time throughout his confinement at the asylum he remained logical, coherent, intelligent, and intelligible, the classic picture of a paranoid delusional disorder. During this time he busied himself compiling thousands of entries that would make their way into the *Oxford English Dictionary*.

After thirty years, and in failing health, he was discharged to the United States and sent again to St. Elizabeth's Hospital where the paranoid delusions continued. Pygmies, agents of the underworld, lived beneath the floors and would hammer his fingernails while birds pecked at his eyes. He was re-diagnosed with the newly coined term *dementia praecox*, what we today recognize as schizophrenia. Eventually he was discharged to the equivalent of a nursing home in his native Connecticut. There, suffering from what appeared to be dementia, he died at the age of eighty-five.

Unlike those with simple delusional paranoia, people with paranoid schizophrenia have a variety of other problems beyond their paranoid delusions. They typically hear voices and have problems with thinking. For example, they may jump from topic to topic, which would suggest that their thoughts bounce around, unfocused. What they say can be quite bizarre and make little or no sense. And they are often manifestly strange and peculiar in appearance and mannerisms.

PARANOID THROUGH AND THROUGH: PARANOID PERSONALITY DISORDER

Personality is something we all have, all know about but would have a hard time defining if put to task. To save the reader the frustration of having to do so, it is defined here as a complex pattern of psychological characteristics: thinking about things, perceiving events, emotional reactions, and so on. These characteristics are deeply embedded in who we are. They begin with a biologically determined temperament that interacts with the environment from the earliest moments of birth.

Personality reflects habitual ways of psychological functioning that is expressed somewhat automatically in diverse circumstances. It is, to a large extent, like your eye color: you take it wherever you go. Unlike your eye color, it can vary, to some degree, within a range.[13] The expression of these behaviors is not consciously dictated and so the term *unconscious* is often used when explaining where the behaviors come from. Because the features of one's personality are etched onto the very fabric of our being, from the earliest moments of life, they are largely unamenable to change. Any of you who have had a relationship with someone whom you tried to change by altering their personality know the near impossibility of this task.

So now that we have a working definition of (normal) personality, what is a personality disorder? Well, when those psychological characteristics or traits become inflexible and reflect chronic patterns of maladaptive thoughts, emotions, and behaviors to the point that they cause us distress or significant impairments in our interpersonal or occupational functioning, then we have a personality disorder. The facets involving personality disorders reflect *degrees* of normal functioning. We all experience dependency needs, or fear of abandonment, or suspiciousness to some degree. When those needs and fears and suspicions become extreme and begin to significantly interfere with our lives, then we call them a personality disorder (dependent personality disorder, borderline personality disorder, and paranoid personality disorder, respectfully).

Given that paranoid personality disorder reflects a dimension of personality that exists on a continuum, where we choose the dividing line between normal and disordered is somewhat arbitrary, and there is a great deal of gray area between the two. In between the poles of naïveté and paranoia is found the cautious (normal) individual who listens carefully to others and looks for subtle cues and hidden meanings. Such cues and meanings are not taken out of context or blown out of proportion. The so-called normal person places great value on trust and loyalty. When criticized, they consider what is said, and their response is measured. We see elements of these responses in paranoid personality disorder; however, whereas in normal individuals they are seen to a more reasonable, adaptive degree, in the paranoid personality disordered individual, they are more extreme and maladaptive.

We have all felt degrees of suspiciousness, sometimes at a pretty high level. At what point do I, as a clinician, determine if the amount of suspiciousness is sufficient to warrant a diagnosis of paranoid personality disorder? Well, when the suspiciousness and accompanying behaviors are persistent, pervasive, and cause disruptions, predicaments, and impairments in my patient's ability to get along effectively with others, study at school, or do his job. Or when they cause him to feel sad, anxious, and other negative emotions.

These personality disorders are typically revealed in interpersonal situations or when under stress. The "inflexibility" part of the definition indicates that such individuals don't have alternative ways of behaving or coping and are, therefore, not resilient under stress. Like it or not, if you have a paranoid personality disorder, or any other personality disorder for that matter, the behaviors and characteristics will manifest themselves despite your efforts to suppress them.

FEATURES OF PARANOID PERSONALITY DISORDER

People with paranoid personality disorder are characterized by their significant levels of unwarranted suspiciousness and distrust. In this regard, they have many of the classic features of generic paranoia described previously (see chapter 2). What distinguishes paranoid personality disorder from other paranoid disorders is that the person's paranoia rarely crosses the line into delusional levels. They are chronically mistrustful individuals. What strikes you most when meeting them is their unpleasant, frequently hostile, angry, suspicious nature, which, though it can vary to degrees, is present virtually all the time. And it is not uncommon. Keeping in mind the caveats noted previously (see pp. 25–27) about the difficulty of researching paranoid disorders, the most recent study that looked at a very large sample of noninstitutionalized Americans, the rate of paranoid personality disorder was found to be 4.4 percent of the population.[14]

WHAT DID YOU SAY AND WHO IS THAT MAN OVER THERE?

It has been noted clinically for many years that older paranoid individuals frequently suffer from hearing and/or visual deficits. Such deficits may not *cause* paranoia, but they are significant risk factors for the development of paranoia for those at risk.[15] Hearing loss appears to be the more important of the two based on the scientific literature. The magnitude of the situation is underscored by statistics that say that up to 60 percent of elderly persons living in their home or in a retirement facility have significant hearing defects. The number is closer to 80 percent for those in nursing homes.[16]

Interestingly, the type of hearing loss seems to be important. Specifically, *conductive* hearing loss—failure of sounds to be conducted through the ear canal, ear drum, and bones of the middle ear—is more associated with paranoia than is *sensorineural* hearing loss, which involves damage to the nerve fibers to the brain from the inner ear. This is particularly important, as conductive hearing loss can be caused by something as simple as impacted ear wax and is, in general, more easily corrected. There is even evidence that such correction, for example, a hearing aid, can reduce paranoia. Importantly, the vast majority (70 percent) of older individuals with hearing impairments don't realize they are impaired.[17]

Part of the evidence linking hearing loss and paranoia comes from some truly clever psychological experiments. Dr. Philip Zimbardo, of Stanford University, who would go on to become president of the American Psychological Association, hypnotized research (undergraduate) subjects and gave them a posthypnotic suggestion that they could not hear well. He did the same to a different group of subjects but told them that the source of their hearing problem was the posthypnotic suggestion.[18]

The setup of the first group, in a sense, resembles what actually happens to individuals as they age and lose their hearing—they don't realize they are hearing less well. The second group, on the other hand, were aware that they were having problems hearing. The first group became more irritable, hostile, and agitated compared to the second group. When given the opportunity to collaborate with others on a task, almost all declined to do so in comparison to the second group, of which almost all did. Thus, members of the first group developed relatively quickly many of the characteristic features seen in paranoia. A similar study using cotton balls coated with petroleum jelly to reduce hearing found similar results.

Research into the hearing impaired and deaf individuals reveals that they undergo a variety of changes. They become bitter; brood; are suspicious of people, even friends; and develop anger. They perceive those without hearing deficits to be impatient with them. More to the point, they often believe they are regarded as being inferior and are treated accordingly. They are patronized, or they are the treated with hostility and taken advantage of. Such are the raw materials for the development of paranoia. Many who refuse to invest in or wear hearing aids do so in order not to draw attention to their defect.[19]

So what is it about sensory deficits that actually contributes to paranoia? The first step appears to be the failure of the individual to perceive that they are having problems. Rather than thinking "Gee, I can't really hear what he is saying, it must be that I am losing my hearing," the future paranoid person thinks "Gee, I can't really hear what he is saying, therefore, he must be whispering so I can't hear him." So the blame for not being able to hear goes from the listener to the speaker, suggesting that the speaker is whispering because he doesn't want to be heard. Confirmation of that suspicion is provided by their denial that they are whispering. The paranoid individual can see their lips moving and this, coupled with the fact that they can't hear what they are saying, is the "evidence" that clearly points to proof that the person is lying. Needless to say, we all mistrust people who lie. The other features of paranoia, such as irritability, hostility, and so on then begin to emerge. As a result, the whisperer tends to avoid the paranoid individual, who then enters into social isolation.

Social isolation plays a key role in all of this. We all use our contact with others as a corrective mechanism. Just think about your eating habits in public versus when you are alone. How many of you are plate lickers? Certainly, or at least hopefully, none of you do this in public. Well, the paranoid person becomes isolated based on the process detailed above and thus lacks the corrective feedback that being with others provides. Others help disavow us of our more peculiar and erroneous beliefs. Without the feedback from others, such beliefs can flourish, nurtured by compelling evidence, at least to the paranoid individual, eventually developing into full-blown paranoia. Over time, as with all delusions, the ability of contrary information to alter perceptions diminishes.

Such impairments could result in reduced contact with others, failure to completely understand people when contact is made, misinterpretations, and a detachment from reality. So when light dims and shadows rule, the tall floor plant in the corner takes on the form of a person. Because that "person" is unknown to the individual and was not let in by them, a logical conclusion is that they are up to no good. The plant-turned-person then becomes a thief out to steal their possessions. From within this matrix paranoia emerges.

DANA'S GRANDMOTHER

My friend Dana expressed concern about her grandmother. "I think she is losing it. She keeps complaining that the neighbors are always calling out to Beverly at all times of the day and night." Dana became alarmed when she saw her grandmother for the first time in a while; she was disheveled, bags under her eyes from lack of sleep. She did indeed look like she was "losing it." She didn't know what her neighbors were up to, but she suspected that they and Beverly were up to no good. Ever the sympathetic granddaughter, Dana reassured her grandmother that it was probably nothing and not to worry.

One night while standing vigil, Dana heard her grandmother complain: "They're at it again . . . again with Beverly." Surprisingly, Dana heard something as well and began to think that maybe her grandmother was not as crazy as she first imagined. A faint sound of someone talking could indeed be heard. Zigzagging across the room attempting to locate the origin of the sound, Dana zeroed in on her grandmother, which is where the sound appeared to emanate from. Cautiously moving closer to her grandmother so as to not alarm the poor woman, Dana began to discern the message more distinctly and located the origin of the sound. There, hanging around her grandmother's neck, was a signaling system that would alert a security company should she fall and be unable to get up. Coming from the small device was the occasional warning: "Battery . . . battery." One small battery later, and Beverly and her coconspirators disappeared.

PRISON AND PARANOIA

Proof that reductions in sensory input and social contact are linked with the development of paranoia is provided by our penal system, and in particular the so-called *supermax units*. These units were developed ostensibly to ensure the safety of staff and other prisoners by segregating those deemed most dangerous.[20]

Prisoners in supermax confinement can spend twenty-two to twenty-four hours per day in a sixty- to eighty-square-foot cell. Many units do not have a window, and if they do, the window does not afford a view of the outside. There is virtually no sensory input beyond that provided from within the cell itself. Dimly lit, the cells contain little in the way of amenities unless you consider a toilet, a sink, and a concrete sleeping slab amenities. There is little in the way of interaction with others, and length of stay is often measured in years.

One of the most common outcomes among prisoners in such facilities is the development of paranoia.[21] At some level this is surprising. In the general-population prison setting, inmates might have good reason to fear that someone is out to get them. But in supermax solitary confinement there is no one to plot against them because they are alone. However, at another level this outcome is quite predictable. Experiments in sensory deprivation, often measured in hours not years, revealed significant psychological changes, including disorientation, confusion, and distress. Further, it has been known since at least the late nineteenth century that solitary confinement results in serious psychological disturbances, such as depression, anxiety, and even psychosis. And, of course, paranoia.[22]

Chapter 4

WHERE ELSE DO WE FIND PARANOIA?

For paranoid individuals, paranoia is saliently the predominant psychological problem and remains so no matter what else might change. The conditions covered in the previous chapter—paranoid schizophrenia, delusional disorder, paranoid personality disorder—are examples. But the fact is that paranoia emerges in a variety of conditions, two of which deserve specific mention based on how prevalent they are: delirium and dementia.

The paranoia found in conditions such as depression or posttraumatic stress disorder is heavily "flavored" by the condition it is associated with. Depressed individuals may feel that people are looking at them and making fun of them. This kind of treatment is deserved because they believe they are bad or inadequate human beings. The individual with posttraumatic stress disorder is, not surprisingly, overly suspicious of people or situations that reminds him of the traumatic event that triggered his disorder. And so on.

"THE TREATMENT STAFF IS OUT TO GET ME"

By the time Julia was finally hospitalized for anorexia nervosa with prominent bulimic tendencies she was a mere wisp of her former self. At five feet six, her eighty-eight-pound frame showed naught but bones. The inpatient treatment center where she was eventually admitted was like most eating disorder units. It was locked, preventing patients from leaving at will. Newly admitted patients were carefully monitored—especially in the bathroom. Every bite of food is observed.

As with most people suffering from anorexia nervosa, Julia's greatest fear was gaining weight. Unfortunately this was at odds with treatment goals of increasing weight as rapidly as possible before the insurance company cut short the stay. Required to eat a bit more than she was accustomed—three thousand calories versus four hundred calories—Julia came to believe that the staff was secretly putting something in her food. "Poison?" I asked. "Worse than that. They're putting extra calories in my food; not that of others, only mine." No joke was intended, as she truly believed her food was being "spiked" with extra calories.

BRAIN STORM

Delirium is one of the most common mental conditions, especially in older individuals, and is commonly referred to as *acute confusional state*, a term that captures quite nicely exactly what delirium is. Approximately 10 to 15 percent of all patients, regardless of age, admitted to the hospital suffer from delirium. Some studies have found as many as 35 to 55 percent of all hospital patients over the age of sixty-five develop delirium, although more conservative estimates put the number at around 20 to 30 percent.[1]

This condition comes on suddenly and causes considerable confusion in the afflicted person. I believe that delirium is best described as a "brain storm" in the sense that a storm often develops quickly, moves through an area rapidly, and while present all hell breaks loose: wind, rain, lightning, and hail. Just as quickly the storm passes, the sun comes out, and all is well on the other side. Similarly, delirium typically develops rapidly. While the condition is present, the person suffering from it is extremely confused and impaired. She may fail to recognize familiar people, think she is somewhere else, and experience visual hallucinations and delusions. Just as storms tend to blow over quickly, so does delirium, usually within hours or days. However, if the underlying cause is not identified and corrected, it can persist.

People with delirium can awaken at night and have difficulty distinguishing a nightmare from reality. Thus, they may react to a nightmare while awake as if it were real. Indeed, for most of us dreams feel very real, but most of us are able to distinguish them from reality upon awakening. The boundaries between reality and this dream state are blurred in delirium. The confusion is only worsened when one awakens in a strange bed, like in a hospital.

During the early development of delirium the individual may only experience difficulty concentrating, a tendency to wander off topic when talking, and confusion about the relationship between events—events that occurred a year ago feel like they happened earlier this morning.

The condition can fluctuate markedly. At times the person may be coherent, and conversation will reveal little if any disturbance, although typically things get worse at night. As the delirium progresses speech becomes more disturbed to the point of incoherence. I saw an elderly woman who perceived me to be a long-time friend. Outside the hospital window was the family farm and people in cars arriving to see her. (In actuality, only the other side of the hospital building could be seen from the window, and I had never met the woman before.) Bewildered and disoriented as to where they are, few delirium sufferers know they are in a hospital. Because the underlying cause is medical, these individuals are most often hospitalized not only to provide treatment but to protect them from themselves. Many of these individuals, who are elderly, wait for their parents, long since dead, to arrive. Where they believe they exist in time can only be guessed at and is likely to change even if you were to figure it out. The elaborate tales of where they are and why they are there represent their brain's best attempt to make sense of a confusing situation. Despite being surrounded by the obvious trappings of a hospital room they imagine they are in their home or waiting for the train to arrive so they can visit their brother, just like they did last night.

If you have ever suffered from a high fever that left you confused and made it difficult for you to think or express yourself articulately, then you have experienced a mild form of delirium. Like looking through a thick fog, you see the world as cloudy and shapes are not clearly identifiable. You do the best you can to identify what is out there, but you may make many gross mistakes. Rather than struggle with the task, it is easier, and preferable, to lapse into sleep.

Delirium sufferers are highly distractible; they have difficulty focusing their attention. The task is made even more difficult when one is competing for their attention with a hallucination. For whatever reason small furry animals are popular hallucinated objects. Running across the bed or lurking in the corners are rats, dogs, cats, birds, and other beasties. Insects are also common. Justin Kaplan, a Pulitzer Prize–winning author of books on Walt Whitman and Mark

Twain saw "thousands of tiny little creatures, some on horseback, waving arms, carrying weapons" all attempting to turn people into zombies. He was in a police helicopter tracking fugitives and did not recognize—and threatened to kill—his wife.[2]

Some patients experience lethargy and have difficulty maintaining alertness. They can be seen muttering to themselves even while seemingly unconscious. Others are in an excitable state of hyperactive confusion that not infrequently results in violent behavior. Rarely is the violence severe; rather, the patient will thrash about or swing wildly at others, including those who aren't there, that is, they will have visual hallucinations.

Paranoia is a common feature in all these facets of delirium. The patient is confused and not sure of where she is or who she is with. Attempts to soothe the patient with reassuring words don't always work, in part because the person is not processing language adequately while delirious. Because delirium is often caused by some sort of medical condition, patients are typically hooked up to IVs, which they then frequently rip out. Agitated, yelling at their tormentors, they often make no sense at all. At that point they represent a danger to themselves and others, and tranquilizers are often administered to calm the individual.

PARANOIA WITHIN DELIRIUM

The paranoia found within the context of delirium is poorly formed and not very elaborate. Simple themes of people out to poison, rob, or kill the sufferer are common. When a family member of mine became delirious he asked me repeatedly about the smoke detectors on the ceiling: what are they there for and who put them there? He was clearly scared by the detector and believed he was being watched.

The paranoia can change and is rarely long lasting. Like all delusional experiences in delirium, it tends to change in response to perceived or real changes in the environment. Because delirium itself changes, being worse at times than at others, so does paranoia, which can disappear then reemerge with similar or new themes. The situation is made worse by the failure to recognize familiars.

A delirious mother sees her adult daughter rooting through her purse in search of a hairbrush and does not recognize her. She therefore identifies her as a thief. Interestingly, although children develop delirium, often as a result of a high fever, they don't experience paranoia.

There are two non-exclusionary explanations for paranoia in patients with delirium. The first is that critical brain regions where paranoia is thought to "live" are directly affected by whatever caused the delirium in the first place, turning it on like a light switch. The second is that the paranoia is derivative of the overall mental state. In other words, as the person's ability to reason, perceive, and otherwise make sense of the world diminishes, the brain engages a primitive circuit that essentially decides "If I can't make sense of this situation it is best to be suspicious and not trust anyone, as they might pose a danger." If there was no real danger then no harm has occurred, with the exception of a bruised ego on the part of those accused. If there was a real danger, then the delirious person was in a position to protect himself by not trusting his fate to someone, thereby increasing his chances for survival.

BEER MAN

On my way to the track where I run routinely is a small one-story house occupied by a stooped elderly man. Unlike most people in this friendly small community he never greeted me as I walked by him on the way to the track or ran by him on the way back. Eventually, enough comments regarding the weather on my way past him softened his crustacean-like demeanor. He came to recognize me as a denizen of the neighborhood and would nod his acknowledgment of my existence.

One day as I walked by he was bent over the recycling bin with an obvious look of displeasure on his face. "Damn college students. They put their beer bottles in my bin to make it look like I'm a drunk." Indeed, it is common in this university town for college students majoring in alcohol to put their spent beer bottles and cans in the recycling bins of the locals. I have always silently thanked the students for doing so, since it beats the alternative form of disposal: broken bottles in my driveway. Not yet realizing the depth of his paranoia, I sought to reassure him that foreign beer bottles in one's recycling bin were not unusual and that "it happens to me all the time." He eyed me cautiously stating, "They also remove my empty cans out of the bin. How do you explain that?" Not wishing to reveal the contents of this book, then in preparation, I replied: "Beats me," and gave him a sympathetic shrug.

THE PLAGUE OF THE MODERN ERA: DEMENTIA

When former president Ronald Reagan and actor Charlton Heston announced to the world that they were suffering from Alzheimer's, they put a public face on a terrible affliction. For many people Alzheimer's is synonymous with *dementia*. In fact, dementia is a category, like cancer is a category. Although the underlying problem might be the same in all cancers—unregulated growth of new cells— there are considerable differences between pancreatic cancer and prostatic cancer, for example. Similarly, all twenty or more different dementias involve the premature or accelerated loss of cognitive abilities. But each is different in a variety of ways, and some are treatable.[3]

I will focus here on Alzheimer's, as it is the most common form of dementia.

AUGUSTE D.

The case of Auguste D. is remarkable, as it is the first written case description of the disorder we now call Alzheimer's. As it happens, the case was initially described by a physician named Alois Alzheimer.

Auguste was a fifty-one-year-old woman who lived in Frankfurt, Germany, in 1901. Following her death, Alzheimer wrote the famous case history that introduced Alzheimer's disease to the world. At the onset of her illness she came to believe that her husband was having sexual relations with a neighbor. Then she began hiding things. Her paranoia and other behaviors escalated to the point that her physician diagnosed her as suffering from "persecution mania," among other things, and she was admitted to the Municipal Asylum for the insane and epileptic in Frankfurt am Main.[4]

Upon admission she feared the attending physician was out to harm her and refused the routine physical examination. She believed staff members were going to stab, harm, or violate her in some way. In the case notes written by Alzheimer, which were found remarkably preserved in 1996 despite the destruction of the original institution during World War II, it is revealed that paranoia ranked high among the many symptoms Auguste D. suffered from. Alzheimer noted "as one of her first disease symptoms a strong feeling of jealousy towards her husband. . . . Sometimes she felt that someone wanted to kill her and began to scream loudly." After five short years she died from the disorder, and the subsequent examination of her brain revealed the characteristic changes in the cells that we now identify as Alzheimer's.

CHARACTERISTICS OF ALZHEIMER'S

Most people recognize that memory loss is the primary feature of Alzheimer's. Even in the early stages of the disorder memory is quite impaired and becomes more so as the disorder progresses. What is being lost is the brain's ability to store information in memory. If that were not bad enough, memories from the past start to disappear, beginning with the most recent ones, then march back in time. Along the way memories of having children, of marrying, of working, and all else disappear. Individuals in their nineties cry and fret that their mothers are waiting for them and will be worried if they don't go home. Very old memories are preserved. I saw a woman who was able to remember the name of each horse on the horse-and-buggy team from when she was a child in the latter part of the nineteenth century. She had no recall of having any children.

At the same time there are impairments in virtually all other aspects of cognitive functioning, such as language and the ability to recognize people and the things around them. Because the brain is essentially rotting away, eventually all aspects of truly human behavior are lost. Significant alterations of basic personality also occur.

DAMN COLLEGE STUDENTS

Bill was not unusual in that he was one of an army of uncounted individuals with Alzheimer's who continue to function independently in their own home. Long since widowed, his presentation to the emergency room was the result of intervention by Adult Protective Services. In the ER he complained about the five college students who were following him around and telling him what to do. They peered in his window at night and were stealing the heating oil in the tank that he had long ago forgotten to have filled. As a result, he had essentially barricaded himself in his home, using the kitchen stove to heat his small house. Failing to bathe for what smelled like months, his aroma nauseated all staff that ventured within one hundred feet of him. As is typical for Alzheimer's, the five tormentors were quickly forgotten when a pleasantly confused state descended upon him as the result of his change in location.

Hiding their money from ne'er-do-well family out to steal from them results, predictably, in forgetting that they hid the money in the first place. This reinforces the thought that family is stealing from them because money is missing.

PARANOIA WITHIN ALZHEIMER'S

About 35 to 50 percent of patients with dementia will develop paranoia.[5] Given that between four to six million people currently suffer from dementia, and that number will likely double within the next decade or so, there are going to be a lot of demented paranoid individuals out there for families, medical personnel, and nursing home staff to deal with.

When paranoia develops in Alzheimer's patients, it generally occurs in the later stages of the disorder and is probably related to the prominent cognitive impairments. These problems affect the individual's ability to make sense of incoming information and to remember it later. Themes typically involve people stealing their money (usually family), pathological jealousy, and being poisoned. Related themes involve the presence of impostors masquerading as their spouse or loved one.

EVEN PARANOIDS HAVE ENEMIES

Famously attributed to former secretary of state Henry Kissinger, the above words were actually said to him by former Israeli prime minister Golda Meir in 1973 after he accused her of being paranoid in not granting concessions to the Arabs. It illustrates the fact that everything suspicious is not necessarily paranoia. Take the case described by Dr. Ronald Hamby involving an elderly woman, Liz, and her exasperated young neighbors (the Browns), who nightly are called upon by Liz to help apprehend the ne'er-do-well trying to break into her house. A very wealthy widow, Liz owns a house that is a thief's dream: full of antiques and other valuables.

On initial examination, Dr. Hamby noted the accompanying diagnosis of Alzheimer's and, consistent with that diagnosis, a low score on a routine mental status examination given by a resident. (This exam is a crude measure of functioning and is somewhat akin to placing your hand on someone's forehead to determine if they have a fever: it is not precise, cannot tell you the extent/degree of impairment, and can be affected by a wide variety of factors that have nothing to do with an illness.) His interview with the afflicted women confirmed the neighbors' report. She indicated the would-be thief comes two to three times a night and attempts entrance through the windows. Calls to the police result in no apprehension as the thief is long since gone by the time of their arrival. With no other options, she calls her well-intentioned but out-of-patience neighbors.

Dr. Hamdy did what most primary care physicians would do in a similar set of circumstances, he ordered a consultation with a psychiatrist and ran a few lab tests. Troubled by the case one sleepless night Hamdy drove to Liz's house. Parking his car he saw the lights turn on at the beleaguered neighbors' house, saw them emerge from their nearby home and walk the short distance to Liz's house. His logical conclusion: she was once again having a paranoid delusion and had called her neighbors. Closer observation revealed the neighbors behaving in peculiar manner. Instead of looking for the "thief" or going into Liz's house to comfort her, they were observed banging on and throwing stones at her windows.

A bit of detective work by this sharp physician revealed that in gratitude for past kindnesses, Liz had promised the Browns her home after her death or should she be institutionalized. Not willing to wait for either to occur naturally, the Browns connived to accelerate the process of institutionalization of this "paranoid" demented woman.[6]

GETTING OLD

To be clear, dementia is a pathological condition reflecting significant changes in the brain. But what of normal aging that doesn't involve dementia? The evidence suggests that as much as 14 percent of otherwise normal older individuals are highly suspicious, with about 7 percent having frank paranoia and 5 percent with paranoid delusions.[7] Given the aging of our population, this reflects a potentially large number of individuals.

Chapter 5

WHERE DOES PARANOIA COME FROM?

There are two levels of explanation for paranoia. Proximal explanations are very specific events and factors that result in paranoia. Delirium and dementia are but two examples of a proximal explanation and a few more, such as use of amphetamines and cocaine, will be discussed shortly. There are a bewildering number of things that can proximally result in paranoia, some of which I've listed in Appendix 2.

Yet these proximal causes only serve to trigger a circuit in the brain, here-after referred to as the *suspiciousness system* (This is the *ultimate* explanation). So proximal causes are those that we can readily identify, such as dementia, but these proximal causes really just hit the button of the ultimate cause. This sus-piciousness system developed in response to situations faced by our ancestors and, under normal circumstances, exists in a kind of dynamic balance, leaving us feeling safe and trusting. Circumstances that alter that dynamic balance, such as seeing your partner in an animated discussion with someone of the opposite sex or being an immigrant, cause changes that result in increased suspiciousness/ paranoia.

Some people, by virtue of brain chemistry or neural defect, are out of balance to begin with. Others condition their suspiciousness system, via training by our family, to view the world in a particular way, leaving them equally off-balance. Finally, major life events, including traumatic events, can also tip the balance. It will be proposed that this suspiciousness system is the result of evo-lutionary processes.

ORIGINS OF SUSPICIOUSNESS

Many human behaviors and characteristics were shaped and developed over the thousands of generations that humans have existed. Since the goal of all life, from an evolutionary perspective, is to survive and reproduce, the behaviors and characteristics we humans have now are the result of those evolutionary processes. Those ancestors of ours who possessed certain characteristics or traits were better able to survive and reproduce, thereby passing on their genes, which included those characteristics. It will be argued here that like many human characteristics, both normal and abnormal, the origins of suspiciousness—paranoia's normal sister—are to be found in the distant past of human evolution.

Perhaps an example will help to illustrate this idea. Most people have a natural fear of snakes. For some of us this fear is quite severe, and we call that a *phobia*—a pathological condition. For the rest of us, we tend to avoid snakes when we see them. Imagine that two of our *Homo sapiens* ancestors, Wheege and Thorp, are walking along doing whatever early *Homo sapiens* did a million or so years ago. Suddenly they come across a brightly colored coiled snake. Wheege is intrigued by the creature and is naturally drawn to the bright colors. Thorp is terrified and just wet his *Homo sapiens* pants . . . or skins. Which one do you think is going to survive the encounter with that snake? Well, we are all descendants of Thorp, since he was the one who did *not* get close to the snake, get bitten, and die. He was able to survive and reproduce little Thorps, all of whom were, generally speaking, fearful of snakes. Through countless generations this characteristic of being afraid of snakes—as well as heights, the dark, and many other things—helped our ancestors survive and reproduce. Funny, isn't it? Seems we are the collective descendants of a bunch of cowards!

It will be argued that paranoia emerged in much the same way as snake phobias, although the route was a little less straightforward. Before starting that explanation, however, a bit of background about our evolution is in order.

GOVERNMENTAL DENTAL WORK

It began as a vague idea, growing slowly. Tony was convinced that the government was increasing its intrusion into the lives of Americans, his in particular. Despite being in his sixties, Tony followed developments in computers and technology, although he didn't trust computers enough to own one personally.

Slowly he began to realize that the government was capable of placing computer chips in human bodies. If veterinarians were able to implant chips beneath the hides of dogs and cats to be used to identify them should they run away, then certainly the all-powerful US government could do the same. Rather than under the skin, however, the government had learned how to implant computerized listening devices in teeth; more specifically—in his teeth. Consultation with his dentist confirmed his suspicions that his dentist was also involved. His dentist's reassurances fell on truly deaf ears. Taking matters, and a pair of pliers, into his own hands, Tony systematically pulled and yanked until one by one the government-issue computer-listening teeth were extracted.

WHO WE ARE

About six million years ago humans diverged from monkeys and continued to develop a variety of features on the way to who we are now. Around 1.2 million years ago the brains of our ancestors began a period of significant expansion during the archaeological epoch known as the *Pleistocene* period. Then, roughly 100,000 to 200,000 years ago, our modern form emerged, which has been labeled *Homo sapiens sapiens*. Although this book is not about human evolution, that topic is important to the study of paranoia. We will be looking especially at life during the Pleistocene period, which lasted up until about ten thousand years ago when agriculture arrived on the scene. During that period we were hunter-gatherers, and it was that lifestyle that helped develop many of the characteristics we all possess today.[1]

LIFE AS A HUNTER-GATHERER

Think for a minute about what life was like as a hunter-gatherer. The term defines itself, and the image that comes to mind is of someone who went around gathering fruit, nuts, berries, roots, and occasionally killing something. Anthropologic studies of hunter-gatherers suggest that food appeared to be very abundant and that many of the foods eaten during that era were drought-resistant, which would have guaranteed adequate supplies no matter what the climate.[2]

The average daily caloric intake of these hunter-gatherers was about two thousand calories, which is what we today would consider a healthy amount of food. They had plenty of protein and ate a wide variety of foods, all without benefit of a food pyramid for guidance. What is even more remarkable is that it only took on average twelve to nineteen hours a week to obtain that food! At most our ancestors spent about thirty-two hours collecting food a week, which contrasts with the typical modern American, who works on average forty-six hours per week. A whopping 39 percent of us work more than fifty hours a week.[3]

So there you are, a dirty little hunter-gatherer. You are well fed, adequately proteinized, working between fifteen and thirty hours a week (we must have been picking a *lot* of bugs off each other and having a *lot* of sex, given all the free time on our hands . . . and no cell phones to text with). So you decide to give up this lifestyle and switch to agriculture to improve your health and reduce your workweek even further. The outcome of this switch: more health problems, a reduction in lifespan, poorer nutrition, longer hours of work, and more worry. What were you thinking?

OUR HUNTER-GATHERER GROUP

Ours is a social species in which individual survival depends on being part of a group. This is probably the result of several factors, the most compelling being mutual protection; a kind of "I've got your back covered" deal.[4] Mutual protection was vital since there were a variety of predators that saw us as lunch. As professor of archaeology Steven Mithen eloquently notes about the situation facing early humans, "At just under 1.5 m [5 feet] tall and 50 kg [110 lb] in weight at most, and with no more than a few lumps of stone to throw, they were not particularly well equipped for hand-to-hyena combat."[5] And it was not only animal predators they needed to worry about but also other (human) groups. Also, food was more easily found in large quantities by more individuals searching for it, then to be shared among all.

During the Pleistocene epoch, a "group" consisted of between eighteen and one hundred individuals; most scholars believe that groups of twenty to fifty were the norm.[6] The actual size of the group might change on a day-to-day basis, as some come and go. Having few possessions, men and women would settle in an area, hunt and gather in the region until their source of firewood was exhausted, then pick up and move elsewhere, perhaps a half dozen times each year.

Stop and think about the implications of this situation from a psychological standpoint. For thousands of generations humans lived in small groups in which they knew intimately every other member: what they had done, their personality characteristics, and so on. Privacy was neither valued nor sought. With no possessions there were no conflicts over property. Fail to get along with the rest of the group, and you risked being voted off the island, so to speak.

Several interrelated events emerged out of this situation that provided the necessary ingredients for the development of suspiciousness. First was language, which developed anywhere from fifty thousand to two million years ago.[7] According to anthropologist Leslie Aiello and psychologist Robin Dunbar, the size of the neocortex of the brain—the top wrinkly layer that is the smart part of the brain—is directly correlated to the size of a species' social group and how much time is spent on grooming, an important social behavior.[8] As our brains grew over the course of evolution, so did the size of our group, to the point that we could not effectively socialize with everyone by just picking bugs out of each other's hair. Aiello and Dunbar argue that language emerged initially to supplement, then eventually replace, grooming as a more efficient mechanism for socialization and bonding.

The bigger the groups became, the more resources were needed to feed everyone in the group. Competition for these resources would naturally arise between groups, and the biggest group was likely to win. Just as important as group size was the ability to understand one's adversary. Just as today's professional athletes often speak of "getting inside the head" of their opponent, so, too, did our Pleistocene ancestors enjoy a competitive advantage if they understood the thinking or intentions of their competitors. What emerged was *social cognition*, the human ability to perceive the intentions of others.

Two facets of social cognition are important to this discussion. The first is social knowledge about others, such as whom we can trust. The second is the ability to understand our own mind and use that as the basis for understanding the minds—the thoughts, feelings, intentions, and so on—of others. This is called *theory of mind*. With those we trust this is somewhat easy. Part of what we don't need to consider about the mental state of those we trust is whether they are out to harm us. In contrast, that is exactly part, a large part, of what we need to consider about non-friends.

What we get when we understand the mental state of others is predictability of their behavior. All other things being equal, those who were best able to predict the actions of others enjoyed an adaptive—survival and reproductive—success over those who were clueless in that regard. However, this is the classic dual-edged sword. As Lawrence Weiskrantz, psychologist and professor emeritus at Oxford University, noted, "The fact that we have the capacity to think about what others might be thinking produces a condition that is probably species-specific to humans: namely, paranoia."[9]

The bigger our brains became, the bigger our groups, and the more complicated life became. As Mithen points out, "As a general rule the more people that one chooses to live with, the more complex life becomes: there is a wider choice of possible partners with whom to share food or sex, and each of those partners will have a greater number and more diverse relationships with other members of that group. It is a considerable challenge to keep track of who is friends with whom, who are enemies, and who bear grudges or desires, and then try to decide with whom to make friends without upsetting your other friends."[10] One of the outcomes, it seems, of all of this social confusion is a big brain. There is a solid relationship between how social a species is and how big its brain is. Mithen says further, "The more complex the social scene, the more devious you are going to need to be to win more friends without winning more enemies."[11] Indeed, research has indicated a relationship between the size/complexity of the brain and the use of deception in social strategies.

The other ingredients that will contribute to the development of suspiciousness have, to some degree, been there all along: fear of being the victim of an attack, being taken advantage of, being cuckolded, and so on. But now arises the ability to intuit, accurately or not, the motives of others, which gives rise to the feelings of trust and suspiciousness.

In a social environment where reciprocal relationships were important, the ability to detect cheaters— *I do for you, but you don't do for me*—would be important. Those who developed more refined aspects of trust/suspiciousness had an adaptive advantage as they more readily were able to identify friends (those who could be trusted) who would cover your back versus those not to be trusted, who were more interested in putting a flint hand ax *in* your back. It is this evolved *adaptation*, a term to be defined below, that we carry around with us today. It is hardwired, or built into to the brain *to an extent*. That extent is the degree to which it is calibrated during the course of our lives. A child born to an inattentive, uncaring mother will not strengthen the trust side of that adaptation. Similarly, a child with chronically paranoid parents or joining a neo-Nazi group will strengthen the suspiciousness side.

LOSING MY FRIENDS

The young student who sat in the back of my class the entire semester appeared no different than the other thirty students sitting around her. If anything, she stood out as being particularly attractive, and her comments and questions in class were always appropriate and gave no indication of the reason for her visit to my office. "I need to find help" was her opening remark upon entering my office. "I'm feeling very suspicious of everyone, including my friends, and it is causing me troubles." Knowing of my interest in paranoia she came seeking advice and help. I made a suggestion for medication, and she was started on one of the new antipsychotic medications that had recently arrived on the market. Unfortunately, her symptoms did not respond, and she dropped out of college. Occasional calls from her over the years have provided a sad picture of her never regaining a sense of trust in the world. She remains paranoid, alone, and afraid.

WHERE WE WENT WRONG: AGRICULTURE

The last ice age ended somewhat abruptly around eleven thousand years ago, ushering in the era in which we now live: the *Holocene*.[12] Climatic changes to both flora and fauna facilitated a shift away from hunting-gathering to an agrarian society. When we started growing food we became less mobile, creating sedentary groups of people and significant increases in the size of groups. Now it was impossible to know intimately everyone in the group. While our hunter-gatherer predecessors traveled fast and light, unencumbered by many possessions, our agrarian relatives stuck to an area and accumulated possessions, like plows and grinding stones. Now strangers presented threats at a number of levels; they might steal the best scythe, the women, and the crops that took so long to grow. Even more reason to become suspicious of others. Then trading began, and with it the risk of being taken advantage of.

As our ancestors moved to larger groups the importance of complex social skills increased as well. Over the course of evolution primitive behaviors, such as aggression, were replaced with these social skills. Those who possessed them enjoyed increased reproductive fitness and were the winners in the pass-on-your-genes contest that is life. Instead of simply mounting a female when the sexual urge struck, the emerging society now expected the man to woo her because such wanton sexuality was no longer tolerated.

ADAPTATIONS

As noted previously, the overall goal of all life is to survive and pass on one's genes. The problems of living in a group as well as surviving during the Pleistocene period resulted in the development of a variety of characteristics and behaviors known as *adaptations*, each of which somehow increased the chances of surviving and passing on one's genes. Each adaptation solved a specific problem faced by our ancestors, thereby increasing survival/reproductive chances. Those who had the behavior in their repertoire were able to survive and pass on their genes, including the adaptation. These adaptations have been likened to a Swiss army knife, which is comprised of a multitude of very specific implements: a large blade, file, scissors, and so on. Each one has a very specific purpose, but you carry them all around so that when a specific situation arises you are equipped with the tool necessary to suit that purpose.

So, too, we carry around a virtual Swiss army knife of adaptations. Specific adaptations are pulled out in response to specific situations. As Dr. David Buss, one of the preeminent leaders in the field of evolutionary psychology, points out, we are all descendants of people with the necessary adaptations for survival/reproduction, for those without them failed to make it in the great evolutionary crapshoot.[13] For example, there are very few toxins in nature that taste sweet. Someone with a preference for sweet things would therefore eat sweet (nonpoisonous) foods, survive, and reproduce. When given a choice between foods with or without sugar—for example, peanut butter—we naturally prefer the taste of the one with sugar. This is an adaptation. Some of these adaptations emerge immediately, such as eye contact between a mother and infant, which increases bonding and hence survival. Others, such as jealousy or suspiciousness, will emerge later when faced with the situations that require those adaptations.

To be clear, adaptations do not simply fate us to act in particular ways, like some genetically programmed robot. Rather, the behaviors increased survival and reproductive success for our ancestors during the Pleistocene age *on average*. Adaptations simply mean that we will have certain traits or tendencies that are either dampened or exaggerated by our environment. A good example is hunting. Our ancestors who enjoyed the thrill of the hunt and kill were able to have more to eat and *on average* survived better than their squeamish colleagues who did not like all that blood and gore. Many people today still enjoy hunting even though food is widely available. I, on the other hand, think deer are cute and don't derive pleasure at the thought of killing them. (Although if they don't stop eating my bushes during the winter, that could change. Consider yourselves warned, deer.) So many of us deviate from our ancestral past.

Keep in mind that today's environment is a far cry from that of our hunter-gatherer ancestors, making some adaptations downright *mal*adaptive. The example of a preference for sweet food is a good case in point. The sweeter something is, the more calories it has. Given that 69 percent of Americans are overweight or obese,[14] preferentially seeking out and consuming sweet foods is, for most Americans, not adaptive behavior, as doing so will lead to ill health, shorter longevity, and poorer reproductive success. Unfortunately we have only had about a hundred years to deal with this issue, while the sweet preference adaptation developed over literally millions of years.

Adaptations are an evolutionary advance over instincts, as they provide greater flexibility in dealing with problems. If all you had was a corkscrew on your Swiss army knife, getting rid of a splinter would not be easy or effective. Having the ability to choose several options, including those handy little tweezers, makes the Swiss army knife so much more flexible and adaptive in solving life's little problems. Unfortunately, the adaptations we carry around with us were developed during the Pleistocene period, and the rapid change in our social environment within the last ten thousand years has not given evolution enough time to update our Swiss knife with a few more tools. In many respects we are poorly equipped, or tooled, to face the problems of modern life.

One major adaptation was the development of sociality or social drive (to be with others). This increased survival/reproduction for reasons noted above. Let's take a common present-day behavior: adolescent cigarette smoking. By now all adolescents know the dangers of smoking. So why do they do it? The proximal cause (the identifiable factor that ultimately triggers the ultimate cause) is because of "peer pressure" or "trying to fit in." The ultimate cause (adaptation) is the need to be part of a social group, in this case by engaging in a behavior that results in admission to a group, even if it is the "wrong" group, from a parent's perspective.

CAN YOU MAKE YOURSELF PARANOID?
THE CURIOUS CASE OF SIR FRANCIS GALTON

After reading a brief biography of Sir Francis Galton (1822–1911) one would walk away with the distinct feeling that he had encountered a true Renaissance man—or a total loon. Yes, he did believe in eugenics, the reviled art of creating better people through selective breeding embodied by the Nazi quest to develop a super race of Aryans. But he was also a world traveler and explorer, a meteorologist, and a statistician forever hated by undergraduate psychology majors for having invented the correlation coefficient (hey, if he hadn't, someone else would have). Cousin to Charles Darwin, he also pioneered the use of fingerprint identification. But there is a little-known aspect of his talents that merits inclusion in this book: his brief experiment to make himself paranoid (children, don't try this at home). Rather than paraphrasing, here are his words:

> A later experiment was to gain some idea of the commoner feelings of Insanity. The method tried was to invest everything I met, whether human, animal, or inanimate, with the imaginary attributes of a spy. Having arranged plans, I started on my morning's walk from Rutland Gate, and found the experiment only too successful. By the time I had walked one and a half miles, and reached the cabstand in Piccadilly at the east end of the Green Park, every horse on the stand seemed watching me, either with pricked ears or disguising its espionage. Hours passed before this uncanny sensation wore off, and I feel that I could only too easily re-establish it.[15]

Given that I was writing a book on this topic, I decided to try the same experiment as Sir Francis. I, too, walk about a mile to my office at the university, and while I don't pass any horses, I do pass all sorts of electronic devices affixed to telephone poles and traffic signals, and lots of students. Try as I might I could not conjure the feeling of true paranoia described so ably by Galton. To my disappointment, not even a twinge. So either I'm less imaginative than Sir Francis or less paranoid. Or maybe it *was* the horses!

So we evolved adaptations during the Pleistocene epoch that continue to be with us today. Some of these adaptations continue to be "adaptive" while others, not so much. Importantly, the adaptations that involve how we relate to each other are based on our life as hunters-gatherers: small intimate groups of semi-nomadic people. It is clear that our current environment is different than during the Pleistocene epoch. The environment can exert considerable influences on our behavior, influences that can be contrary to adaptations. For example, through most of human existence, mainly before the twentieth century, we males generally preferred heavier females, as they were viewed as being more fecund. A thin female may not have had enough body fat to support the development of a fetus, or her thin frame might have been the result of an illness like cancer. The preference for heavier women is certainly not the case today, generally.[16]

Chapter 6

THE ENGINE OF PARANOIA: THE SUSPICIOUSNESS SYSTEM

In the previous chapter I described the foundational adaptations our Pleistocene ancestors left us with. But where does paranoia fit into those adaptations? To be clear, paranoia is a pathological state, not an adaptation. What is adaptive is the ability to trust some individuals and to be mistrusting of others. I termed this ability the suspiciousness system previously.

This suspiciousness system is an adaptation in the sense that those ancestors who developed the ability to form a trusting relationship with the right individuals and to be correctly suspicious and wary of other individuals were better able to survive and pass on their genes. This has wide-ranging implications and applications. For example, females have always had to be suspicious of males and their motivations regarding sex. Since developing and delivering a baby is hard work and requires a substantial commitment of time on the woman's part, she needs to have reasonable assurance that the male will be there through it all, providing her with the resources she needs. That support will ensure that her genes are passed on.

The male, on the other hand, is interested in passing on his genes largely by impregnating as many females as he can. Females possessing a suspiciousness system would more likely screen out the males looking only to spread their seed but having no intention of sticking around and providing resources. As a result both she and her offspring survive.

When the suspiciousness system is functioning optimally, all aspects of the system are in balance. Inputs into the system, in the form of events occurring in the real world, cause the system to shift its dynamics in a particular way, much like a rheostat that brightens or dims the lights in your house. When we arrive at our relatives' home for a holiday the inputs of family, safety, love, and so on cause the system to increase the tonus of the trust side. More threatening inputs, for example from an angry neighbor, increase the suspiciousness side. This prepares us to engage in behaviors that will protect us, including the use of violence. Thus, increased suspiciousness in response to events that occur around us is perfectly normal and adaptive. The big question is why and how the rheostat in some people becomes stuck at paranoid levels.

PARANOIA BY ANY OTHER NAME

The official diagnostic manual used by mental health professionals, the *Diagnostic and Statistical Manual for Mental Disorders* (DSM), just went through one of its periodic revisions. The process whereby a particular condition is promoted to a disorder is a bit like the elevation of a priest to a cardinal, but without the colorful robes. Poor PMS (premenstrual syndrome) tried for decades to achieve disorderhood and was finally promoted.

Many other conditions sought recognition; among them was *posttraumatic embitterment disorder* (PTED). I'm not making this up. Presumably, following a traumatic event of some sort—say you don't get that promotion you wanted, only to find out that the person who did get it is having an affair with your wife—you become, well, embittered. A deep sense of injustice settles in followed by anger and pessimism. Revenge emerges as a motivating drive.

According to Dr. Michael Linden, a German psychiatrist who is championing this disorder, approximately 2 to 3 percent of the German population suffers from it.[1] Elements of PTED include feeling let down, taking the event as a personal insult, a sense of injustice, and a desire to fight back in some way. The feeling feeds on itself and snowballs. The precipitating event remains a perpetual thorn in the sufferer's side, and the mind repeatedly goes back to it and seems unable to let go.

These symptoms appear to be quite similar to those seen in paranoid individuals. In fact, there is little to argue that PTED is not simply a form of paranoia, the difference being that it is initiated by a single (traumatic) event.

Nothing described in this book thus far precludes paranoia developing from a single event. In fact, there are case reports of individuals developing paranoid delusions following the events of 9/11. Posttraumatic embitterment disorder does share one other salient element with paranoid conditions described in this book: those who allegedly suffer from it also do not seek help for it. In typical paranoid manner, it is the world that needs to change its unjust ways, not the individual. A rose by any other name . . .

PARANOIA AND THE SUSPICIOUSNESS SYSTEM

The suspiciousness system does have some "defects" at a number of levels, any one of which could result in paranoia. For example, one can misperceive the intentions of a neighbor, which can thereby activate the suspiciousness system. One could be raised in a home where everyone outside the family is mistrusted, resulting in a more or less constant activation of the suspiciousness system. Release of neurotransmitters, which are responsible for activating brain functions, can be excessive, or the brain structures involved—for instance the limbic system—could be overly sensitive to normal amounts of neurotransmitters.

There are also potential interaction effects. Subtle shifts in the equilibrium of the suspiciousness system can result in a sustained state of paranoia. Biochemical changes, such as increased release of dopamine, can result in increased attention/arousal, which could distort one's interpretation of environmental events. The same action by the annoying neighbor can be interpreted very differently based on the individual's biochemical state. This has been demonstrated with chemically altered mood states.[2] When given a mood-lowering drug research participants interpreted events—such as a college lecture—as more boring than those not given the drug. Conversely, when given a mood-elevating drug, subjects report the lecture and professor to be more interesting.[3]

Suspiciousness and paranoia arose out of more basic and primitive emotions such as fear, which we have in common with all animals. The ability to be concerned about someone else's actions in relation to ourselves requires *theory of mind*, the process by which we are able to intuit or understand the actions and intentions of others through introspection into our own thoughts and actions.

Animals experience a general wariness that evokes the same mechanisms as fear, albeit to a lesser degree. Even as I type this, the chipmunk outside my office door that has entertained me for days, successfully distracting me from writing this book, is eying me with trepidation. Its tiny little brain is not capable of wondering if I poisoned the pistachios I left out for it. Paranoid individuals not only perceive danger, like my chipmunk friend, but they are also able to determine the reasons for that danger. I saw a patient once who believed that his neighbors were pumping poisoned water into his basement in order to kill him. The reason for doing so was that his daughter, a physician, was not providing narcotics to them, as they wanted her to do. In retaliation (or as blackmail) they were poisoning him. Both theory of mind, in this case determining the reasoning of the neighbors, and language abilities are necessary for the development of paranoia.

The same is true for suspiciousness. As noted previously, it is a healthy emotion and represents, therefore, an adaptation. Those of our ancestors who were without a sense of suspiciousness were easily duped and killed or had their mates stolen from them. Either way, they didn't leave any descendants behind.

THERAPIST MISSES POINT

While on my internship I ran across a particularly inept psychologist. He had been treating a woman in her early twenties for over a year. Being proud of his ability to memorize the diagnostic criteria in the American Psychiatric Association's diagnostic manual for mental disorders, he felt confident that his diagnosis of delusional disorder, persecutory type, was an accurate one. His patient had ongoing paranoid ideation regarding her sister's lover, who she was afraid was going to kill her sister, then come after her. She often discussed at length what she was going to do the day he came to the door armed with a gun: where she would hide, how she would defend herself, and so on.

One day the psychologist was seen shaking his head sadly after a session with this client. "An unfortunate therapeutic setback," he lamented. "It seems that her sister's lover shot her sister yesterday. This bad coincidence will only strengthen her paranoid delusion!" The therapist never stopped to consider that perhaps her paranoia was not pathological but based on a realistic fear.

TAYLOR SWIFT—THE SUSPICIOUSNESS SYSTEM IN ACTION

Perhaps an example of suspiciousness contrasted with paranoia is in order. For those of you who have been living in a cave for the past several years, Taylor Swift is arguably the most popular pop music artist at the time of this writing. Her life, like that of many famous people, is lived in an electronic fishbowl where her every move and utterance is immediately shared via the ether of social media.[4]

Interviews with Ms. Swift quickly point to elements that are likely to cause our—or her—suspiciousness system to become activated. Just a few quotes will suffice to illustrate this point:

It's strange because my life now is really abnormal. I get used to the fact that when I go out, there's gonna be a line of people wanting pictures on their phone, and there's gonna be crowds everywhere, even if there weren't crowds when I walked into a store. I realize the only privacy I'm really entitled to is when I'm in my own apartment or my own home, 'cause everything else is kind of—I'm looked at as sort of public property. And there's nothing I can do about that perception except control my mental perspective on it, which is, I need to treat people well. I need to be grateful. I need to take pictures with people when they ask for one. So if I'm not in the mood to do that, I don't leave my house (Swift).[5]

But sometimes you don't want to have a camera pointed at you (Swift).[6]

"Don't even get me started on wiretaps," Swift says seriously. "It's not a good thing for me to talk about socially. I freak out."[7]

"She also told me she didn't trust reporters, ever since she caught one (a female) rifling through her purse."[8]

"Swift has a 24-hour security detail. 'It's because of the guys who write and say they want to chain me up in their basements,' she said. 'One was in California and drove all the way to Nashville and tried to get into this building.'"[9]

There's someone whose entire job it is to figure out things that I don't want the world to see. They look at your career, they look at what you prioritize, and they try to figure out what would be the most revealing or hurtful. Like, I don't take my clothes off in pictures or anything— I'm very private about that. So it scares me how valuable it would be to get a video of me changing. It's sad to have to look for cameras in dressing rooms and bathrooms. I don't walk around naked with my windows open, because there's a value on that (Swift).[10]

It is not surprising that Taylor, along with many other high-profile individuals, has security teams charged with keeping her physically safe and keeping her feeling safe. Her recent purchase of a $15 million apartment in New York City also included the purchase of a $5 million apartment across the hall just for her security team. A simple walk back from the park takes on the air of a commando operation. "One of Swift's bodyguards, Jeff, a former Marine Corps anti-terrorism specialist, comes over to brief her. 'OK, we've a six-minute walk to the exit. Twitter is going like wildfire, so some of the more obsessive fans . . .' He trails off. 'We're gonna close the gap on you and keep them back.'"[11]

The reaction of many individuals to such descriptions is a form of schaden-freude or mock sympathy: "Oh, the poor little rich thing." Many envy the lives of the rich and famous. Yet think about just the limited information presented above and how you would feel if that was your day-to-day existence. We don't know about many aspects of her life, like the number of files her security team must have on obsessed fans. One man was arrested crawling out of the ocean in front of her Rhode Island home after swimming two miles to meet her.[12] I'm sure that dialed up her suspiciousness system quite a bit.

So is Taylor Swift paranoid? Probably not. Is her suspiciousness system often activated during the course of the day? Probably yes, and far more so than the average person. Few of us feel the need to check to see if there are hidden cameras before we go to the bathroom. And few of us worry that powerful camera lenses are trained on us, aiming to capture us in an embarrassing or compromising situation. When someone walks toward you making eye contact, do you immediately wonder or worry what their intentions might be? I suspect Taylor might. Cue the suspiciousness system.

CAUSES OF PARANOIA

Like a rheostat adjusts electrical current, different events cause the level of our trust or suspiciousness to increase or decrease, as noted in the example of Taylor Swift above. In normal individuals each level increases or decreases in response to environmental events. These events include such things as how we are raised; the immediate actions of those around us; and factors that affect the brain, such as injuries, diseases, or chemicals. As discussed previously, delirium caused by a variety of medical conditions can also increase the suspiciousness side of the system. But ultimately what all of the above are doing is tapping into an existing network that is "hardwired" in our brains to serve the purpose of increasing or decreasing feelings of suspiciousness or trust. Certain abnormal conditions appear to be able to ratchet the suspiciousness side up to paranoid levels and keep it there.

Given the sheer complexity of the brain, it is a wonder that any of us develop normal brains at all. Throw on top of that the unique nature of our individual experiences—each of which helps shape the brain—the stress of modern life, and it is not much of a stretch to see how abnormalities in normal brain functioning can arise and result in pathological conditions such a paranoia. There are a large variety of events and conditions that can result in paranoia by overactivating the suspiciousness system. Among these, one in particular merits discussion, given its prevalence in our society: drugs of abuse.

Chapter 7

DRUGS AND PARANOIA

In chapter 4, I discussed the nature of delirium and noted that just about any drug, legal or illegal, taken to excess or withdrawn from after a period of use can result in delirium. But certain drugs, such as cocaine, amphetamines, and cannabis, deserve special attention, as they are able to produce paranoia in the absence of delirium.

AMPHETAMINE SCARS

I vividly recall my first encounters with amphetamine addicts. I was working at a Veterans Health Administration hospital after I graduated from college but before going to graduate school. As a research assistant in a substance-abuse unit I was permitted to sit in on the staffing sessions for veterans with substance-abuse problems as each of their cases was reviewed. A determination was made concerning the appropriate treatment setting.

One day a male in his early twenties came in and sat down. He proceeded to describe his deterioration into amphetamine abuse, culminating in an abortive suicide attempt using his stove. Images of the young man setting himself on fire or sticking his head in a gas oven entered my mind. Those images were quickly erased, however, when he lifted his shirt over his head. In their stead, to this day, remain the images of large bull's-eye-like scars left from the concentric circles of the electric coils he had laid his chest on in an attempt to kill himself.

Another veteran was reviewed, also a young male. He became paranoid following an amphetamine binge and in an attempt to escape from his (imagined) tormentors ran from his house and began climbing a telephone pole. Unfortunately, in his paranoid state, he had neglected to put on any clothes. I'll leave it to the reader to imagine the outcome of that naked vertical ascent.

HISTORY OF AMPHETAMINES AND COCAINE

The history of drug taking among humans is a long one indeed; evidence for use of stimulants dates back some five thousand years. Of course, people at that time were not taking amphetamines or cocaine but rather were ingesting the plants from which those modern drugs were derived. These include the *ma huang* plant, which the Chinese enjoyed and from which ephedrine, a stimulant drug, was extracted, and the *coca* plant whence cocaine is derived.

You might expect that with such a long history of use, there would be an equally long history detailing the many problems associated with these drugs, paranoia especially. Surprisingly, up until the 1950s, most of the information found in medical and lay publications did little but sing the praises of these drugs. The Conquistador invaders in South America (around the sixteenth century) found the coca leaves to be highly enjoyable, and their accounts, as well as those that followed, are downright glowing in extolling the many benefits. Of course, their rave reviews about its ability to increase stamina, decrease appetite, increase energy, and so on were self-serving because it made the native Indians laboring in the silver mines work harder and longer.

When cocaine was initially synthesized the medical community was equally impressed with its many salubrious effects. Scientific legitimacy was added by the enthusiastic endorsement of none other than Sigmund Freud, who prescribed it to a good friend as a treatment for addiction to narcotics. He also believed it to be an efficacious treatment for depression. So healthy and helpful, cocaine was quickly made into a wide variety of elixirs that promised cures for a multitude of maladies. A particularly popular drink mixed cocaine with extract from the kola nut, producing a refreshing beverage known as Coca-Cola, which is obviously still available today, even if not quite so "refreshing" as before.

As late as 1946 a scholarly review of the use of amphetamines came to largely positive conclusions and noted that thirty-nine different conditions could be treated with them.[1] The study noted that "with the passage of years and the ripening of experience Benzedrine sulphate [the original amphetamine] has found a rationally established place in clinical medicine as a drug with divers and valuable indications."[2] There was only one short article in 1938 that noted a small number of patients seen by the authors had developed psychosis as the result of amphetamine use. This untoward reaction at the time did not appear to be headline-type news.[3]

All that changed rather quickly following the end of World War II. During the war all combatant countries supplied their soldiers with amphetamines to improve stamina and fight off fatigue. The last thing anyone wanted to do was to fall asleep at the wheel while flying over the English Channel from a bombing run on the Continent. Britain and the United States combined to produce over 140 million tablets for use by their armed forces.[4]

No country embraced the drug quite like Japan did. Both soldiers and civilians working in war-related activities were given it freely. After the end of the war Japan had tons of the stuff left over in ampoule form, which found its way into the domestic market. The result was a virtual epidemic of addiction and paranoid psychosis.[5]

Concerns over such epidemics turned to US shores. In July 2005 the Drug Enforcement Administration declared amphetamines as this nation's most serious illicit drug problem at the time.[6] Evidence of this is seen in hospital emergency rooms. Over recent years 73 percent of regional hospitals have seen increases in the number of patients with amphetamine-related problems. The upper Midwest has been particularly hard hit by this problem, and the vast majority of emergency rooms in those states indicate that as many 10 percent of all emergency visits are related to amphetamine abuse.[7]

Government statistics indicate that up to 13 percent of emergency admissions are amphetamine-related.[8] Amphetamine-treatment admissions increased fivefold from 1992 to 2002, and it is estimated that twelve million Americans have used the drug.[9] Not surprisingly, given the topic of this book, is that one of the many problems amphetamines cause, and for which hospital treatment is sought, is paranoia.

ANOTHER CASE AGAINST ABUSING CHEMICAL SUBSTANCES

Country-Western singer Doug Supernaw ("Reno," "I Don't Call Him Daddy") is no stranger to the court system, having colorful encounters with law enforcement while intoxicated and for other drug-related episodes. His April 2007 court appearance merited his appearance in this book, for while in court, and presumably sober, he revealed some classic signs of paranoia.

According to Supernaw, the police were trying to ruin both his music career and professional baseball career (never mind that he was forty-six at the time). There was a "political economic conspiracy" against him that allegedly began back in 2002. In that eventful year he was reportedly "held hostage in Paris" for two weeks in a "mentally retarded home for terrorists." The connection between his drug use and baseball career apparently revolved around being a "test monkey" in order to determine if someone could simultaneously play baseball and smoke marijuana. After listening to such statements the judge in the case decided that the jury pool would not be needed, but that a psychiatric evaluation would.[10]

WHAT DOES IT DO?

Like all drugs of abuse both cocaine and amphetamines produce a number of seemingly positive effects. Both provide the user with a mild euphoria (or a whopping euphoria, if injected or smoked). Mental clarity is increased while appetite and need for sleep are decreased. People become more loquacious and report having more energy. That's the good news. The bad news is that both drugs can lead to hallucinations, delusions, and thinking disturbances—all of which are elements of what is commonly referred to as *psychosis*, with paranoia being the most prominent symptom, in 90 percent or more of cases.[11] The symptoms of paranoid psychosis look virtually identical to what is seen in paranoid schizophrenia. Certainly not everybody who uses cocaine or amphetamines develops severe psychosis, and, as is the case with all drugs, there is huge individual variability. In a study in which research subjects were given amphetamines, one subject developed a paranoid psychosis following a dose of 100 milligrams, while another, who took close to 1,000 milligrams, did not.[12]

In the case of cocaine use paranoid psychosis usually appears to develop after about three years of use. Half of those who use it regularly will develop paranoia within about two years. Close to 70 percent of cocaine users develop transient paranoia during the course of their drug use, in which the paranoia recedes following abstinence.[13] The more cocaine you use, the more paranoid you become. Prominent themes include being busted by the police or ripped off by others. It is hard to tell if these are true paranoid thoughts or legitimate concerns regarding the pitfalls of such a lifestyle. Within five to ten minutes of ingesting cocaine around 60 percent of individuals report paranoid feelings that persist even after the cocaine high has gone away. Half who develop paranoia act on it in some way. Many individuals find the paranoia upsetting and troubling, and about 40 percent will attempt to "treat" it by the use of narcotics.[14] Yet the powerful effect of cocaine is attested to by the low rate at which users spontaneously stop taking it.

As with cocaine, the majority of individuals who abuse amphetamines (50 to 90 percent) develop a paranoid psychosis. One of the big differences is that the paranoid psychosis that develops after regular cocaine use typically goes away with abstinence. With amphetamines the outcomes of those who develop paranoid psychosis are more variable. It appears that most (roughly 65 percent) experience a transient paranoid psychosis that disappears within a week of abstinence. However, about 18 percent develop a prolonged psychosis that may last for up to a month. Another 18 percent have a persistent psychosis that lasts longer than a month and can last for years, even with continued abstinence.[15] Themes of being watched or plotted against predominate.

The chances of amphetamine-induced paranoid psychosis increase with use, although it can occur with even a single ingestion. Research subjects given modest doses of 5 to 10 milligrams an hour reliably developed psychosis even without extensive abuse histories.[16]

WHAT'S GOING ON IN THE BRAIN?

The effects of any drug of abuse on the brain are complex. The only thing simple about the effects of cocaine and amphetamine will be the explanation given here. In terms of the topic of this book, the most significant and important effect is that both drugs increase the neurotransmitter *dopamine*. The role of all neurotransmitters is to facilitate communication within the central nervous system. Neurotransmitters are released within the brain, which causes electrical events to send the intended signal down the neural line. Like most neurotransmitters dopamine wears a variety of hats depending on where in the brain it is working. In many regions it facilitates muscle movement. Its absence, as in the degenerative condition known as Parkinson's disease, causes abnormalities in movement, such as tremors or shuffling gait. Dopamine is also the major neurotransmitter involved in the brain's reward system. If something feels good—like sex or eating or snorting cocaine—then you can be sure that dopamine is what is causing that good feeling. For our purposes here, the important point is that dopamine is increased as a result of using these drugs.

The problem with dopamine is that when excessive amounts of it are produced, psychosis is the result. Long ignored among the scientific community, the importance of dopamine, especially in understanding schizophrenia, was skillfully revealed by Professor Arvid Carlsson of Sweden, who would be rewarded for his efforts with the Nobel Prize in Physiology or Medicine in 2000. Based on his research, drugs that blocked dopamine quieted the psychotic storm in the heads of patients with schizophrenia, including those with paranoia, and freed them from the straitjackets, wet packs, and lobotomies that were used to control, but not treat, their illness.

In the case of paranoia the role of dopamine becomes more focused. One of its many functions is to highlight important elements in our environment, both good and bad. With elevated levels of dopamine there is an increase in the salience of environmental stimuli, even when the stimuli are not all that important. A candy wrapper left on a table is normally overlooked when dopamine levels are normal. But the same wrapper takes on new, hidden meaning and significance when levels of dopamine are high.

The evidence that cocaine/amphetamine-induced increases in dopamine are responsible for paranoia and other psychotic symptoms is underscored by the efficacy of antipsychotic medications in preventing and treating such psychosis. These drugs, to varying degrees, all share the same mechanisms of action, which is to block the effects of dopamine.

PHILIP K. DICK

Anyone who has seen the futuristic films *Blade Runner* (1982) or *Minority Report* (2002) will appreciate the unusual and creative mind behind such science fiction. P. K. Dick was an extraordinarily talented and prolific writer who was capable of cranking out twelve novels during a two-year stretch. That's one novel every two months! *Crank*ing is a good word, for Dick was a prolific user of amphetamines, the old street term for which was *crank*. Swallowing as many as a thousand pills a week he would remain awake for days on end, then crash and sleep for days.

Such a lifestyle, and abuse style, facilitated the completion of an astounding forty-plus novels and two-hundred-plus stories—all in a fairly short period of time, considering Dick died of a stroke at the age of fifty-three. It must be remembered that at the time Dick's addiction to amphetamines began, such drugs were legal and were prescribed for a wide variety of conditions.

One of the conditions for which he was prescribed amphetamines (ephedrine) was asthma. During a seven-year stretch he completed an incredible thirteen novels and over eighty stories. While the amphetamines facilitated his artistic productivity, they also fueled a raging paranoia involving the FBI, CIA, and US government, as well as visual hallucinations. Interestingly, some of his paranoia was not delusional; he apparently was questioned by the FBI under the guise of a radio interview, and the CIA did have a file on him based on a letter he sent to the former Soviet Union during the Cold War years.

The years of abuse took their toll, and Dick eventually required psychiatric hospitalization. Amphetamines probably contributed to his untimely death, given their known deleterious effects on cardiovascular functioning. Interestingly, in one of Dick's lesser-known novels, *Clans of the Alphane Moon*, a colony of mentally ill patients on a distant moon revolt and take over. What emerges is a psychiatric caste system where individuals with a particular illness are given tribal names of sorts: Ob-Coms (obsessive-compulsives), Deps (depressives, who are disliked by all the other groups), and at the top of the heap—the leaders—are the Pares, who suffer from . . . you guessed it: paranoia.[17]

SENSITIZATION

An interesting phenomenon develops when amphetamines are abused: *sensitization*. Basically, neural tissue becomes sensitized to repeated use of the drug. Much like when you burn yourself and that area of your skin becomes overly sensitive to heat, so, too, nerve terminals become overly sensitive—and over-react—to subsequent use of amphetamine, making it more likely that paranoia will emerge. Even after considerable periods of abstinence, psychosis, including paranoia, can quickly reemerge, suggesting that this sensitization reflects permanent changes in the brain, a condition documented in research studies.[18]

It is noteworthy that trauma—for example, rape—or severe stress can have a similar effect. They, too, cause increases in dopamine and can result in sensitization. This may explain, in part, the persistent nature of paranoia. If you believe there is someone out to harm you, then you are under stress and your brain is secreting dopamine. The more dopamine release you have, the more likely you are to feel paranoid, causing more stress, and a vicious cycle develops. Mind you, much of this is speculative, given the paucity of information in this area and the trouble of using nonhumans to test our theories. Yet even monkeys appear to display paranoid-like behaviors. They seem to be perceiving nonthreatening behaviors by their monkey colleagues as being threatening and respond with either submissive or aggressive behaviors.[19]

One final aspect is worth highlighting. This sensitization via amphetamines or traumatic stress is a bit like *reverse tolerance*. With many drugs, like heroin, your body adjusts and becomes *tolerant* to the drug such that you need higher and higher doses to get the same effects. With reverse tolerance, you now need less to get the same effect because your brain has become sensitized, as described above.

AMPHETAMINES STRIKE AGAIN

While delivering the Sunday newspaper, newspaper carrier Jennie Stricker's attention was caught by three people inside a house in clear distress. These unfortunate individuals had been held hostage and shot at. They had gone to great lengths to protect themselves, including tearing out a toilet and the bathroom sink and heaving them out the window—which had also been torn out—in an attempt to hit their attackers on the ground. Jennie called police, who quickly arrived on the scene. Despite the presence of law enforcement the three hostages feared that their abductors were still on the ground floor of the house and they refused to come out.

The police soon realized that there were no attackers. The presence of methamphetamine and a meth lab pointed to amphetamine-induced paranoid hallucinations. Numerous bullet holes were found, as the three had apparently shot at their hallucinated assailants. Between the bathroom and window deconstruction, as well as damage done by the bullets, the total damages to the residence exceeded $10,000.[20]

BATH SALTS

In 2011 bath salts hit the United States like a plague, resulting in horrific psychiatric consequences. The powerful "designer drug" (so named because of how it was disguised for sale) is cheap and was at one point legal. Related to amphetamines, synthetic bath salts have resulted in severe psychosis and paranoia. According to the *Journal of the American Medical Association*, in 2011 alone over six thousand calls were made from hospital emergency rooms to poison centers seeking help on how to handle these psychiatric emergencies.[21]

Like amphetamines and cocaine these drugs flood the brain in the same paranoia-inducing neurotransmitter: dopamine. The difference is that it results in significantly higher levels of dopamine. Even when a person stops taking the drug, levels of dopamine remain high. Although illegal in most US states, they apparently remain in circulation under a variety of aliases and pose a very serious public health concern, given the often violent nature of adverse reactions. Yes, these are the same drugs that turn ordinary people into face-eaters, like something out of a bad zombie movie. More often, they result in severe paranoia and often violence as a consequence.

REEFER MADNESS—NO, REALLY

Cannabis is perhaps the most widely used drug of abuse in the world after alcohol. In the United States 44 percent of twelfth graders have used it, with close to 6 percent using it daily. In the eighteen-to-twenty-five-year-old group, over 50 percent have tried it, with close to 20 percent having done within a month of the study.[22]

At the time of this writing four states have legalized marijuana for recreational use. Many other states have passed legislation allowing medicinal use of cannabis, and many cities are reducing the criminal penalties associated with possession of small amounts of cannabis to the level of parking tickets. The federal government has signaled its intentions to *not* target marijuana possession for enforcement. The arguments for these measures are compelling and include a decades-long failure to eliminate marijuana use—similar to Prohibition-era failure to end the consumption of alcohol, the billions of dollars spent incarcerating individuals arrested under previous laws, and the perceived benign nature of its use.[23]

This book is not the proper forum to debate the relative merits of decriminalizing marijuana. The obvious issue, as it was for amphetamines and cocaine, is whether marijuana is capable of triggering the suspiciousness system. The short answer is yes, it is.

Starting with the broad impact of increased marijuana use, the current data would appear to indicate increased visits to the emergency department for marijuana-related psychiatric problems. In states that have legalized marijuana for recreational or medicinal use the increases are in the 50 percent range.[24] The symptoms seen in those visits can vary from increased anxiety to psychosis, which is where paranoia is commonly embedded.

There is a growing body of evidence linking early marijuana use with an increased risk of developing psychosis and schizophrenia. Paranoia is a common feature of both. This risk is substantial—as much as a threefold risk for those using cannabis compared to those who don't—and depends, in part, on how much was ingested.[25]

But the most direct way to establish a relationship between marijuana use and paranoia is to give cannabis to research subjects and see if they become paranoid. This was first done in the nineteenth century by French physician Jacques-Joseph Moreau, who extracted a THC-rich syrup that he then administered to research subjects, including himself.[26] After one such experiment he came to believe that his colleagues had poisoned him and that one of them was an assassin.

The advantage of administering cannabis to research subjects under controlled conditions is that we can screen out those who were paranoid from the get-go. In other words, it is possible that those individuals who used marijuana and ended up in the emergency department were psychotic or paranoid to begin with, before they ever ingested the stuff. So research studies eliminate this possibility by selecting normal, non-paranoid individuals. When this is done and they are given doses of the active ingredients in marijuana—comparable to what might be ingested smoking a standard marijuana cigarette—many experience an increase in paranoia.[27]

The trend toward increased legalization of marijuana is gathering momentum, and it is likely that more and more states will decriminalize it. This will benefit the large numbers of otherwise law-abiding citizens who simply enjoy the buzz they get from marijuana. The cost, at the individual and societal level, may be increased rates of paranoia.

Chapter 8

OTHER WAYS TO TURN ON PARANOIA

There are a variety of ways the rheostat mechanism involved with the suspiciousness system can be turned up. Some may be situational, in which case the resulting response is unlikely to be paranoia. For example, you may receive the same e-mail message that I do from a kind gentleman in Africa with poor written English skills who has thirty-five million dollars he wishes to share with you, a complete stranger. I suspect both of our suspiciousness systems ramp up when we receive such a message, but not to the level of paranoia. Others are more likely to activate the suspiciousness system to paranoid levels. These are the conditions that interested us in previous chapters, at least one of which is worth revisiting in light of our discussion of the suspiciousness system.

DELIRIUM REDUX

You will recall that delirium was described as a brain storm, with a wide variety of causes: fever, medications, urinary-tract infections, and others. The paranoia that emerges within the context of delirium can be considered the default setting for the suspiciousness system. As noted in chapter 4, when a person becomes delirious, the brain's ability to make sense of the environment is impaired. Things, including people, are not recognized for what or who they are. Memories are unavailable to guide perceptions or to make important judgments. When a delirious person experiences these changes, it makes sense to become suspicious and to assume that those around her are out to harm her and to act accordingly. Given the person's weakened cognitive state, failure to do so could result in a potentially fatal outcome.

Prior to his death a family member of mine believed his nurses were out to get him, vast government conspiracies were afoot, and the sprinkler overhead was spying on him. All this emerged quickly as he became delirious.

Paranoid feelings aren't the only result. In addition, the brain attempts to create some meaning out of the situation. The resulting paranoid narrative usually makes little sense, but it really doesn't matter. Most important is that the suspiciousness system ratchets up and lifesaving defensive measures are taken. Ironically, such "lifesaving" measures often include tearing out IV lines or refusing medications, both of which are designed to save the person's life by treating the underlying cause of the delirium.

HOW TO BE A PARANOIAC

The goal of this book is certainly not to inspire readers to become paranoid. Yet should you find yourself curious about what it would be like and perhaps want some guidance about pulling paranoia off, then look no further than H. Michael Sweeney's book *The Professional Paranoid*.[1] A more honest title can scarce be found. This book contains all you'd ever need to know should you find some government agency coming after you.

The story starts when Mr. Sweeney becomes privy to a document detailing various crimes that somehow tie together such disparate events as the Kennedy assassination and Watergate. Showing the information to a "former intelligence agent" appears to have set the government on Sweeney's trail, and within days his "life began to fall apart." "They" messed with his computer, which they eventually stole, attacked his business and family, made attempts on his life, seized his mail, observed him via low-flying aircraft, and put his home and business under electronic surveillance. The classic black vans with big antennas sat outside his house. He was victimized by police, followed by a Cuban, and witnessed his business destroyed to the point that he was forced to declare bankruptcy. Rather than accept these abuses he fought back and left this book so that others could fight back against the likes of the CIA, FBI, IRS, DEA, BATF, DIA, MJTF, and other unnamed acronyms.

Among Sweeney's concrete recommendations: always be looking out for the unusual; document everything, make copies and then put them in a safe; use electronics: cameras, tape recorders, security cameras; have multiple routes to work; have contingency plans; take changes of clothing for disguise, leaving such changes of clothing at work should you need them; be unpredictable; set booby traps; wrap your computer in chicken wire to prevent the electronic impulses sent from the keyboard to the computer from being detected or, better yet, embed said chicken wire in the walls, floor, and ceiling of the room in which your computer sits; and "Don't assume any person, thing or event is what it seems to be. Be suspicious, and verify everything." Be wary of those who are friendly as "anyone who goes out of their way and becomes very talkative and overly friendly is probably trying to convince you of something." As insurance, gather all the information you can on your oppressors, make copies and put them in fifteen mailing envelopes. Get a copy of mailing lists from, for example, churches affiliated with your church. Take fifteen random names—of people who don't know you—from these lists and send them your documentation with instructions to monitor the news in case something happens to you, in which case they are to open the packet and follow the enclosed instructions regarding whom to contact and release the information to.[2] Think Mel Gibson in *Conspiracy Theory*.

Even more sinister are the government's mind-control attacks by which it monitors your brain waves, identifying your individual brain wave patterns when you are happy, sad, angry, and so on. These identified patterns are then broadcast back at you, thereby inducing the emotions associated with the particular wave pattern. Eventually, via this subliminal methodology, words and sounds themselves can then enter the victim's mind directly. Insanity is the result of this process, and the mind is fragmented so that latent personalities can be awakened at will by the mind controller. Think Matt Damon in *The Bourne Identity*.

Extensive appendices provide the reader with all the technical information regarding various listening devices (bugs), Internet resources, and others. The main text contains page after page of details to consider when protecting yourself from those out to get you. In words of true advice from an admitted paranoid, Mr. Sweeney tells the reader: "Don't fear being called a paranoid. That is a much better alternative than being caught off guard and attacked by an unseen opponent."[3]

PERCEIVING THE WORLD

Delirium results in an extreme case of perceptual disturbance in which the normal ability to see objects, search one's memory for a template for what that object is and then to correctly recognize it, is severely disturbed. But what of other, more mild, cases of perceptual disturbances? For example, imagine someone born with a subtle defect in his ability to read people's faces. Such a defect may lead him to misinterpret your puzzled expression as a frown or a smirk. His subsequent interpretation of your intentions or thoughts would lean in a more negative direction, and paranoid reactions might emerge.

Now imagine that instead of a narrow defect, such as the inability to read facial expressions accurately, the person has a defect in most areas of perception. He is unable to correctly perceive vocal inflections and the proximity or spatial relations between objects. These deficits would be most severe in the social realm, where subtle cues of all sorts are vital to establishing social relations and are interpreted. Misinterpretation of these cues could lead to a variety of downstream misunderstandings. A wink intended as a flirtatious gesture is misinterpreted as a conspiratorial gesture and the subsequent (mis)interpretation is that a conspiracy is afoot.

What types of conditions can bring on this wholesale reduction in perceptual process? Well, as my fellow boomers and I can attest, one is old age. As noted in chapter 3, hearing loss, which might occur because of wax buildup, or vision loss due to cataracts can contribute to paranoia. Both of these conditions may result in failure to adequately make sense of the world, which leads to the suspiciousness system dialing up.[4]

Another way perceptual processing becomes reduced is by traumatic injuries to the brain. Such injuries are prevalent among American troops in the Middle East. Not only do the concussive blasts from IEDs (improvised explosive devices) result in damage to the brain, but they can also damage hearing and impair vision. Damage of this sort has the potential to decrease the quality of sensory input and affect how accurately the brain interprets that input. Add to that the traumatic stress these soldiers experience—and the effects of stress and sensitization of brain tissue to traumatic stress noted earlier, and you have a full recipe for paranoia.

THE FAMILY

For much of the century past, Freudian conceptualizations of mental illnesses held sway. In a nutshell, feelings experienced early in life—such as wanting to possess one's mother sexually—are the foundations of both mental health and ill health. Actually, according to the way Freudians see the world, we are all pretty much screwed-up no matter how healthy our families were. Therefore, we are all in need of the cure: psychoanalysis. How convenient, label everyone as ill and in need of treatment—a treatment you just so happen to be an expert in! The important point, according to Freud, is that all your problems—cigarette smoking, bad relationships, depression, anxiety, and so on—are all the result of your family. Even schizophrenia, which is clearly a brain disorder, was blamed on the mother, aptly named the *schizophrenogenic* mother, in the sense that the mother caused the schizophrenia in her offspring.

Fortunately such Freudian notions have largely been swept aside. We now have a better understanding of how events during the course of development result in mental illnesses later in life. However, regarding paranoia, we again find a hole in the research literature. We simply do not have any evidence about how childhood events shape an individual who develops paranoia later in life. That being said, it is not much of a stretch to imagine the effects of growing up in a household of suspicious or paranoid individuals. If from a very early age your parents taught you to not trust strangers, or neighbors, or anyone else except close family, you might be likely to adopt such an attitude. Face it, Democrats raise Democrats and Republicans raise Republicans. But the message passed on from parents to offspring is probably a bit more elaborate than just that. It probably includes the fact that it is a "dog-eat-dog" world, so you had better get your bite in before you are bitten. Family members passing along paranoid ideas might identify the government as an organization that cannot be trusted. They would also repeatedly demonstrate through their own actions how to misinterpret benign events in paranoid ways, such as others whispering. Multiple locks on the doors, loaded weapons, and so on signal that the world is not a safe place, and you need to be vigilant. *They* are out there, and if you do not spot them first, and if you are not prepared, *they* will get you.

There are some indications based on less-than-systematic research to suggest that children with severely authoritarian parents who were harsh, cruel, and controlling experience repressed rage. These future paranoiacs typically shy away from social interactions, which prevents them from fully understanding how others think and feel and from being able to adopt the mindset of others. This same research, guided, not surprisingly, by a Freudian viewpoint, unfortunately found paranoia to also be associated with repressed homosexuality, a favorite topic of Freudians, as well as with constipation—perhaps second to homosexuality in Freudian popularity—and hypertension.[5] Fortunately virtually no one takes these notions seriously anymore.

At least one study that examined thirty-four cases of paranoia in people living in a kibbutz (a communal farm in Israel) found evidence for family factors as a contributing cause. In five cases there were multiple family members who were paranoid. A shared delusion between two people is called folie à deux (madness of two), however in this case it was *folie à familie*. When looking at family dynamics it was found that the father was prejudiced, critical, and suspicious as well as dominant and rigid. While the father was authoritarian and enforced oppressive rules, the mother was passive and submissive.[6]

Extending these findings into a greater cross-cultural domain, similar results are found. When interviews with paranoid individuals were conducted in Boston and Burma, the same authoritarian, dominant father emerged. Whether he was Bostonian or Burmese, he gave orders and expected them to be obeyed with no expression of pride, concern, or fondness for the kids.[7] A harsh, critical individual, the paranoid-building father engendered a sense of fear in family members.

There is no direct causal evidence for this although there is evidence that if your parents are liberal (or conservative) you tend to see the world that way yourself. In fact, evidence exists that parental attitudes in a variety of domains significantly influence the personalities, attitudes, beliefs, and behaviors of their offspring. Keep in mind that those offspring are also wearing their parents' genes, making them biochemically predisposed to elevated levels of dopamine in the brain. With both of these conditions in place, a suspicious attitude toward the world will have fertile ground in which to develop paranoia.

"I KNOW THIS SOUNDS CRAZY"

In her early fifties and with no previous psychiatric history, Joann appeared distraught and somewhat bemused. "I know this sounds crazy, but I think that the doctors have been treating me like a guinea pig." When asked to provide reasons for this belief, she offered only vague inferences and unproven assumptions. More concretely, there was a lump in her side that she felt was a computer chip implanted to keep track of her. She believed that people broke into her house while she was out because "things look slightly out of place when I go home." "I know this all sounds crazy, but this is what I think and feel." She was postmenopausal, so I inquired about her estrogen status and whether she was taking a hormone supplement. "I don't take it anymore because I think they gave it to me just to make me docile so it would be easier to trick me." With gentle encouragement she went back to her physician accompanied by a note from me. A very low dose of antipsychotic medication was provided, and her husband reported that the paranoia diminished to tolerable levels.

It makes a lot of sense that our earliest experiences tell us something about the world. And because these experiences occur before we have language available to us, we do not store them in our memories in quite the same way as we would if language were more fully developed. If my spouse cheats on me now, I am able to store that experience, along with the emotional pain, in my memory with the aid of language. In a future relationship, should I find myself distrusting the fidelity of my partner, I have a way of accessing, via language, that stored memory that explains why I don't quite trust this new partner. Our earliest infancy experiences simply leave us with predilections, attitudes, and tendencies toward trust or distrust without the ability to articulate them.

TRAUMA AND STRESS

It was noted in the previous chapter that a phenomenon known as sensitization can occur following use of amphetamines. Brain tissue essentially becomes more sensitive to the effects of amphetamine with each use. Sensitization also occurs following traumatic stressful events.[8] At a biological level neural tissue also becomes more sensitive to the effects of various biochemicals released during stressful events. So the same amount of a particular chemical, such as dopamine, will now have a stronger or more exaggerated effect following the stress or trauma.

As discussed in chapter 7, dopamine is perhaps the major biochemical implicated in fueling psychosis, of which paranoia is often a part. In light of this it is not surprising that paranoia is often seen within the context of posttraumatic stress disorder, although not as prominently as many of the other features of that disorder. Dr. James Scott and colleagues in Queensland, Australia, found that individuals who had been exposed to traumatic events were more likely to have delusions, and while the nature of those delusions was not specified, based on previous research we would expect a substantial percentage to be paranoid ones.[9] Further, the more traumatic events one had experienced, the more likely the individual was to have had delusions. In the United Kingdom, Dr. Daniel Freeman, one of the leading experts on paranoia, found that previous traumatic experiences, especially in childhood, increased the risk of developing paranoid thoughts 2.5 times that of those without such trauma.[10]

These findings suggest the possibility of a stress sensitization similar to that seen with amphetamine use. They would also provide support for developmental theories that emphasize early experiences. So a traumatic, significantly stressful event in childhood could cause the same type of sensitization. However, as with most things in life, not everybody will react the same way to the same traumatic or stressful event.

THE GREAT KETCHUP CONSPIRACY

The good people of Santa Ana, California, have had the opportunity of learning about paranoia by watching the exploits of Steve Rocco (not to be confused with the skateboarder and businessman), a previously elected member of the school board. Attending board meetings dressed in his usual attire: black clothing, dark sunglasses, and black knit cap, he railed on against "the partnership," a group of politicians out to take over the United States. The same group also planned on killing him. When the rest of the board attempted to censure him for his rants, he sued—and lost.

But his history of eccentricities—or, some would say, paranoia—preceded his election to public office. In 1980 he shoplifted sausages and rolls of film from a grocery store and was caught. To vent his spleen, he began handing out fliers in which he reported, using the clever conceit of a self-interview, that the film manufacturer, grocery store chain, and sausage maker were all involved in a conspiracy against him.

Even greater revelations regarding conspiracies, including "the partnership," are to be found in his self-published autobiography: *R.O.C.C.O: Behind the Orange Curtain.* Rocco reveals the "secret chronicles and public-record accounts of corruption, murder, and scandal of corporate and political California, written by America's premier legal technician." His explanation for his wrongful conviction of shoplifting is also provided. He had purchased the items previously and had returned to the store with the items in a bag but without a receipt. (I'm sure the police never heard that one before.)

His second shoplifting conviction, for a bottle of ketchup from a local university, had a more paranoid-sounding explanation. The police allegedly had planted the ketchup bottle near him, in order to make it appear that he had stolen it. He was on campus trying to find a professor who, in cahoots with the university's president, was trying to have him killed. Rather than accept an agreement to stay away from the university he demanded a jury trial. He lost again.

After censure from the school board he continued to pursue governmental posts, including a run for the Santa Ana City Council. On the application he listed his occupation as: "Prevent the further incursion of PARTNERSHIP/ORGANIZED CRIME into the OUSD, as represented by MEXICAN MAFIA . . . their CAUCASION PUPPETMASTERS . . . JUDICIAL MISCREANTS . . . REGISTER . . . Law Enforcement." In his latest attempt (2012) he ran for Orange County Supervisor, listing his occupation as "retired educator."

Among other things he has alleged that powerful others have conspired to prevent him from gaining employment; beaten him from head to toe; kidnapped his parents; murdered his father (with the drug Lopressor); had him "set up"; stalked him; and made death threats against him. According to Rocco, we are "living in the time of secret organizations." Many of his behaviors have been caught on video and can be watched on YouTube.

He also believes that comedian Andy Kaufman is not dead. This was apparently important enough for him to start a website, cleverly called AndyKaufmanlives.com. On that site is a message, by Andy Kaufman himself, posted on the twenty-fifth anniversary of his death. Rather than paraphrase, here are "Andy's" words:

As many of you have figured out over the years, I am not dead. I did not fake my death, I performed an illusion. I have spent the last 25 years creating my art, my way, on my terms. In 1984, I was unemployable. I was considered a liability. My agents could not get me work in television, film, theater, or comedy clubs. A tour of colleges was cancelled due to lack of interest. In the summer of 1983, my wrestling matches were cancelled due to lackluster ticket sales. I could not get backers for any of my screenplays. No publisher had the slightest interest in the books I had written. I was the boy who cried wolf too many times. I was considered a has-been. I was accepted in the TM movement but not welcome. The only reason I was accepted was my many monetary contributions over the years. My closest friends had no use for me since they could no longer advance themselves through me. I was no longer profitable to my friends or management. My family was done with me as well since I would not reach out to my child that *they* had given up for adoption. In 1983, I was alone and could not even find menial work since washed up celebrities are considered over qualified. My agents and family put me in therapy. I did the only thing I could do short of killing myself. I killed the Andy Kaufman character and buried him with a man named Nathan McCoy. With the deceased Nathan McCoy's identity, I moved on. I have spent the last 25 years producing television, making films, writing books, and keeping journals of my daily activities. I have hundreds of hours of home video. All this has been done my way, on my terms. All my work is in storage and will be destroyed upon my death. I have spent the last 15 years haunting the internet. People ask when I am going to "return." You do not seem to understand. You left me 25 years ago. I have no use for you now. My message to the world is this . . . fuck every last one of you.

Were it not for the fact that thousands of dollars of taxpayers' money have been spent battling Rocco's legal problems, he would be rather amusing.[11]

HOW WE THINK

Our brains process a tremendous amount of information, continuously and simultaneously. Right now your brain is aware of all sorts of things in your environment; for example, the temperature, sounds, how bright it is, and so on. It is also simultaneously aware of your internal environment, including how hungry or thirsty you are, whether you are in pain, and so forth. Fortunately, there are brain structures that filter out the unimportant stuff, like the position of your feet on the floor. This occurs automatically and unconsciously in the sense that you don't have to actively think "I've got to ignore the feeling of this cotton shirt and focus on this computer keyboard." But what about more sophisticated screening of information?

At a higher level, one way we reduce the amount of information we attend to is by focusing on and processing information that is somehow consistent with our beliefs. We pay attention to aspects of the environment from which judgments and inferences are drawn. A belief emerges that subsequently guides the individual's search for and interpretation of other information. Typically, as with all individuals, it involves paying attention to information consistent with our beliefs and ignoring inconsistent or contradictory information. This is referred to as *confirmatory bias* and is a perfectly normal process found in all of us.

When I was looking to get a new dog and was reviewing various breeds, I quickly honed in on Anatolian Shepherds. I considered all the positive attributes of the breed: loyalty, protection of family, long lifespan, intelligence, and so on, and made a decision to get one. I felt great about my choice and brought home a cute twenty-pound puppy—that quickly morphed into a one-hundred-and-fifty-pound behemoth—that was apparently bred directly in hell by Satan himself. I had fallen victim to a confirmatory bias.

I then went back and saw reviews of the breed that I had somehow not seen or did not process adequately. They dig, and with great skill and enthusiasm. Mine was halfway back to the center of the planet—presumably to be reunited with Satan—before I could stop him. They are also destructive, but nothing that a whole house full of new furniture couldn't fix. And they are stubborn, to the point that I really thought he had been bred without any brain material whatsoever.

Confirmatory bias reflects a systematic error in the way our minds gather and process information in order to guide our decisions and judgments. Mind you, this error is one you have to *consciously* avoid making, otherwise this "unconscious" process will proceed along its merry way.

Within the context of the development and persistence of paranoid thinking, the confirmatory bias suggests that the more entrenched or fixed an idea becomes (*She is trying to poison me*), the less likely new, contrary information will alter that belief because that information will be ignored.

Much of this occurs quickly and is often referred to as an *automatic process*, in the sense that we are not consciously aware that we are doing it. We all have mental processes, like filters, that occur automatically in response to incoming information. Dr. Brendan Maher at Harvard University has argued that delusions develop because biological dysfunction renders the normal filtering mechanism of the brain inoperable.[12] The resulting perceptual intensities of experience beg the individual to make sense of what is going on, a normal human cognitive activity. That "making sense of" employs the regular (automatic) cognitive processes that we all use. Whereas most individuals will examine an ambiguous situation by collecting more information, including reflecting on past experiences, the paranoid individual is more likely to focus only on the situation at hand. Doing so they quickly draw a conclusion the correctness of which they have high faith in. Then they gather information supporting that erroneous conclusion while ignoring contradictory information.

A cadre of researchers from the United Kingdom, including Drs. Richard Bentall, Philippa Garety, and David Hemsley, has found that delusional beliefs begin in the same way that all beliefs begin.[13] The starting point is the individual—each of whom has a unique amalgam of prior experiences, current emotional states, and personality traits. This amalgam "primes" us to experience our world in a particular way. Like colored glasses, they change our perception of the world. An event that occurs, which can be internally or externally generated, is then seen through these colored glasses. The event in question can be different than what we typically encounter, or it can be consistent with our expectations.

Particularly important as far as delusion formation is concerned is the individual's tendency to ignore previous patterns or frequencies of events and instead focus prominently on the single event in front of her. This is where the molehill transforms itself. The single event—such as an ambiguous, menacing facial expression from a coworker—is given much greater importance and weight in making a final decision that it does not merit. All previous facial expressions that were not menacing or ambiguous are forgotten or ignored so that the single one takes on greater significance.

Other aspects of thinking that contribute to the development of paranoid thinking include the tendency to quickly arrive at decisions and to be *extremely* confident in one's judgment. The final ingredient is for the individual to seek more information about the situation, which he does by utilizing the confirmatory bias noted above. This process guarantees that information consistent with the hastily drawn conclusion will be found and contradictory information ignored, the end result of which will be a deepening of the conviction. It bears repeating that this bias is normal. It is the degree to which paranoid individuals employ it that is abnormal.

The above model is very useful in understanding paranoid delusions, but it fails to adequately explain why paranoia emerges as the most common delusion. If I'm seventy years old with a urinary tract infection and develop delirium, a very common occurrence among the elderly, why is it that I believe that my daughter is stealing my money? Why don't I have a delusion that I have just found a cure for cancer, and my daughter, who I fail to recognize, is a grateful cancer survivor here to thank me? I believe the reason is that the threshold for the suspiciousness system to kick into gear is low in cases of ambiguity, as is seen in delirium.

PUTTING IT TOGETHER

The paranoid individual is "primed" to be sensitive to—or have radar for— certain events and situations by virtue of previous experiences, genetic vulnerability, exposure to certain drugs or a variety of other events discussed previously. As a result, only selected aspects of an event are abstracted and focused on. These are not random but conform to the person's belief system (confirmatory bias). Then, *previous* events are reinterpreted in light of this new information. Thus, events or situations that seemed innocent enough at the time are now (retrospectively) reinterpreted as being malicious in some way. The frequency of an event is ignored, and judgments are made quickly with a high degree of certainty on the part of the paranoid individual.

Unfortunately, these individuals don't have the ability to talk to others about their growing suspicions. As a result there is no correction factor, which would help set right deviant thinking. By definition they keep their suspicions to themselves. Other people are not willing to enter the world of the typical paranoid individual, given their less-than-warm-and-fuzzy nature. Instead others dismiss the delusions as "crazy" and don't bother to listen. As a result, they are classified by the paranoid individual as untrustworthy.

It bears repeating that in many respects paranoid individuals use the same cognitive mechanisms that we all use in trying to tie pieces together and make sense of situations. We all make mistakes when we do this. In other words, we all fail at times to come to the same conclusions that other individuals do. The difference is that we have the ability to go back, reexamine the situation, and draw different conclusions. The paranoid person is typically unable to do this.

PARANOIA-GENERATING EXPERIENCES

Paranoia has been described as a pathology to be contrasted with reasonable levels of suspiciousness. However, that does not mean that the process that results in paranoia must also be "pathological" or abnormal in some way. Shin splints are a pathological condition involving the swelling of the sheath that surrounds tendons in the shins, resulting in significant pain. One way to develop shin splints is to simply run too much. Running is not a pathological condition; it is a healthy activity that can improve cardiovascular functioning, maintain muscle mass, lower cholesterol, maintain cognitive functioning in the elderly, and may protect against the development of dementia. Yet too much of it can cause shin splints. You can see where I am going with this.

Paranoia can develop out of processes and events that, in and of themselves, are not specifically pathological. For example, many African American writers over the years have described circumstances they experienced that resulted in paranoia. Poet and sociologist Calvin Hernton describes quite eloquently how his paranoia of white policemen developed even before his negative encounters with police. "Then suddenly I remember being afraid of the police. The fear, through the process of social contagion, must have been socialized in me by merely living on Slayton Street." He then goes on to describe numerous direct encounters with the police in which he is wrongly accused.[14] I would like to believe that Hernton's experiences, occurring in the 1960s, are now an anachronism. Unfortunately, recent events of unarmed African American youths, such as Walter Scott, shot by Michael Slager, a white police officer, on April 4, 2015, in South Carolina,[15] and Michael Brown (also African American, also unarmed, shot in the back by police in Ferguson, Missouri, on August 9, 2014[16]) being targeted by police suggest otherwise.

Why some individuals develop paranoia while others in similar circumstances do not points to an even larger issue: paranoia is probably multiply determined in most cases. A combination of unique life events—for example, police profiling—individual personality characteristics, genetic disposition, biological status, traumatic events, and early environment all conspire to produce paranoia in those for whom these factors come together. This is probably the case for most paranoid individuals, yet any one of these factors may be enough for some individuals to develop paranoia.

AN AMERICAN IN BELGIUM

As a junior in college I had the opportunity to spend a year studying philosophy in a medieval university in Belgium (University of Leuven). Rich in philosophical tradition it counted among its alumni classical scholar Erasmus. As this was my first time in Europe, I found my days there to be filled with a mixture of fascination and appreciation for the differences between European and American culture, especially the Belgian ales, yet I was sadly nostalgic for the familiarity and comfort of things American. In addition, the nagging feeling that one was being looked at and talked about often occurred. Not speaking

Flemish or French didn't help the situation. Fortunately, a large ex-patriate American community and many other English-speaking students made my daily life less paranoid. However, this was not the case for some of the students. It was well known that by the end of the first month perhaps one out of ten students who came to study for a year would be gone. Homesickness was the ostensible reason, and it is difficult to determine the relative contribution of paranoia to "homesickness." It was not difficult to determine in Sam's case.

For all appearances Sam was no different than any other American abroad. There was certainly nothing about his appearance, demeanor, or way of talking that would have presaged the onset of paranoid ideation. By the end of five months he was noticeably strange. He complained about the "frogs" who were always talking about him and that the "flems" (Flemish-speaking Belgians) were actively trying to make him look foolish. He no longer hung around the student bars with us and rarely made it to lectures. Shortly before his premature return to the States he could be seen yelling at Belgians as they passed him on the street. Paranoia had claimed another young victim.

Chapter 9

THE MONSTER WITH THE GREEN EYES: JEALOUSY

O, beware, my lord, of jealousy;
It is the green-ey'd monster which doth mock
The meat it feeds on.
—William Shakespeare, *Othello*, act 3, scene 3

Most of us have experienced that horrible feeling called jealousy.[1] It hits you in the pit of your stomach and causes your face to flush, your heart to beat hard, and your emotions to reach Vesuvian levels of passion. In some it can lead to eruptions of violence and even murder. It is here considered a special form of paranoia, born of the same evolutionary stuff whence paranoia itself emerged. Dr. Thomas Arnold, who wrote one of the earliest textbooks on mental illness (circa 1786) noted that suspicion (paranoia) and jealousy "are so nearly allied that the former may be considered as differing from the latter chiefly in degree."[2]

In a sense jealousy is, like suspiciousness and paranoia, a normal human emotion on a continuum. The complete absence of jealousy can be unhealthy for some relationships, as it might signal a lack of concern or commitment on the part of the person devoid of it. Studies show that relationships in which there was minimal if any jealousy do not survive in the long haul. In the middle range of the continuum are varying healthy degrees of jealousy. At the extreme, so-called *pathological jealousy* (aka Othello syndrome, morbid jealousy, conjugal paranoia, psychotic jealousy) resembles paranoia to a marked degree. The same irrational preoccupations, persistence of the belief in the absence of credible evidence, spurious use of logic, and twisted combinations of "evidence" characterize pathological jealousy, just as they do paranoia.[3]

Jealousy and paranoia are sides of the same evolutionary coin. That coin is on one side survival, the other side reproduction. Paranoia is the pathology of the former, jealousy the latter. The universal nature of jealousy argues for its evolutionary, not cultural, origins, although cultures can certainly uniquely season their form of it.

Our focus here will be on *romantic jealousy* as opposed, for example, to the jealousy one sibling might feel toward another who has managed to garner their parents' affections. Community surveys reveal that as many as 40 percent of all people have experienced jealous feelings without good cause, and that 20 percent report that our partner's jealousy has caused us problems. For three out of one hundred the problem, either ours or our partner's, drove us to seek counseling.[4] The extent of how common and problematic jealousy can be was underscored by a large study of university students currently in a relationship in which fully one-third indicated that jealousy was a significant problem.[5]

About 30 percent of couples seeking marital counseling do so because of jealousy affecting their relationship.[6] Surveys among college students indicate that half have had relationships end due to jealousy.[7] Jealousy begets anger problems, alcohol and drug problems, reductions in self-esteem, and other mental health issues.[8] Keep in mind that actual rates of infidelity within marriages are quite high. Estimates of extramarital affairs range from between 20 to 40 percent for women and 30 to 50 percent for men.[9] Further, DNA analyses indicate that 10 percent of children are not of their putative father's making. The partners of these philanderers have good reason to be jealous. Yet that is not what this chapter is about. Just as paranoid individuals can have real enemies, the jealous can have unfaithful partners. This chapter will focus on those people who have no basis to be as jealous as they are. These are the pathologically jealous.

AMY AND RUDY

Amy was a beautiful woman fresh out of an Ivy League school where she graduated summa cum laude. Her incredibly high intelligence was matched by an equally impressive physique. She possessed the slim athletic figure and large breasts that often cause males to rubberneck and whistle, with no chance of garnering serious attention. She entered the dating scene and quickly grew to know the value of her "commodity," attracting wide attention from males of all stripes and calibers.

Amy's favor finally came to rest on Rudy, who was quite handsome and came from family money. Early into his career as a stockbroker he had already shown great potential. They were a perfect couple . . . almost. Hidden within Rudy was the hurt born from his mother's betrayal of his father, who had been caught in bed with a neighbor. The infidelity proved to be the death blow for the marriage. The seeds of jealousy had long since taken root in Rudy and needed only some provocation to erupt. The attention Amy received from all men who laid eyes on her was more than sufficient. Although Amy did not dress seductively, she did not shy away from stylish or comfortable clothes that highlighted her natural endowments. Still not completely out of "playing the field" mode, she was quick to flirt at parties, especially after a drink or two, and not infrequently her hand would come to rest on a man's arm to emphasize her laughter over a droll remark.

Waiting until they reached home after such an outing, Rudy erupted into a torrent of abuse in which the word "whore" figured prominently. Cowed by his anger she apologized and promised no such further behavior. True to her word, she subsequently curtailed her flirtatious behavior and became the model partner. Unfortunately the monster had been unleashed, and Rudy found countless evidence of her infidelities. Her clothing was inspected for hairs from her lover when she returned home from an outing. He called her dozens of time a day to ask who she was talking to. When this failed to reduce his jealous feelings he required her to keep a daily diary of all the men she spoke to. Surprise visits at work, opening her mail, checking her cell phone, and searching deleted e-mails were but several of the many techniques Rudy employed to catch Amy in the act.

All the while the verbal abuse continued until Amy's once buoyant spirit was broken. Rudy's distrust had long since alienated her friends, and the relationship became a prison. Her sister, realizing the extent of Amy's distress, urged her to "leave the jerk." Summoning up her remaining courage and dignity she began to fight back. Unfortunately her high IQ was no match for his right hook, and a visit to the ER and a woman's shelter resulted in a restraining order against Rudy, which, like most batterers, he ignored. He continued to harass her at work. Legal intervention failed to curtail the harassment, and eventually Amy moved out of state to rid herself of Rudy.

PATHOLOGICAL JEALOUSY

Paranoia represents one (pathological) end of a continuum. The same is true for jealousy. Because a certain level of jealousy can be construed as healthy, it becomes difficult to determine at which point we would identify it as "unhealthy" or pathological.

Research has shown that jealous feelings are common among people in relationships.[10] Normal jealousy is elicited when a provoking event occurs, such as seeing one's partner in an animated discussion with a potential rival. Normal individuals typically react with anger and distress, followed by confrontation of his or her partner. An explanation and reassurance are usually sufficient to allay the concerns. Even if these thoughts persist, the jealous person will rarely act on them by, for example, inspecting their partner's clothing, opening their mail, and so on. The jealous reaction remains an internal event without subsequent behavior. In contrast, pathologically jealous individuals are not reassured by explanations from their partners. They act on their erroneous conclusions, which are largely divorced from what others would considerable credible evidence.

One way to determine when jealousy turns from healthy to unhealthy is to pinpoint when it begins to significantly affect a person's happiness or interferes with his or her relationship. At any level the feeling of jealousy is unpleasant and will at least temporarily lower one's mood. Moreover, when these feelings are verbalized, they will likely cause friction with one's partner. A temporary feeling of jealousy is not a problem; it is when the feelings are persistent and significant that this becomes an issue. When the term *pathological jealousy* is employed several factors serve as indicators to support this categorization. First, the preoccupation with infidelity is unfounded. Second, the thought process would be identified by most as being irrational. Finally, the level of jealous concern is in excess of what is considered normal in those circumstances or in one's society.

LOW-LEVEL PATHOLOGICAL JEALOUSY

At the lowest levels of pathological jealousy we find a person who is obsessed with the notion that his partner is being unfaithful ("low level" should not be interpreted as being mild, as these individuals have considerable jealous pathology). This condition resembles obsessive-compulsive disorder in the sense that the thoughts (obsessions) are unwanted and intrusive. Like someone with an obsession about leaving the lights on, the jealous partner cannot rid himself of the thought or, in particular, the image of his partner enjoying sex with someone else.

The person with a germ obsession tries hard not to think about all the germs that are covering her hands, yet the thoughts push their way in, intruding into ongoing thinking and causing a considerable amount of distress in the process. Imagine for a moment that I just dumped a vile of blood on your hands that had been taken from someone who was HIV positive or who had the Ebola virus. To what extent do you think you would be able to continuing reading this book? Obviously all your thoughts would be directed to your now-infected hands. You would be quite upset, and the only way you could reduce your anxiety would be to wash your hands thoroughly. Yet ten minutes later the thought crosses your mind that you might have missed some blood. That thought grows until again you can think of little else except your infected hands. A second trip to the bathroom, and you might begin to feel normal, because you are—presumably. In the case of obsessive-compulsive disorder, no amount of washing eliminates the distress. At best it temporarily reduces the anxiety until the obsessive thoughts return.

Low-level (obsessional) pathological jealousy works in much the same way. The individual cannot help but think about it. Doing something—like calling her at work to see if she answers the phone immediately or has to push her lover off her before answering it—temporarily relieves the stress. But the thoughts will return. Normal jealousy might involve seeing your partner smile coyly at a colleague and wondering if there is something going on between them. That evening while having sex she suddenly tries a new sex position, which really rings your jealousy alarm. You confront her with the "evidence" demanding an explanation about what is happening between her and the colleague. A spat might ensue, and even if she provides a convincing denial of any infidelity, the thought might remain with you and make you more vigilant. In the absence of further evidence the feeling subsides. Not so in obsessional jealousy.

Low-level obsessional jealousy might bring someone in for psychotherapy as the thoughts and images are alien and unwanted.

OTHELLO SYNDROME

When I first encountered him on the inpatient geriatric psychiatric unit, Jim was one year post-stroke. The stroke had occurred in the right hemisphere of his brain, resulting in mild (partial) paralysis of the left side of his face, arm, and leg. As is common among males who have suffered strokes, he became impotent, which is also not unusual for men his age (eighty-three). Unlike many of the patients on the unit it was not apparent what his problem was. He was articulate, intelligent, and not depressed or demented. However, he appeared to not know why he was there. (Many patients with Alzheimer's can't answer the same question due, in large part, to the fact that they can't remember how or when they got there or where *there* really is)

After I read his chart it was clear why he was there. In a fit of anger he had thrown his walker at his wife. Why? Because she was having a torrid love affair with the high school checkout boy at the local supermarket. He was absolutely sure that the sexual liaison had taken place and that it continued.

"Proof" of this tryst came from the way the boy always looked at his wife ("lustfully"); her frequent awakenings in the night, not to urinate as claimed, but to meet her lover; and the secret signals she sent her young paramour—for example, hanging the laundry in a specified manner to indicate the time of their next rendezvous.

The large age discrepancy (seventeen versus eighty-one) did not seem apparent to him or cause him to alter his belief. A quick call to his wife dispelled my notion that we were seeing an "accentuation of premorbid characteristics"; in other words, Jim had always been the jealous type and the stroke had simply made it worse. To the contrary, she described a warm and loving relationship before the stroke, and noted that this one isolated symptom—pathological jealousy— appeared only after the stroke. In most other ways, he was the same Jim, only now he did not trust her, and she could not trust him.

This phenomenon, the de novo development of pathological

jealousy in older individuals following strokes, is not common, nor is it exceedingly rare. It is seen often enough to merit the designation of Othello syndrome.[11]

PATHOLOGICAL JEALOUSY IN EXTREME: DELUSIONAL JEALOUSY

Delusional jealousy is far less common than low-level pathological jealousy, with its obsessive-compulsive features. Estimates are that 25 percent of people with delusional disorder have the jealous type.[12] It is therefore statistically rare; only about 1 percent of all patients admitted to hospitals are reported to have it.[13] We do not know how many people in the general population experience delusional jealousy because most do not necessarily come in for treatment, although their spouses might.

The previous description of delusions applies to delusional jealousy. This is someone whose level of jealousy is truly delusional, as the case example above illustrates. Moreover, the disorder persists for years. It appears that both males and females suffer from pathological jealousy to the same extent, although males are more likely to end up hospitalized or imprisoned for it, largely as a result of violence due to the jealousy.[14] There is evidence that the disorder is found frequently among older males.[15]

At what point do we promote low-level pathological jealousy to the status of delusional jealousy? One criterion would be when the "evidence" is highly dubious to someone else. Like all delusions, it is unmodified by counterargument or evidence, is unremitting, and often persists for many years. Not uncommonly such delusional individuals were noted to be "suspicious" *premorbidly* (that is, before the onset of the condition), suggesting a progression from lower level to the more extreme (delusional) form.[16]

PATHOLOGICAL JEALOUSY: THE FULL PICTURE

The pathologically jealous individual engages in similar behaviors as does the paranoid person. Exquisitely well-tuned to the nuances of any situation, the pathologically jealous individual can see "evidence" of their partner's infidelity everywhere. A carpet stain or splotches on a blouse are immediately assumed to be semen stains from her tryst. A rogue hair, rumpled shirt, or tie askew is as close to a smoking gun as it gets. The partner's desire to try a new sexual position, the discovery of a new musical artist, or beginning a new hobby are all seen as indications of another's influence.

Their partners are in a no-win situation. Denials of unfaithful behavior are "just what I'd expect you'd say" and "Methinks thou dost protest too much." The pathologically jealous are inordinately preoccupied with their partner's past relationships. Even something as innocuous as putting on perfume or cologne is interpreted as an attempt to cover up the smell of their paramour and/or an enhancement in order to seduce another. Attempts to look good are for the sake of the other. No thought is given to alternative explanations such as "I want to look good for you" or "I want to feel good about myself and look my best."

Trips to the tanning salon, hairdresser, or gym are seen as attempts to attract and lure potential partners. Their lives are fraught with anxieties that most of us never think about. Getting stuck in rush-hour traffic and arriving home twenty minutes late is merely an inconvenience for us. The partner of the pathologically jealous knows that accusations and an angry tirade await them. Social situations are not times to relax and enjoy the company of others but are impression-management exercises. How much you smile, whom you look at, how much you talk, whose body you bump into become the evening's interrogation fodder.

The pathologically jealous are no happier than the paranoiac is. Keeping your wanton partner's sexual appetites in check is tough work. First you must gather the evidence sufficient to indict and convict your partner. Just a few of the duties include checking through their purse or wallet, reading their journal and e-mails, checking their cell phone for calls made and received, opening their mail, rummaging through the trash for incriminating evidence, and examining their clothing. They also must examine their partner's body for telltale signs of sex, such as bite marks or abrasions from a beard. The next stage may require more significant actions. Showing up at their workplace unexpectedly, arriving home in the middle of the day to catch them in flagrante delicto, and surreptitiously listening in on their phone conversations are common. I saw once saw a man who hid a video camera in the bookshelf to record his wife's indiscretions. It was a testament to the pathological jealous individual's persistence that countless hours of uneventful videotape did not deter him from continuing to record each day.

Failing to catch them with basic procedures, the pathologically jealous up the ante by following their unfaithful partner or even hiring detectives to do the dirty work for them. Their own interrogations may be supplemented with trips to a polygraph lab. Odometer checks are compared to reported excursions and distances between points measured so precise comparisons can be made. The time it takes to reach certain destinations is determined. Friends and even children may be questioned about what they have seen or heard. They may "leave for work" only to park down the street and slip in the back door, hiding somewhere in the house to catch their unfaithful partner. Some have been known to feign a business trip and hide in the attic, which had been provisioned for days of spying.

A paradoxical phenomenon often occurs with the pathologically jealous as far as sexual behavior is concerned. There can be a significant increase in sexual activity with their partner despite that individual's presumed infidelity. This may include not just an increase in the amount of sexual encounters but also the types of those encounters. New positions, "toys," pornography, and such may suddenly appear. Keeping their partner sexually sated will presumably decrease his or her interest in having those desires satisfied by another.

While all of this is going on, there is a program of restriction and control under way. It is not enough for them to catch you in the act. They must also prevent you from engaging in your infidelities. One of the first restrictions is who you can associate with. The first victims here are your friends, for they are in a position to introduce you to others, one of whom you might find as a suitable replacement partner. Often friends see what is happening and try to help by pointing out how pathological the behavior is.

A frequent method of control is over finances. You are provided with what amounts to an "allowance," which is calculated to provide you with sufficient gas and lunch money, but not enough to rendezvous for dinner or drive to your lover's place. I have encountered a number of women in therapy who are not "allowed" to possess a credit or debit card, and who are essentially denied access to the couple's financial resources. Sometimes the true motivations for this are acknowledged; sometimes they are disguised under the justification of needing to "stick to a tight budget."

In addition, restrictions are made on answering the phone, talking to people at work, and even the location of one's job. Some are required to keep a log of any conversations with the opposite sex. Even the pursuit of higher education will be questioned as having the hidden motive of extensive contact with members of the opposite sex, including the professoriate. Where you go, how long you stay, who you meet, who you talk to, and what you do are all increasingly dictated until your life becomes smothered to the point that it barely resembles a real life. Lost along the way are your friends, family, and self-respect.

One might justify remaining with a pathologically jealous individual if their life together was for the most part happy and harmonious. Rarely is that the case. The issue is not a real infidelity but a pathological mental condition that does not require an actual infidelity to keep it fueled. As a result the accusations, recriminations, and restrictions continue. It is like living in a densely packed minefield. Try as you might to tiptoe around the mines, sooner or later one will go off, and the final result is often violence. On a day-to-day basis, this kind of life is stressful for the accused, and the pathologically jealous are usually depressed, as would be most people who believed their partner was unfaithful.

ALCOHOLIC JEALOUSY

As alcoholism is far more common in males, this section will focus on male alcoholics.

It has been observed for centuries that a significant proportion, perhaps 30 to 40 percent, of alcoholics are pathologically jealous, with higher rates among males.[17] The degree of jealousy seen in alcoholic jealousy is proportionate to the degree of marital discord. One caveat to these statistics is the fact that many long-suffering spouses of alcoholics may indeed have found solace in the bed of another.

The nature of alcoholic jealousy is probably multiply determined. Long-term heavy alcohol consumption significantly impacts a number of biological factors associated with sexual performance, including reduced sexual desire (libido). Often the alcoholic will project his own lack of desire onto his partner, who is accused of not wanting sex because she is "getting it elsewhere."

Certainly the symptoms of alcoholism causes marital tensions that spill over into the bedroom. Disinhibited by the effects of alcohol, the man may become rough and uncaring in his lovemaking. A woman's natural reaction would be to avoid sex, thereby confirming the potentially erroneous suspicions that she is cheating on him. Angry with her, he resorts to drinking even more to quell the distress and drown the anger and pain. And the cycle begins anew and deepens in severity.

JEALOUSY AND VIOLENCE

The association between jealousy and violence is well known. Indeed, in the past, when a man found his wife in flagrante delicto her subsequent murder was treated as a lesser crime or even dismissed entirely. Historically women have typically not enjoyed the same legal protections, being viewed for many centuries as mere property of the husband to do with whatever he wants.

It is difficult to determine the percentage of pathologically jealous individuals who become violent. What can be said with some precision is that jealousy is an important factor in many violent crimes, most perpetrated against women. In the United States jealousy ranked as either the second or third leading cause of homicides in several major metropolitan areas. The UK statistics are very similar. In cases in which someone is killed by their partner, the vast majority (80 percent or more) involve jealousy.[18] It is noteworthy that these studies often show that a female accused of killing her husband did so in order to protect herself from his abuse, which was typically fueled by jealousy. Studies of dating relationships have found that between 14 and 45 percent of males admit to being physically violent, and women are no slouches themselves: between 10 and 59 percent admit to being so. Jealousy is the most commonly identified factor in such violence among both sexes.[19]

Most research on men who batter women suggests that jealousy is perhaps the primary "cause" of such brutality.[20] Studies examining violence in marriage find 90 percent or more of male batterers were jealous.[21] Compared to nonbatterers in general, the batterers are more jealous but no more so than other men who are unhappily married. While it is generally the case that young males are more violent than are older ones, the reverse is true among the pathologically jealous who murder their partners. In one British study the average age was over forty. Fully 12 percent of these (male) British murders (3 percent of females) had definite delusions of jealousy that caused the murder.[22] These delusions persisted even after the death of the spouse. Not surprising is the fact that about 50 percent of these murderers were quite paranoid, often believing they were being poisoned by their soon-to-be-deceased spouse.

Anger is the predominant emotion among pathologically jealous individuals. Premorbidly many are described as being angry and hostile. They have poor attachments to others and are generally mistrustful.[23] Yet at the onset of a relationship these characteristics, plus the jealousy itself, are often kept tightly in check. A quick perusal of the personal ads in any publication or online will reveal that while many singles identify themselves as "tender" or "romantic," no one admits to being the "jealous or possessive" type.

The progression of violence usually begins with verbal assaults and moves to non-personal violence, such as throwing objects or punching walls. Destruction of property moves from anything within arm's reach to possessions of either monetary or emotional value to the accused individual; for example a prized stuffed animal or cell phone. From there low-level physical violence begins—pushing, grabbing, squeezing, shoving, and shaking. Then more serious forms of violence emerge—slapping, punching, strangling—including the use of lethal weapons. The ostensible "purpose" can be simple punishment for a perceived transgression, as a "warning shot" designed to give a hint as to the consequences of any indiscretions that might occur, or to elicit a confession.

Not uncommonly the partners of pathologically jealous individuals tire of the incessant harassment and interrogation process and confess to something just to stop the assault. Often, the real (physical) assault then begins: shoving, grabbing the throat, slapping, shaking, and so on. Although the pathologically jealous claim that the truth will eliminate their jealous distress, it does so only temporarily. As with the hand-washing preoccupation of someone with a germ-related obsessive-compulsive disorder, the thoughts and feelings return quickly.

Indirect evidence for this progression of violence is provided by the fact that 16 percent of jealous murderers had prior convictions for assault, and 25 to 30 percent had previously attacked their partners before eventually killing them.[24]

In 30 percent of cases the couple had separated at some point, only to reunite, after which the partner was killed. About one-third of these murderers attempt suicide, and the majority of murder-suicides (50 to 75 percent) are jealousy-related, as best as can be determined by psychological postmortems.[25] As was noted previously, pathological jealousy takes its toll on the mental health of those who are afflicted. Jealous murderers are typically depressed, and alcohol/drug abuse is common as well.[26]

R. R. Mowat's classic study of pathologically jealous murderers in Britain remains one of the best descriptions of the progression from jealousy to tragedy. Based on an extensive review of records and interviews, the picture that emerges is of a normal married male who after a period of time in an unremarkable marriage comes to feel that his wife no longer cares for him. The thought of infidelity creeps into his mind, at which point he begins to see "evidence" for it in much the same way the paranoid individual will accumulate evidence. Minor details such as a piece of lint become conclusive evidence—in his mind—for the wife's wayward behaviors. Accusations are made, which result in a predictable fight. The seriousness of the fights escalates and eventually become physical. She typically leaves at some point, only to return to "work it out."[27]

He may develop classic paranoid delusions involving being poisoned or having contracted a sexually transmitted disease from her. The situation escalates until in a classic "fit of jealous rage," he kills her then tries to, or does, kill himself. The process usually takes about four years, on average.[28] A curious aspect is that when someone becomes jealous, they rarely are violent toward the perceived interloper. For both males and females the partner becomes the target for violence.[29]

JEALOUSY AND DEATH

Dr. Robert Ferrante, a professor of neurologic surgery at the University of Pittsburgh, was convicted of killing his wife, Dr. Autumn Klein, chief of women's neurology at the University of Pittsburgh Medical Center in 2014. Toxic levels of cyanide were found in her system, and Dr. Ferrante had previously done online searches for the phrases "cyanide poisoning," "how would a coroner detect when someone is killed by cyanide," and the definition of "malice of forethought." He also purchased, for the first time and just before his wife died, cyanide using a university credit card. Two months before her death, Dr. Klein confided to a friend that her husband had accused her of cheating on him. Ferrante had acknowledged that fact and confronted her three times shortly before her death regarding alleged infidelity. On the stand he admitted to reading her mail, including letters of a "flirtatious nature."[30]

JEALOUSY ON THE ROAD: STALKING

When we hear the word *stalking*, thoughts of celebrities hounded by obsessed fans come to mind. Such celebrities as David Letterman, Madonna, Leonardo DiCaprio, John Lennon, Jennifer Aniston, Rihanna, Sandra Bullock, Justin Timberlake, Gwyneth Paltrow, Halle Berry, and Rebecca Schaeffer have been the victims of stalking, sometimes with tragic results. The deaths of Lennon and Schaeffer are sad testimony to this. Yet most stalkers, probably 65 percent or more, know their victim personally and in most cases had been intimate with the individual—for example, ex-partners. More often it is males who do the stalking, and it is estimated that about 8 percent of females and 2 percent of males will be stalked at some point in their lives.[31]

LIKE IT IS RIGHT OUT OF A STEVEN SPIELBERG MOVIE

The plot is pure Hollywood: an evil member of a satanic cult places an electronic microchip called a *soul catcher* in the head of a hapless victim to control her. These despicable satanists have been engaging in ritual sexual abuse of children as well. But the victim turns the tables on the leader by stalking him to expose his wickedness.

The evil genius behind these shenanigans? None other than filmmaker Steven Spielberg, who allegedly performed these deeds out of his basement where the cult was headquartered. The "victim" was psychotherapist Diana Napolis, who was subsequently slapped with a restraining order for stalking the filmmaker. This didn't stop her; she simply changed her target to actress Jennifer Love Hewitt, whom she stalked and sent death threats to. In addition to Spielberg and Hewitt, Napolis named actor Sylvester Stallone, the CIA, the Illuminati, NSA, Livermore Laboratory, the Russians, NASA, University of California, and space aliens as being involved in conspiracy.[32]

The terms *paranoia* and *jealousy* conjure up definitions for most of us that do not differ significantly from more technical definitions, as might be found in a psychology textbook. Stalking is somewhat different and a bit trickier. Those of you who have recently fallen in love, do you not find yourself thinking about your loved one? Did you try to position yourself in places where he or she might "bump in to you" early in your relationship? Do you want to talk about them when you are with others ad nauseam? Are these all signs of early stalking or just the normal obsessional activities of Cupid's victims?

If I ask you out on a date and you turn me down only to find flowers on your desk the next day with a note asking you again to go out with me, along with assurances that "I'm really a nice guy," am I stalking you? If I "happen" to bump in to you at your favorite bar at happy hour a couple of days later and ask to buy you a drink, and again ask you out, am I stalking you then, or am I being the persistent romantic? Now, if the next day, after having shot me down three times you find your favorite childhood stuffed animal, Snuffles, on your desk, decapitated with a note indicating that "you got what you deserve, you castrating bitch . . . and there is more of this to come," then you would probably have no problem deciding you are being stalked. So the difference between "romantic persistence" and stalking is that the latter involves persistent, unwanted intrusions or communications that are malicious or threaten the victim's safety in some way. It is a step up from harassment, which "merely" involves behaviors that annoy, torment, or alarm the other person without a legitimate purpose.

WHEN JAMIE MET DOUG

When Doug first approached Jamie and asked her out, she felt a reticence that she could not describe. There was something mildly "creepy" about him, although nothing manifestly bizarre. She declined and he persisted. After several attempts during the span of a couple of weeks Jamie decided that perhaps she was being too judgmental and relented. The date was relatively unremarkable—lots of small talk, and since she felt no spark, Jamie kept the banter superficial. She thanked him at the end of the evening and, when he hinted at further contact, demurred that she had just ended a relationship recently (a lie) and was not interested in jumping into another. Hoping to soften the blow she added that "maybe we can do lunch sometime."

Within a week a thank-you card arrived from Doug expressing how much he enjoyed their "romantic evening" and that he hoped that "the lunch" would not be too far off. Choosing the "ignore it" route, Jamie did nothing. Within another week flowers arrived at her place of employment with a card from a "not so secret admirer" asking her to "call me about that lunch." He left a message on her answering machine later that week asking her to call him.

Sensing that Doug was not getting the message, and a bit annoyed by this point, she called him the next day. Fortunately she got the answering machine and left a blunt "Don't call me or send me gifts—I'm not interested" message. The tenor of Doug's next communication had taken a decidedly ominous tone. His note, left under her door, began with "Dear Stuck-up Bitch" and was filled with vile invectives. Charging her with leading him on and having sex with multiple other males he ended his tirade with "You'll get what you deserve."

Despite advice from friends to call the police Jamie chose to ignore the message. Then she began seeing him standing outside her place of work. Gifts ranging from chocolates to a dead cat were left on her front porch. The police were called and a restraining order issued, which Doug ignored. Veiled threats were made against her family—for example, "I know where your niece gets off the school bus." Calling in some favors, she asked her friend Kyle to play the role of her boyfriend. The ploy did not go unnoticed. Although she had gotten an unlisted number, Jamie received a chilling message on her answering machine: "I guess both of you like to live dangerously." The message/tirade sounded like one from a jilted lover, and themes of infidelity, betrayal, and mistrust were prominent.

Over the course of a three-year ordeal Jamie's house was broken into, mail stolen, pet killed, relationships ruined—all under the constant threat of violence. Anonymous calls to her employers with information about her "character" resulted in layoffs or a palpable change in demeanor toward her. Frustrated by the inability to "catch him in the act" and prosecute, Jamie chose to take a job elsewhere and start over. Unfortunately the memories went with her, and like most people who have been stalked she suffered from posttraumatic stress disorder–like symptoms, all for the price of a single date. And not unlike many stalking victims, she became paranoid about people she met.

The statistics on stalking are stark: about 25 percent of stalkers become violent, and 2 percent kill their victims. Yet only about 30 percent of victims actually report stalking to the police. And with good reason: police intervention often serves to further enrage an already angry stalker.[33] Among college students, both in the United States and in the United Kingdom, about 20 to 30 percent of students are victims of stalkers.[34]

The behavior of stalkers includes many of the characteristics of paranoid individuals and the pathologically jealous. They follow their victims, call and confront them, attempt to approach them, and watch them in their homes. The big difference is that for the paranoid or pathologically jealous person, these behaviors are more information-gathering maneuvers. For the stalker they are intermixed with other behaviors, the goal of which is to intimidate, coerce, frighten, or seduce the victim. The pathologically jealous person calls at a time when a tryst between their partner and another is suspected. The call of the stalker comes in the middle of the night and is intended to harass. They may leave "gifts," including flowers, dildos, and dead animals, often to serve as warnings. They break into the victim's house and move some furniture in order to "leave a message" or call their target's family, friends, or employer. One of my students found semen splattered on her door upon returning from class.

As interesting as stalking is as a topic, why include it in this book? Perhaps not surprisingly, the vast majority of stalkers are jealous and/or suspicious to the point of being paranoid.[35] A significant proportion (35 percent) of stalkers are psychotic, and of that group many have paranoid delusional disorder. The effects on the victim are often devastating and resemble the posttraumatic stress disorder reactions seen in returning war veterans or those who have been raped. Sadly, about 50 percent of victims develop significant suspiciousness and/or paranoia as a result of their ordeal.

STALKING AND PARANOIA MEET

The overlap between paranoia and stalking is perhaps best exemplified by the book *A New Breed: Satellite Terrorism in America*, written by anesthesiologist John R. Hall.

According to Hall, the government has satellites capable of hearing what you are thinking and even seeing what you are seeing. They are able to see you indoors, to alter your moods, and to put thoughts in your mind. These thoughts sound like voices that make the victim appear crazy, which is the intent of those controlling the satellites. Because the satellites use microwave technology, they can cause gastrointestinal maladies including vomiting blood, heartburn, and blood in your stool. But it doesn't stop there; they also use ultrasonic technology that can cause sedation, runny nose, and confusion as well as pressure on your heart (thereby mimicking cardiac problems), urethra, and bowels, causing elimination difficulties.

Based on this premise, one might think that the government is using this diabolical technology to control us all. Perhaps, but according to Hall, common criminals have successfully hacked into this system and are now using it for their nefarious activities. He should know, because apparently he has been the victim of these attacks, perpetrated by a fellow physician and the rogue detective agency he hired to discredit Dr. Hall and ruin his life.

Not only were these ne'er-do-wells targeting him; they also went after the women in his life. First came Mary. Soon after moving to San Antonio to be with Hall her apartment was broken into and ransacked. Further, she appeared to be drugged at times. Next came Priscilla, whose house was also broken into and her possessions rifled through, although nothing was taken. They took apart household appliances only to reassemble them and repainted rooms in her residence while she was at work. Doors were shortened in length "thus allowing one to look under bedroom or bathroom doors with baseboard-mounted pinhole cameras."[36] He and Priscilla also found a battery-operated pinhole camera embedded in her bedroom closet door.

Next up was Mallory, who experienced the same scenario: furniture tampered with, doors dissembled, and so on. More ominous were the drugging and rapes that she could not recall. So in order to "protect" her, Hall began keeping watch on her—sitting in his car outside her residence, placing recording devices in her condo, and basically, well, stalking her.

He examined the contents of her refrigerator only to find puncture holes in her bottled water, like those that might be caused by a syringe. Tea bags had been opened then glued back together (that was how the date-rape drugs were ostensibly being administered to her). Her parents began to suspect and accused him of being the source of their daughter's problems. But he knew that they, too, had been targeted by those controlling the satellites, and had had their minds altered. When Mallory began to suspect him of having schizophrenia based on his strange explanations and beliefs, he attributed that to their mind control of her.

Next came a "female friend" who helped type his book. She, too, had her home invaded, air-conditioning vents removed, and computer destroyed. Finally, there was Cynthia Vurbeff. She was dating one of Hall's friends, and on the day she met Hall he claimed he'd been told that she would be the next victim of stalking. True to his "prediction" her computer, car, and motorcycle were vandalized, and her residence was broken into on numerous occasions. Her safe was drilled open, furniture was moved, the gas oven was left on, clothes dryer was disassembled, doors were left open, lights were left on, and Vurbeff was reportedly drugged and raped.

Dr. Hall's descriptions of his experiences were quite telling, and the picture of paranoia clearly emerges through them. He acknowledged hearing voices even when in the operating room with a patient under anesthesia! Of course these are not hallucinations, according to him, but satellite technology that can turn even the aquarium in your home into a broadcast device. The satellites were used to deprive him of sleep and continued almost nonstop. Like most auditory hallucinations, the voices were not pleasant and threatened to kill him, his girlfriend, and even his pets. The ultimate goal was to make him appear delusional, a task they appeared to have achieved with flying colors. Cars followed him, people stared at him from behind window blinds, strangers walked across his roof at night and watched him twenty-four hours a day. They put bleach in his water system and drugged him in an apparent attempt to kill him. His socks and shoes began to emit a strange odor, and metal chips were placed in his shoes. Why metal chips in the shoes, you may ask? Well, when the microwaves from the satellite are turned up, the chips heat up and burn his feet. As a result of the chips and the stench, he started to wear sandals.

The ultrasonic waves he was bombarded with caused his jaw to be displaced, and the microwaves caused his genitals to be burned. Electromagnetic energy beamed at him burned out his lightbulbs within days of being replaced and caused his car transmission to shift at inappropriate times. He also installed infrared cameras and began to carry all personal hygiene products with him rather than risk having them tampered with. (This was the result of finding his deodorant tampered with and ground silica placed in his toothpaste, which caused his gums to bleed.)

He checked his food for signs of tampering, filed complaints with the local police, FBI, and "National Intelligence Service." The latter agency doesn't exist in our country; perhaps he sent complaints to Greece, for they have a National Intelligence Service. Eventually, his employers noticed that he was not quite right and suspended his privileges. This prompted the Texas Medical Board to investigate him, and he was eventually found to be suffering from a delusional disorder.

He described to them everything that was happening to him, then mocked them for the "dumbfounded looks on their faces," as if *they* were the crazy ones. He alluded to his attorney being "enamored" with the medical board's attorney, hinting at a possible conspiracy there. Drug monitoring was mandated, which eventually resulted in a positive urine test for cocaine and the suspension of his medical license. According to Hall, all of this was rigged, of course, by others. So why was this happening to the good doctor and his female friends? Well, according to him it was an effort to discredit him, to ruin his career, to bankrupt him, and to repeatedly rape his female friends.[37]

Let's put this all together. We have someone who hears voices, believes he is the target of harassment from evil-doers who have hijacked a government satellite, has access to sedatives, tests positive for cocaine, believes that the Texas Medical Board somehow managed to tamper with his urine sample so it would test positive for cocaine, and has had at least five female acquaintances suffer the same fate of being stalked and possibly drugged and raped. What conclusions might someone draw from this? Investigative reporter Joe Conger at KENS Channel 5 in San Antonio saw these as "interesting connections," to the point that he bluntly asked Dr. Hall if he was the one doing the stalking. Not surprisingly, he did not acknowledge doing so.[38] He certainly appears to fit the pattern of someone suffering from a delusional disorder, although the possibility of cocaine-induced paranoia can't be ruled out.

So if you ever find yourself in surgery in the San Antonio area you may want to ask the person who is about to administer the anesthesia and place you in a delicate balance between life and death if they are hearing voices that day. Why should you ask? Well, the Texas Medical Board reinstated Dr. Hall's license. He is out there somewhere.[39]

ALL YOU NEED IS LOVE . . . AND A LITTLE JEALOUSY

Previously I defined an adaptation as a solution to a problem involving our ability to survive or reproduce, which occurred repeatedly throughout the course of human evolution. Suspiciousness was identified as one such adaptation, and jealousy will be added as suspicion's sister. But much like the understanding of suspiciousness required identifying the situation(s) that prompted its emergence, so, too, understanding jealousy behooves us to determine what problem it solved—that is, what it was an adaptation for.

The issue with jealousy involves the question "Whose child is it"? Not to put too fine a point on it, the real issue is that we guys can't trust you females. You see, you women know whose child it is. It is half yours because it grew inside of you. We guys hope that it is ours, but hope does not guarantee that we have successfully passed on our genes by impregnating a female. As the saying goes, "Mommy's baby, daddy's maybe." Not only must we gain sexual access to a female—step one—but we must then make sure that our seed, and only our seed, is the one to fertilize the egg. Given that a human male's sperm can remain viable inside a woman for up to seven days, it is important to ensure that no one else has sex with her.

As if this problem was not enough, you clever females over the course of evolution have figured out a way of disguising when you are impregnable. Unlike our baboon cousins, females of our species do not walk around with bright-red asses advertising the fact that they are ovulating. This hidden ovulation is itself an adaptation designed to prevent a male from simply showing interest during estrus, then running off with his resources to find another red-assed female to impregnate. Because of this hidden estrus we guys have to hang around and provide resources, because we are never sure when ovulation takes place.

Now, out of all of this we must also make sure that no other male attempts to impregnate our female. Jealousy is the adaptation that arose out of that situation. Jealousy in males serves to impel behaviors that protect access to their partners by other males, thereby increasing their confidence that the child is theirs. More specifically, what evolved was a disposition to distrust competitors who hover around our females. The behaviors that emerged are the careful observations of other males with *our* females. The casual touches, quick smiles, degree of engagement during conversations all signal to males that we are in danger of having our females go off with someone else and become impregnated by them instead of us. We look for these signs vigilantly, and when we see them, the feeling of jealousy emerges.

In and of itself the feeling of jealousy does us no good. It is the behaviors that result from it that make it a true adaptation. In the case of jealousy there are a number of options. Most simply, heightened awareness to cues of infidelity occurs. Alternatively, we can threaten the rival male; at prior times in history this was done with threats of bodily harm or a duel. This works fine if you happen to be the bigger of the two. In Woody Allen's movie *Love and Death* he competes for the affections of a particular woman. When her paramour attempts to protect the relationship by insulting Woody, the quick-witted Allen states that if a man had made such a comment he'd do him bodily harm, to which the larger rival replies, "I *am* a man." Flustered at the failure of his threat the hapless Woody replies, "Well, I mean a much shorter man."[40]

So if your proportions are more Woody Allen and less Arnold Schwarzenegger you might try plan B, which is to threaten the typically smaller female. Not a good solution, and in real life this unfortunately often takes the form of violence, as noted previously.

A third possible response to your jealousy is to redouble your efforts to woo your female. Buy her flowers, drop an antelope carcass at her hut entrance, and give her unlimited affection and attention. Psychologist David Buss, one of the foremost experts on the evolutionary perspective on jealousy, has proposed that a woman's flirtations may often be purposely motivated in the sense that they result in renewed interest, affections, and commitment on the part of the jealous individual.

The bottom line is that whatever response strategy is ultimately chosen, it has the effect of preventing the female from consorting with another male. Buss has nicely likened jealousy to a fire alarm. The fact that the alarm sounds does not invariably mean a fire is present. But you want a low threshold so that if there is one, you are not burned, figuratively or literally. Jealousy only signals the possible infidelity on the part of your partner. It tells you to be careful and to be ready to spring into action lest you be cuckolded.

THE GREEN-EYED WOMAN MONSTER

Up until now I have focused on men as the jealous party. What adaptation does jealousy provide the female, given that she is assured that the baby is half hers? The answer is resources. From an evolutionary standpoint finding a guy who is willing to have sex and impregnate you is about as hard as getting wet in the ocean. In fact, trying to keep such willing participants at bay is the real chore. So what is important from a female's viewpoint is picking the "right" guy. Both sexes look for particular qualities in the other. For example, males find younger females more attractive because they are more fertile and likely to become pregnant. Females typically prefer older males who have had the time to accumulate resources that they can devote to the woman and her/their offspring. While males fear most the possible impregnation by another male, the female fears most the withdrawal of resources, which would then be devoted to a rival female. Jealousy signals the female of that possibility.

The same cues and situations that cause jealousy to arise in males occur with females as well. Females observe the degree of emotional involvement with the other female, something they are arguably far better at than males. This involvement is a pretty reliable indicator of whether the male is going to withdraw and reinvest his resources in another female.

JEALOUSY AND GENDER

Research on jealousy reveals that males and females tend to be equally jealous, but that the nature of that jealousy is different and in keeping with the evolutionary view noted above.[41] Not surprisingly, males are much more focused on and concerned about their partner having sex with a rival. This is a paternity issue. Females are more attuned to their partner sharing nonsexual intimacy and attention with a rival. This is a resource issue. That is not to say that males don't become upset by their partner sharing intimacy with another male or that females don't much care if their partner is having sex with another. On average males are more focused on sexual infidelity, females on emotional infidelity. When a valued relationship is threatened in some way, motivated behaviors designed to counter that threat are set into motion.[42]

That being said, there are those who argue that culture shapes males to be more promiscuous. The import of this is that males are more likely to engage in sex without a strong emotional component being involved. Women, on the other hand, are said to be culturally programmed to require intimacy along with sex. So when a female has sex with someone else, the male should be doubly upset because it is assumed that it is sex plus intimacy, whereas women are less upset at finding their partner with someone else because they assume that only sex is involved. If she were to find that intimacy was also part of the encounter, she, too, would be doubly distressed. In the 2003 movie *Love Actually*, the character played by Emma Thompson discovers that her husband has given a necklace to a young woman that she believed was intended for her. Confronting him she tearfully ponders if "it's just a necklace, or if it's sex and a necklace, or if, worst of all, it's a necklace and love?"[43] Unfortunately this viewpoint fails to take into consideration the fact that evolution has provided males with a good reason to be promiscuous. If they do "sleep around" they are more likely to pass on their genes, a fact that women are assured of.

CARVING JEALOUSY AT ITS JOINTS: CULTURE

If evolution and its adaptations were the only considerations when evaluating jealousy, then human cultures throughout the planet should be about the same when it comes to that issue. Those arguing against the importance of evolutionary factors point to wide variations in how cultures deal with extramarital sex.[44] Frequently cited as examples are the Greenland Inuit of the Ammassalik region and the Toda people of India. The Inuit have a quaint little custom called "putting out the lamp." Essentially, once I have turned out the light—put out the lamp—you can have at my wife without fear that I am going to bludgeon you to death with a walrus bone as you mount my mate.

In contrast, the Toda are a clan-based society in which males seem to worry very little as to whether a child is theirs or not. Recreational sex is common, and their language does not have a word equivalent to our word *adultery*. Yet closer examination of these cultures suggests that while they may be more sexually permissive, they do have jealousy and adultery issues. For example, the putting out of the lamp is a ritualized event. Having sex with your host's wife when he has not made the formal offer, as symbolized by putting out the lamp, runs the risk of inciting jealous passions.

It would be safe to conclude that while issues of fidelity and jealousy are probably universal, the expression and form they take are heavily shaped by culture. For example, even within the industrialized countries of Germany, the Netherlands, and the United States there are differing levels of response to partner infidelity. We here in the United States appear to be more upset by it.[45]

Ultimately evolutionary adaptations point us in a particular direction. The unique interaction of culture, family, environment, and neurochemistry can alter the course evolution orients us toward, sometimes to the point of going in the opposite direction. For instance, as noted in chapter 5, throughout most of human history the ideal body type, from a male's perspective, was a robust female with excessive body fat. The Venus of Willendorf, a twenty-thousand-year-old statuette, is a robust woman with large breasts and a sizeable butt. She was the ideal of beauty, because if a woman had enough body fat, then she had enough calories to support the development of a fetus. Therefore, such women were sought after by males who eschewed the waif look of less well-endowed females. Men's preference for fat women was an adaptation because those women were more likely to be able to carry a fetus to term. Very thin women may have been ill and thus would be a risky bet as far as passing one's genes was concerned.

Yet look where we are now! Poor Venus would likely not get asked to the prom and would be making every attempt to reduce the size of that butt to conform to our current conceptions of beauty, which favor extreme thinness. Similarly, it is possible that a particular culture can shape issues of fidelity and jealousy so that it is far removed from the original adaptation. So-called open marriages or polyamory might be examples of this.

WHERE DOES PATHOLOGICAL JEALOUSY COME FROM?

It took a while for me to come up with the notion of a suspiciousness system rheostat that is turned up or down depending on the environmental circumstances—as well as in the internal circumstances—of the individual. I'm going to get as much mileage out of that analogy as I can, so it will be used here again.

In the case of jealousy the evidence from the environment is about as ambiguous as it gets. That is not to say that the evidence used by paranoid individuals is any less ambiguous. In the case of jealousy much of the evidence is played out in the social realm. Nods to another, coy smiles, brief touches all signal possible infidelity. They can all cause the jealousy rheostat to dial up, hopefully proportionate to the observed behavior.

Some evidence, for example, a condom or a woman's lingerie, can result in high levels that are quickly reached. A person's unique experiences with members of the opposite sex can reset the basal level on the rheostat. A background in rocket science or psychology is not necessary to appreciate that if someone has cheated on you in the past, you will be less trusting in the future. The rheostat is ratcheted up, and subsequent events start with that new elevated baseline.

Besides actual infidelity by someone in the past, are there any other factors that appear to contribute to the development of pathological jealousy? Interestingly, there is no evidence indicating that conflict in the family while growing up predisposes one to jealousy. That doesn't mean that it isn't important or can't happen, only that there is no research documenting it.

One factor that does emerge is sexual dysfunction, which frequently accompanies old age. Diminished libido is also a common causality of aging, particularly if the male is significantly older than the female. The chance of cuckoldry increases realistically in such circumstances. Yet pathological jealousy does not need much for the process to become self-perpetuating, much like the case with paranoia. The more one partner accuses the other of being unfaithful, the more conflicted the relationship becomes. One of the first casualties of discord is a reduction in sexual intimacy, which serves to reinforce the belief that you don't want sex because "you are getting it elsewhere." Eventually, if you have been accused and convicted of being unfaithful over and over again, you have nothing to lose by actually being unfaithful.

Chapter 10

TREATING PARANOIA

The history of the treatment of mental illness, including those conditions that are paranoia-related, has been an inglorious story, but no less so than the treatment of medical maladies. In previous centuries many forms of mental illness were simply lumped together under the term *insanity*. That term has since evolved out of the clinical field and into the legal realm.[1]

Past treatments for insanity have included straitjackets, roasted mice (which were to be consumed), whirling chairs and beds, bicycle riding, fresh air,[2] and "more holidays."The latter treatment is going to be a problem for many Americans according to Expedia, the online travel site. We get far fewer vacation days per year than other industrialized countries—a measly average of fourteen days per year. Workers in Great Britain get twenty-four, France thirty-six, Germany twenty-six, and Spain thirty. Were that not bad enough, 20 percent of us take work with us on vacation, and 35 percent of us don't even use all our vacation days.[3]

This chapter will briefly trace the evolution of psychiatric treatments, then discuss current treatments that, though considerably better than prior treatments, remain problematic.

EARLY "TREATMENTS"

Evidence would suggest that humans have been experiencing psychological problems from the earliest vestiges of our species. The treatment of those problems follows in lockstep with how we have conceptualized or framed the question "What is wrong with that individual?" From prehistoric times through the Christian Middle Ages we viewed abnormal behavior as the result of possession by spirits. The prehistoric evidence comes in the form of skulls containing carefully chiseled holes—a process termed *trepanation* and designed, presumably, to allow the evil spirits contained therein to escape. It is obviously not clear whether our prehistoric ancestors employed this "treatment" on their paranoid neighbors.[4]

The spirits eventually developed names, Satan being the most renowned of them, and the Christians came up with some clever ways of eliminating them without having to poke holes in the heads of the afflicted; they were burned or tortured instead. Satan would find the vessel he occupied to be distinctly unpleasant and would flee, leaving a spirit-free but largely charred or broken pile of flesh behind. Certainly those with schizophrenia and other serious mental illnesses were among the unfortunates who suffered these fates.

Now the common perception of the treatment of mentally ill individuals during the Middle Ages and the Inquisition is of cruel and inhumane practices. However, this view is not entirely supported by historical records. Evaluations of the mentally ill in medieval Britain were done by a panel of individuals in a process called an *inquisition*. It resembled to a fair degree the mental-status examinations given to psychiatric patients today, including questions regarding who and where they were, and other factual pieces of information.[5] Other treatments at the time included special diets, baths, perfumes, reading, and the like. But by the Middle Ages there was awareness that biological factors could cause aberrant behavior. Unfortunately, bloodletting and a few other worthless treatments were all that could be done.

TREATMENTS IN THE EIGHTEENTH CENTURY

The treatment of the mentally ill during this period ranged from inhumane confinement in settings barely fit for animals—including leg irons, handcuffs, and being chained to the wall—to enlightened approaches that respected the dignity of the infirmed as human beings and treated them accordingly. Ironically, as medical journalist Robert Whitaker argues in his provocative book *Mad in America*, our current treatments of the seriously mentally ill may be *less* effective than were those of the latter eighteenth century.[6] Some of the enlightened treatments included giving patients a real mattress to sleep on rather than a bed of straw, giving them activities to engage in that were meaningful, allowing them to walk around outside, and letting them listen to music and play games.

Less enlightened treatments of the time included those left over from the Dark Ages; for example, bleeding, often to the point that the poor patient was simply too anemic and exhausted to pitch a fit. The ending of fit-pitching was typically the goal of treatment. Other treatments brought patients to fatigue with other mechanisms, like emetics that would quickly dehydrate the patient, rendering him washed-out and weak.

The use of water as a treatment became popular, and doctors devised various ways of getting patients wet. Some of the methods included dropping them into a vat of cold water while blindfolded, pouring water over their heads, nearly drowning them in confining devices, and high-velocity showers. Believe it or not, water methods of treatment survived well into the twentieth century.

During this century emerged the view that the insane were deranged by virtue of problems with their brain. Dr. Benjamin Rush, the "father of American psychiatry," believed that circulatory abnormalities accounted for insanity. The "treatments" that resulted from this view included bleeding and causing blisters on the ankles (to draw blood away from the head). Rush also invented the "Tranquilizer Chair" treatment, whereby the patient was basically strapped down in a chair with her head in a box. Kept for hours, days, weeks, and even months in the contraption, it was likely pure hell for those being treated.[7]

TREATMENTS IN THE NINETEENTH CENTURY

Treatment of mental illness came somewhat of age during the nineteenth century. For during this time morphine, bromine, and a variety of other drugs were used. Each proved to have some efficacy in stilling the mind or controlling the behavior of the mentally ill. While we can look back and see the earliest vestiges of an informed treatment approach to mental disorders, it was mixed with less enlightened treatment. In 1847, psychiatrist Amariah Brigham wrote of the treatments employed by the New York State Lunatic Asylum:

> No specific remedy for insanity has as yet been discovered. Different cases require very different treatment, and that which would be serviceable at one period of the complaint, might be injurious at another. We have very rarely considered it advisable to have recourse

to general bleeding at this Institution. Only four of the 622 patients that have been here during the past year have been bled by us. In three of these cases the bleeding did not appear to be serviceable; in one we thought it highly beneficial. Occasionally, when there is much cerebral excitement, we have resorted to topical bleeding, but more frequently, even in such cases, we derive benefit from placing the feet in warm water; the application of cold, to the head; and the free movement of the bowels by laxatives. Pouring cold water in a small stream from a height of four or five feet directly upon the head, is generally one of the most certain means of subduing violent mani-acal excitement, we have ever seen tried. But this should be done in a gentle manner and under the immediate observation of the physi-cian, and should not be continued but for a short time; we also advise never to resort to it when the patient's bowels are confined or when he has just been eating and his stomach is full. The warm bath is also serviceable in many cases to calm excitement; but for this purpose it should be long continued at least half an hour and cold water should be gently applied to the head at the same time.[8]

Used in combination, drugs of a variety of sorts—morphine, chloral hydrate, bromine—often worked well in controlling the violent behaviors of psychotic individuals, by keeping them effectively sedated but not cured. Perhaps more importantly, reforms begun in the eighteenth century—labeled the *moral treatment*—supplanted the strange, cruel, and ineffective methods described above. Removed were the swirling chairs used to make patients dizzy, nauseous, and confused. In their stead physicians actually talked with their patients. This was the beginning of psychotherapy, which emerged at the beginning of the next century. No longer beaten by their warders, patients were better fed and engaged in the same activities as those not in asylums.

THE ANTI-PARANOIA HORMONE

Compelling findings regarding the hormone *oxytocin* merit brief mention. A favorite among animal researchers, oxytocin affects a variety of behaviors, such as bonding, parenting, and so on. Presum-ably it influences humans as well. In studies where a human subject received a spray of the hormone up the nose, he was more likely to trust others. In laboratory studies in which money transfer was involved, the majority of those getting the oxytocin gave away most or all of their money compared to those who received nothing but a whiff of placebo.[9]

So perhaps paranoid individuals of the future will be dispensed with an inhaler much like those that people suffering from asthma carry around. All we need to do is convince them to take a snort of this peculiar hormone.

THE BIG SHIFT

A major paradigm shift in the treatment of mental illness came at the beginning of the last century. Among the patients housed in the massive psychiatric asylums of the time were those suffering from *tertiary syphilis* (described below).[10] Up to 20 percent of patients in these facilities suffered from this condition.[11]

The story of syphilis is an interesting one and deserving of more lines than will be given here. It has been called by many names throughout the years, including the *great pox*—as opposed to the *smallpox*—and the *French Disease*, as the Italians were wont to call it. Perhaps not surprising the French term was the *Italian Disease*. It was reportedly brought back from the New World by Christopher Columbus and his crew, along with tobacco, and quickly spread throughout Europe.

The first sign of the infection is an ugly chancre, which develops after a few weeks or so but then goes away on its own. This is *primary syphilis*. In the secondary stage, which arrives a few months later, a rash and flu-like symptoms develop, which also largely disappear without treatment. The spirochete bacterium then wreaks havoc, quietly, over the course of years or even decades before the tertiary form emerges. One of the various manifestations of tertiary syphilis is *neurosyphilis*, which developed in 25 to 30 percent of infected patients circa 1900.[12] The clinical presentation of neurosyphilis involved various psychiatric conditions including personality changes, dementia, paranoia, and psychosis.

It was noted that syphilitic patients who developed a high fever were markedly improved or cured afterward. This led the Austrian psychiatrist Julius Wagner-Jauregg to inject his tertiary syphilis patients with blood taken from patients with tertian malaria. The result was a series of high fevers, which could be controlled via quinine, and the elimination of the syphilis. Subsequently, various heating devices such as cabinets equipped with infrared lightbulbs, electric "mummy bags," and hot baths were used to achieve the necessary increase in body temperature.[13]

This rather clever treatment earned Wagner-Jauregg the 1927 Nobel Prize in Physiology or Medicine and changed fundamentally the way we view mental illnesses. No longer were such illnesses caused by stress, bee stings, black bile, or wandering uteri. Rather, these illnesses were the result of identifiable "bugs" that could be seen under a microscope and—more importantly—killed. Now it was just a matter of determining which bug caused depression and which one caused paranoia, and so forth.

The emergence of a successful treatment for syphilis was not the only event that shifted our thinking regarding the origins of mental illnesses. The problem was that once biology became the culprit of causing mental illnesses, then all sorts of bizarre biological treatments rushed to the fore. Take Henry Cotton (circa 1930) as an example. He began removing teeth, intestines, and tonsils from his patients under the assumption that infections in these areas caused mental illness. He then came to conclude that up to 80 percent of female psychiatric patients had cervical infections requiring—you guessed it—surgical removal.[14] Unfortunately the infection was often reported to have spread to the fallopian tubes and ovaries, requiring their removal as well. Interestingly, this male physician rarely found the male sexual structures to be infected. He estimated that up to fourteen hundred patients were "treated" via these methods. Others focused more exclusively on the endocrine system, removing the endocrine glands to eliminate the hormonal cause of mental illness.[15]

Water, too, became a treatment method of choice and included the use of steam, douches, continuous showers, and *wet packs*, which involved rolling the unfortunate individual up in wet bedsheets that were sometimes layered with ice. Employed well into the 1960s, this treatment reportedly calmed violent psychotic patients. When all else failed, patients could always just be put to sleep. Not in the "we need to put the dog to sleep" sort of way, but in the narcotic- or barbiturate-induced sleep way. Such treatments lasted often for days, weeks, and up to a month. Other methods involved injecting blood from horses directly into the spinal canal of patients, while others put patients in cold conditions such as refrigerated blankets.

At some point electricity became a popular treatment method, and the various treatments were given names that paid dubious homage to those who pioneered the field of electricity, if not the treatment of mental illnesses. These include *faradism*, (named for English chemist Michael Faraday), *galvanization* (named for Italian scientist Luigi Galvani), and *franklinization (for Benjamin Franklin)*. But the most controversial use of electricity, even today, is the purposeful induction of a seizure, known colloquially as *electroshock therapy* or by the professional term used today—*electroconvulsive therapy* (ECT).

ELECTROCONVULSIVE THERAPY

The story of ECT is not so much about electricity as it is about seizures. It did not escape the notice of the ancients that individuals who had an epileptic seizure often felt quite good emotionally afterward—at least after the post-seizure confusion subsided.

The Egyptians and Romans employed the torpedo fish, a type of electric eel, to cure a variety of conditions and improve mood, suggesting the possible first use of ECT. In the 1930s insulin-coma therapy was introduced, in which patients were injected with insulin. This caused a dramatic drop in blood glucose levels, often resulting in a seizure and coma. Unfortunately, too often it resulted in death since the line between coma and death is very thin indeed. To make matters worse, patients were often subjected to these comas for weeks at a time—up to ten weeks in some cases.

The apocryphal event that ushered in the age of ECT was the first use of electricity by two Italians, neurologist Ugo Cerletti and his student, Lucio Bini. The former derived his inspiration reportedly by watching pigs at an abattoir rendered unconscious by a jolt of electricity. According to legend, the two men came across an engineer from Milan wandering around a train station. Muttering naught but gibberish he was subjected to ECT, whereupon he regained his senses and returned to normal life.

To understand the impact of ECT one must keep in mind that in the early

1900s, with the exception of the treatment of tertiary syphilis, there were no cures for mental illnesses, especially the more serious ones like paranoid schizophrenia. Moreover, there was a 1 to 1 ratio of psychiatric beds to medical beds. Put another way, for every hospital patient with a medical condition, there was one with a psychiatric condition. Now, for just a few pennies—or lira—worth of electricity, true cures were being achieved. However, the rates of cures were often exaggerated by those employing the procedures, and rather than subject their claims to scientific scrutiny in professional journals, the methods were often reported in the popular press.

There were problems with electricity treatment, including broken bones and memory loss. These have largely been eliminated in current treatment methods, although it remains controversial. Despite its somewhat barbaric nature ECT does work, especially for severe depression. Better treatments are available for schizophrenia and other paranoid disorders, so it is not used today for those conditions.

As sordid as the history of ECT might be, it pales in comparison to the ultimate biological treatment of mental illness: psychosurgery. More to the point of this book, while ECT was used to treat people with schizophrenia, the paranoid version being the most common, it was mostly employed for depressed individuals. Psychosurgery on the other hand, was used to "treat" a wide variety of conditions, some of which don't even qualify as maladies.[16]

PSYCHOSURGERY

Ironically, it was a sixty-three-year-old women suffering from paranoia, among other things, who became the first *lobotomy* patient. In 1935, Dr. Egas Moniz, a Portuguese neurologist, drilled holes into her skull where the frontal lobes are located and injected alcohol, thereby destroying the brain tissue in that area.[17]

The whole procedure took half an hour. The result was deemed a success, although there was little systematic research. Switching eventually to a *leukotome*, a long probe with a wire loop at the end that could be extended, Moniz was able to cut the connections to the frontal lobes like he was using a melon baller.

Results from his early cases were reported to be significant, and patients, many of whom had resided in state-run psychiatric institutions for decades, were now able to go home. Were they cured of their schizophrenia, paranoia, or melancholy? Hardly, but they were more passive and less likely to hurt themselves or others. Many were calm and zombie-like in the stereotypical way we often think of a lobotomized patient. At the time, this was considered to be a minor inconvenience rather than a significant surgical complication. For his efforts Moniz received the Nobel Prize in 1949 and the attention of one Dr. Walter Freeman. It was Freeman who took the lobotomy ball and ran with it.

Freeman was a psychiatrist by training, not a surgeon. Nevertheless, it is estimated that he performed thirty-five hundred lobotomies. He was able to accomplish this by developing a procedure that did not require the usual trappings of brain surgery, such as a sterile environment, operating table, anesthesia, or the necessity of cutting into the scalp and sawing/drilling the skull away. Instead, he developed the infamous *transorbital* lobotomy, also known as the "ice-pick lobotomy," so named because that is exactly the implement he used for these procedures in the beginning.[18]

The frontal lobes are connected to other parts of the brain by millions of nerve fibers. These can be thought of as telephone lines conveying information to and from the frontal lobes and can be accessed behind the orbit of the eye. A relatively thin, bony plate separates the back of the eye from the frontal lobes. Insert an ice pick or similar device behind the eyeball, give it a tap, and you break through this plate and into the frontal lobes. Sweep the pick back and forth like a windshield wiper, and you sever those telephone line–like connections. As simple as this might sound, and it certainly sounded simple to Freeman, things didn't always go well. One example, provided by Professor Elliot Valenstein of the University of Michigan in his book *Great and Desperate Cures* will explain.

> When visiting the Sykesville State Hospital in Maryland, he [Freeman] attempted to operate on a seriously disturbed woman. She had persecutory delusions and hallucinations and attacked people violently without warning. He had tried to operate on her a year earlier, but her orbital bone was so thick he could not drive the leucotome into her brain, and was forced to give up. This time he managed to

get the leucotome through the bone, but the instrument broke into three pieces when he attempted to force up its handle to make the deep frontal cut. One fragment lacerated the women's eyeball and detached her retina. A neurosurgeon had to be called to remove a piece of metal in her brain, but the eye could not be saved. Because the woman was still very violent, Freeman tried to complete the transorbital lobotomy, but the surgeon objected. On a later visit to Sykesville, Freeman operated on this woman a third time, using a much sturdier orbitoclast, and finally succeeded in completing the operation; he reported a week later, that the patient appeared "calm and accessible."[19]

The "beauty" of the transorbital lobotomy is that it did not require a surgical theater, anesthesia,[20] or the other accoutrements of real surgery. In fact, it didn't even require a surgeon. Freeman did it himself and traveled the country widely teaching other non-surgeons how to do it. And when done efficiently, the procedure took less than ten minutes to complete. The result is that between 1936 until the 1970s, perhaps up to forty thousand people worldwide were lobotomized. In the United States alone, between 1949 and 1952, it is estimated that five thousand lobotomies were performed yearly.[21]

The practice continued well up until the 1970s, even though more effective treatments for paranoia, schizophrenia, and other illnesses were already available.

This treatment became and remained so popular due to a convergence of factors. First, at the onset there were no real treatment options for the seriously mentally ill, many of whom were chronically mentally ill, violent, and out of control. The introduction of the lobotomy changed that. Unfortunately, as Valenstein points out, under closer examination many of the lobotomy patients had not been ill for very long, nor were they necessarily violent.

But Freeman himself was perhaps the largest factor. An inveterate showman, he "hawked" lobotomies at professional meetings like he was selling the latest and greatest toilet bowl cleaner at a county fair. He "systematically" collected outcome data that consisted of his own observations, focusing on those factors he considered important, ignoring those that weren't. These biased data were then published in professional journals with little scientific scrutiny. But like any true huckster, Freeman went to the popular press, knowing its tendency to sensationalize stories. And sensationalize it did, making lobotomies seem as large a public health boon as fluoride. But ultimately it was economic factors that proved the most compelling.

Circa 1900 there were hundreds of thousands of psychiatric patients in state-run institutions, 40 percent of whom had been patients for five or more years. They were costly to maintain, and so any significant reduction in this population would save states millions of dollars. Freeman and his acolytes claimed success rates of approximately 50 percent. Based on those statistics it is no wonder that vast numbers of state psychiatric patients underwent the procedure. (Private hospitals had much lower rates.) By the 1970s we developed a much more "enlightened" way of reducing this population without the need to lobotomize them: we threw them out in the streets under the guise of "de-institutionalization," thereby making them homeless.

The problematic outcomes from lobotomy procedures are legion. With reference to paranoia, there are no indications that the procedure altered the paranoid thinking of these individuals in any appreciable way. What it probably did do was dull the emotional reactions to those paranoid thoughts. Paranoid patients were no longer capable, in many cases, of experiencing anxiety or distress as a result of their paranoid thoughts. "The neighbors are out to get me . . . so what."

WORLD WAR I VET

The patient I was asked to see had been having problems of an acute nature for several months. As is standard in initial evaluations I inquired about any family history of mental illness. She mentioned that her grandfather had been hospitalized for "emotional problems" at one point in his life, but she was unsure of the details. The next week she brought with her a series of letters and documents dating to the early part of the twentieth century, including the military history of her grandfather, a World War I veteran who survived the killing fields of Europe.

After marrying and becoming a skilled and licensed tradesman, he apparently developed paranoid delusions. People were out to get him, and everyone in his family was conspiring against him. In a series of letters to his wife from the various psychiatrists charged with his care, the details of the limited treatment options were outlined. They consisted of reducing stress, which was felt to be the cause of the paranoid ideation. In the era before psychotropic medications, there was little else that could be done to help this poor veteran. Throughout his life hospitalizations were necessary to quell the delusions of persecution that plagued him.

MEDICATIONS

As in others areas of medicine, the development of drugs to treat mental illnesses frequently involved creating a drug to treat one condition, only to discover it treated something else far better. Such was the case circa 1952 when Parisian surgeon Henri Laborit, looking for a drug to reduce shock associated with anesthesia used during surgery, came across chlorpromazine (trade name Thorazine).

In use at the time as an antiemetic, it greatly calmed individuals prior to surgery. Word got around, and psychiatrists began experimenting with it to spectacular success, especially in that most difficult to treat patient group: schizophrenics. Unlike lobotomy, which merely rendered psychotic patients passive, this drug appeared to improve their core symptoms. Patients treated with it were no longer paranoid, stopped talking gibberish, and stopped hearing voices.

CLOZARIL

Tommy was what was commonly referred to as a "back-ward schizophrenic," so named because he was relegated to the "back wards" of the hospital where long-term patients reside. The more correct term for these individuals is treatment-resistant patients. Nothing seemed to silence the voices or decrease the paranoia and agitation experienced by these patients.

In 1989 a new antipsychotic drug was introduced that held hope for Tommy and other treatment-resistant patients. The drug was clozapine and was marketed under the trade name Clozaril. Although the medication was expensive, a significant percentage of patients were responding to it, thereby saving state psychiatric institutions hundreds of thousands of dollars as they no longer needed to be hospitalized. Eager to see if Tommy would respond to this new drug, the attending psychiatrist approached him with high hopes that he might find relief from his paranoid delusions. Excitedly he explained the new medication to Tommy, who listened passively. When no response was forthcoming the psychiatrist finally asked, "Well, Tommy, what do you think?" "No way I'm taking a drug that is a 'closet to hell!'"

The discovery of Thorazine caused a mini-revolution in the treatment of psychotic conditions, paranoid ones included. The first generation of these powerful antipsychotic tranquilizing drugs (Stelazine, Haldol, Loxapine) eventually gave way to newer versions, with reported lower side effects and greater efficacy. However, subsequent research has demonstrated that these newer medications continue to have a very high rate of side effects, cost a great deal, and are no more effective than the older generations of medications. Moreover, these newer medications have side effects even more problematic than the ones that preceded them.[22] For example, they cause metabolic disturbances that result in substantial weight gain and resultant problems associated with obesity: high blood pressure, diabetes, elevated cholesterol, and so on. Nevertheless, the development of these drugs had important implications for the treatment of paranoia. Utilizing lower doses than might be needed to treat the more severe paranoia as found in schizophrenia, now all levels of paranoia could be effectively treated.

The biggest problem with these medications is compliance: patients stop taking them. There are several reasons for this. First—as noted—there are a considerable number of side effects. This is the single greatest reason individuals stop taking any medication prescribed them, for physical or psychological problems.

Second, the psychological/emotional effects of these drugs are not very pleasant. In all my years of working with substance abusers not a single one of them voluntarily chose to use one of these drugs.

Third, there is an inherent conundrum with paranoid individuals. They think people are out to get them and that often involves being poisoned. Such fears are only exacerbated when they begin to experience side effects from medications used to quell their paranoia. As a result many with paranoia won't take medications prescribed to them for fear of being poisoned or other such paranoid reasons. Those who are willing to try often stop once the side effects are experienced.

Finally, many—if not most—individuals with paranoia don't feel there is anything wrong with them. Would you take a medication if you felt there was nothing wrong with you? Perhaps you would if a trusted physician prescribed it. But how long would you continue to take it if it had significant side effects?

The evidence suggests that these medications do work in reducing paranoid thinking. They are particularly helpful with the more severe paranoid delusions found in paranoid schizophrenia. Not only do they bring clarity to paranoid thoughts; they also reduce the anxiety that results from being plotted against, talked about, and so on. They are by far the primary method to treat most forms of paranoia, including those found in people with delirium and dementia. But that doesn't mean they are necessarily the most effective. It is possible that drugs that reduce anxiety, such as Xanax, could prove to be effective and have far fewer serious side effects. However, to address such an issue a clinical trial needs to be done. This entails placing equal numbers of patients on the drug under consideration and on a placebo, then evaluating if the target symptoms are reduced. As noted repeatedly, the conundrum is finding a large enough group of people with paranoia who are willing to participate in a drug study.

PSYCHOTHERAPY

Talk therapy has been used to treat mental disorders since the beginning of the last century. Unfortunately, through most of that century the effectiveness of such treatment, for any condition, was questionable.

In the 1960s psychiatrist Aaron Beck at the University of Pennsylvania, and psychologist Albert Ellis in New York City developed an approach to mental disorders—primarily depression—that focused on the individual's thoughts and subsequent behavior. They found that if they could change the way a person thinks about their experiences, and the way they subsequently behave, then their condition would improve. Termed *cognitive behavioral therapy*, the method was co-opted for use in a wide variety of other disorders, including paranoia.

Research on this form of treatment for individuals with paranoia has been promising.[23] Targeting the worrying that paranoid individuals experience and defusing it has resulted in reductions in paranoia and related distress. It appears to work without directly attacking the paranoid thoughts. Rather, it educates the individuals about the nature of worry and teaches them how better to cope with worries—paranoid or non-paranoid—they experience. To date, there are few studies on this treatment, so it is far from being an established or even a first-line treatment for paranoid conditions. As with many psychiatric disorders a combination of medications plus psychotherapy is generally the case, and I suspect paranoid conditions will likely prove to be the same.

A final note regarding cognitive approaches to treatment of paranoia: It was previously noted that a study by Dr. Daniel Freeman and colleagues in the United Kingdom found high rates of paranoia in the general population. An interesting aspect of their study is that they also looked at how people deal with those paranoia feelings and subsequent distress. Many simply became depressed and isolative. Others, however, were able to gain some emotional distance from their paranoid thoughts and reason their way to a greater level of comfort. In a sense they did their own cognitive behavioral therapy by challenging their thoughts, seeking advice and perspective from others, and generally dealing with their situations. Like all conditions paranoia exists to varying degrees. As such, individuals with milder forms of paranoia are probably in a position to cope with their problems. Think about yourself and the degree to which you might have dealt with depression or anxiety throughout your life. We each use a variety of strategies to keep our emotional heads above water, and it is expected that those battling paranoia do the same.

A second aspect to this involves the remission of psychiatric conditions spontaneously. If we look at a group of psychotic individuals in an emergency room or a hospital who are given no treatment or medication, a portion of them would simply get better and stay better without further episodes of psychosis. Most would go on to have other psychotic episodes, but in between those episodes they would enjoy varying degrees of mental health. Paranoia shows a similar pattern, suggesting that continued treatment, medication, for example, may not be necessary in all cases.

GETTING THEM IN FOR TREATMENT

I will assume that some of you are reading this book because you have a family member or friend who suffers from paranoia, although it is probably more accurate to say that it is *you* who is suffering. So what should you do? Well, it is difficult to talk about the treatment of paranoia without specifying the nature of the paranoia involved. The paranoid thoughts of someone with paranoid schizophrenia will be quite different than those with lower-level paranoia or with Alzheimer's. I have no empirical evidence to support specific recommendations for those with paranoia. However, here are some thoughts to consider.

First, as a family member or friend you are likely in the best position to help this person whom you care about. You are probably acutely aware of the burden of unhappiness this individual feels because of his or her paranoid thoughts. Reassure them as best you can. Appreciate that their suspicions are very real to them. Even though you may see the flaws in their perceptions and conclusions, they do not. A full frontal assault on their logic will, like all frontal assaults, result in defensiveness. Accepting their fears and concerns as valid affirms your position as one who knows and cares about them. You can attempt to provide alternative explanations for what they are experiencing, but do so gently. If they are resistant to even gentle challenges to their logic, drop the issue. Depending on their degree of insight into their problem, they may benefit from a self-help book on mental illness. Dr. Daniel Freeman and colleagues have written a very good guide targeting treatment of paranoia titled *Overcoming Paranoid and Suspicious Thoughts*.[24]

Second, you can acknowledge that there is nothing you can really do about those people who are talking behind their backs, plotting against them, and so on. What you can do for them is support them, let them know you are on their side, and express your concern about the emotional strain you recognize they are under. Help by distracting them from their paranoid thoughts by doing things that draw their attention and are pleasurable for them. Play with the dog, go for a walk, watch a funny movie—anything that provides them with relief.

Third, monitor them for changes. If their paranoia is increasing, their thoughts and behaviors becoming more erratic, disorganized, and bizarre, then seeking professional help may be indicated. Ideally you will make an appointment with a psychologist or psychiatrist in advance, anticipating a possible deterioration. You can always cancel an appointment if they are stable. Waiting until later, when they have more fully decompensated, runs the risk that they will need to be seen on an urgent basis, which usually involves a trip to the emergency room at a local hospital. This is far from a comfortable environment for most individuals, let alone those with paranoia. Believe me, I've been to the emergency room many times with my accident-prone daughter. It is not a soothing atmosphere.

I recommend you avoid addressing the issue of paranoia itself (frontal assault) and focus your concerns on their distress. Acknowledge that you see they are suffering to the point that they need some relief. That relief can come in the form of talking with a professional. It may also take the form of medications that can reduce distress. Liken it to physical pain. I have a broken rib right now and there is nothing I, or anyone else, can do about it except wait until it heals, since there is no treatment. So I can take a painkiller. Similarly, a medication can reduce their distress even if it doesn't address the underlying problem that the neighbors are spying on them.

Finally, if you are concerned that the individual may become violent, take steps to minimize this. Remove guns, knives, and any other potentially lethal implement. Call other family members and friends to help monitor the person and, if necessary, take them to a hospital. As will be discussed shortly, too many horrific events have occurred involving mentally ill individuals who are often paranoid. Stay alert to changes in those you care about and be willing to protect them—and others they might harm—by contacting your local help-line or hospital.

IRONIC TIMING

In order to understand how paranoia evolved over the ages I went to the Oskar Diethelm Library at Cornell Medical College in New York City to examine their outstanding collection of old texts, some dating back to the fifteenth century. I arrived at my hotel on East 62nd Street by midmorning and set off to meet friends in Central Park. Walking down 62nd Street I observed several helicopters hovering just ahead and was puzzled that there would be traffic helicopters at that time of day. After a few blocks I was met by numerous fire trucks, ambulances, and police barricades, which proved to be the reason the helicopters were hovering. Peering between the police I saw a townhouse, or what was left of it, lying in ruins in the street. I asked a fireman who emerged from behind the barricade what had happened. "Either a gas explosion or someone blew the house up."

Over the course of the next several days more and more details about the house, its owner, and the circumstances surrounding the explosion emerged. The owner, one Dr. Nicholas Bartha, had recently lost a bitter divorce settlement with his now ex-wife. The cost of that settlement would be in the neighborhood of $4 million, which would necessitate selling the landmark nineteenth-century townhouse worth between $6 and 10 million. Faced with seeing his house auctioned Bartha chose a more drastic approach to dealing with the situation: he tampered with the gas main and blew up the house, with himself still inside. Over a dozen people were injured as a result, and the perpetrator was severely burned. He was pulled out by firefighters after calling them on his cell phone, only to die several days later due, in large part, to the fact that he was massively obese.

Prior to immolating the building he sent his ex-wife and select members of the media a rambling, paranoid e-mail in which he touched on everything from Jane Fonda to Transylvanian gold mines to the Nuremberg trials. Among his allegations: his deceased brother's wife lied during their divorce with the help of Legal Aid Society, women's shelters, and other organizations; the judge in his divorce—who he stated was a lesbian—should have recused herself since she had worked with his wife's attorney before; the Netherlands, where his wife was born and at whose embassy she is employed, is exporting abortion to other countries and encouraging the sexual exploitation of children; his wife never deposited her earnings in their account but was taking money ($56,000) out of the account and sending it to her bank account in the Netherlands. The judge in his divorce was allegedly against him, and Bartha went so far as to sit in her courtroom in order to listen to attorneys and what they had to say about the judge. His conclusion of this eavesdropping: the judge rules in favor of women.

He railed on about the Dutch and their decadent liberal society; the ACLU; our legal system ("A judge is a [sic] unelected Stealth politicians who concoct lows [laws] in disregard of the Constitution to serve extreme liberal purposes."); restaurants that use coal-burning pizza ovens; the "Building Department" that denied him a permit to make changes to his house; sidewalk food vendors; and even college professors. Apparently we professors fail students who are not politically correct. In true paranoid fashion he ranted at length about his boss, her incompetence, and how she harassed him. While he was wrongly labeled incompetent and blamed for various things, doctors are lazy, stupid, or just plain uncaring. The nurses are just as guilty in his eyes.

One can never be sure of paranoia until it is thoroughly assessed. Although Bartha's thirteen-page diatribe has all the hallmarks of paranoia, ultimately only an interview and significant amounts of background information would permit a confident diagnosis of paranoia. One thing about Bartha we can be relatively sure of is that he intended to die. At one point he stated: "I think I deserve a $7,000,000 crematorium/coffin." In the most oft-quoted line from the entire missive he informs his ex-wife that she will be "transformed from gold digger to ash and rubbish digger" but then ominously goes on to state "You always wanted me to sell the house I always told you 'I will leave the house only if I am dead.' You ridiculed me. You should have taken it seriously."

Chapter 11

PARANOIA AND VIOLENCE

O ver the years I have been working on this book a number of trag-
edies have occurred involving individuals who appear to have been
paranoid. Seung-Hui Cho and the massacre at Virginia Tech University immediately comes to mind. Such events are nothing new; violent events associated
with paranoia have been occurring for centuries, as some of the historical case
examples in this book attest.

Indeed, the legal standard many states employ in determining whether
a person should be held legally responsible for his behavior or absolved of
wrongdoing by reason of insanity stems from the case of Daniel McNaughton.
A woodturner and shopkeeper, he shot and killed Edward Drummond, the
private secretary of the prime minister of England in 1843. During his trial
he claimed that the Tories "follow me, persecute me wherever I go and have
entirely destroyed my peace of mind. They follow me to France, into Scotland
and all over England. In fact, they follow me wherever I go." "They accuse me of
crimes of which I am not guilty. They do everything in their power to harass and
persecute me. In fact, they wish to murder me."[1]

His father testified that young Daniel often spoke of spies who followed
him continuously. They laughed at him, shook their fists and sticks in his face,
and even threw straw at him. In just about every encounter between father and
son the topic of Daniel's persecution arose. No longer willing to suffer these
outrages, he sought to end the persecution by killing the source: the prime
minister. Mistakenly, he killed his secretary instead but was found not guilty by
reason of insanity.

In any given year events like the Virginia Tech shooting occur, although on a
smaller scale. Here is a sample of cases over the recent past:

November 2014: Attorney Myron May walked into the library of his alma mater, Florida State University, and opened fire with a semiautomatic pistol. He managed to wound three students before he was killed in a shootout with police. Online social media posts documented his concern about the government's mind-reading program and the fact that the government was spying on him. He complained to a female friend that he was being targeted and that the police had bugged his car and house. A camera had allegedly been placed in his home, and he could hear the voices of those watching him in the walls.[2]

October 2014: Just one of a series of White House "fence jumpers," Dominic Adesanya was apprehended as he crossed the White House lawn. His father acknowledged that his son was paranoid, believing there were cameras everywhere. In fact, President Barack Obama and the National Security Agency allegedly placed cameras and other devices in his cell phone and lightbulbs throughout his house in order to spy on him. In his initial court hearing he was agitated, asking to represent himself and denying that he knew who his public defender was. After the hearing adjourned, he refused to leave and had to be forcibly removed by federal marshals, yelling: "I'm a target; someone please help me! This is a conspiracy . . . it's a scheme." Adesanya was charged and is awaiting trial.[3]

September 2014: Iraq war veteran Omar Gonzalez scaled the White House fence and made it to the White House door before being apprehended. Although he was found to be carrying only a knife, in his car nearby were two hatchets, a machete, and eight hundred rounds of ammunition. He believed that someone was breaking into his house, so he installed a motion-sensor spotlight and began to carry a gun. Believing that he was always being watched and that the government was attempting to bug his house, he kept his cell phone in the microwave. A friend described his behavior earlier in the year as "strange; kind of paranoid."[4]

April 2013: Paul Curtis was accused of mailing a ricin-laced envelope to a Mississippi senator as well as to President Obama. He had been trying to "expose various parties within the government, FBI, police departments." Why? Because there was "a conspiracy to ruin my reputation in the community as well as an ongoing effort to break down the foundation I worked more than 20 years to build in the country music scene." He denied having sent such letters and claimed that he was being "set up." Apparently, he was right: the FBI failed to find any evidence that he mailed the letters, and charges were dropped. Suspicion turned to someone he'd had a falling out with previously who had sent the letters pretending to be Curtis. Again, even paranoids have enemies.[5]

January 2013: Jimmy Lee Dykes walked on to a school bus and took a five-year-old-boy hostage after first shooting and killing the bus driver who attempted to intervene. He then held the child hostage for seven days before law enforcement rescued the child, killing Dykes in the process. The inevitable interviews with those who knew him revealed the telltale traces of paranoia. Described as an angry survivalist, he was believed to have taken the child hostage in order to have a stage upon which to vent his concerns regarding government conspiracies.

Known to patrol his property with a gun, Dykes would threaten those who wandered onto it, including children. He beat a dog to death with a pipe after it had strayed onto his property and shot at a neighbor in a dispute over a speed bump. Not surprisingly, those who knew him frequently used the words "angry" and "paranoid" to describe him.[6]

February 2013: Former Los Angeles police officer and survivalist Christopher Dorner killed four people, including two police officers, and wounded three other officers. Evidence emerged suggesting he had been stalking his victims before killing or attempting to kill them. Eventually trapped in a cabin in the San Bernardino Mountains following a massive manhunt, he died when the cabin burned down.

His vendetta of targeting of police officers and their families is believed to have resulted from his previous dismissal from the LAPD. The basis for his dismissal apparently involved allegations Dorner had made against a fellow training officer that were eventually determined to be unfounded. Dorner appealed multiple times and was convinced that his dismissal was racially motivated.

Like "Unabomber" Ted Kaczynski before him, Dorner left behind his manifesto—never a good sign as far as mental health is concerned. In it he detailed the numerous racial slurs and inequities he had to endure, starting in childhood. He also described the "conspiracy" that eventually resulted in his termination and the hacking of his bank accounts by a fellow officer.

On one hand, the numerous allegations might be interpreted as evidence of a paranoid individual who sees conspiracies against him and interprets events to conform to his paranoia. On the other hand, what if many, most, or all of what Dorner said was true? Could his actions not be interpreted as a proud and honorable man who was robbed of that honor and could not reclaim it through legal means, eventually giving in to his frustration and seeking to deliver justice, however misguided? Given what is now known about racism within the LAPD during the time of Dorner's complaints, it is certainly not clear whether he was paranoid.[7]

January 2011: Carrying a semiautomatic pistol, twenty-two-year-old Jared Loughner fired thirty-one rounds into a crowd gathered for a meet-and-greet with Congresswoman Gabrielle Giffords, killing six and wounding thirteen. Miraculously Giffords survived a bullet to her brain.

Loughner believed that the government controlled grammar in order to brainwash people and that spaceflights conducted by NASA were faked. He was preoccupied with the US currency, which he felt was worthless, as well as other government conspiracies including the notion that the events of 9/11 were perpetrated by the US government. Loughner pleaded guilty and was sentenced to seven consecutive life terms plus 140 years without the possibility of parole.[8]

May 2010: Jerry Kane Jr. and his sixteen-year-old son Joseph were pulled over in Arkansas by two local police officers, whom the Kanes immediately shot and killed. Reports suggest that it was Joseph who first opened fire. Both Kanes were subsequently killed in the shootout with police.

Believing that illegitimate corporations had taken over the government and were harassing him, Jerry apparently raised his son to believe in such conspiracy theories as well. The father had a long history with local police and government officials in his home state of Ohio. Flouting the law, he'd trim his overgrown grass with a pair of scissors when police arrive to enforce local codes.

Described as having a "mental history," he was a member of the patriot movement and believed that it was every American's right to drive without a license. When jailed in New Mexico for failing to have one he reportedly obtained the arresting officer's name, address, and the name of his wife. In true paranoid fashion, he detailed what the consequences would be if authorities kept harassing him: "I don't want to kill anybody but if they keep messing with me, that's what it's going to come down to. And if I kill one, then I'm not going to be able to stop. I just know it."[9]

February 2010: Dr. Amy Bishop, a Harvard-educated biologist, walked into a faculty meeting of the Biology Department at the University of Alabama in Huntsville and shot six colleagues, killing three, after being denied tenure.

Although many people were shocked by this violent act, many others who knew her were apparently not surprised. Known for her mercurial temperament and—more importantly—her tendency to carry grudges, important clues to her mental status emerged only after her arrest.

She had a history of responding to perceived slights by others with violent reactions. This apparently included her own brother, with whom she had a verbal argument when she was twenty-one years old. She "accidently" shot him in the chest with a shotgun; his death was ruled an accident and never investigated. Subsequent to the shooting in Alabama, Bishop was charged with homicide in the 1986 shooting of her brother in Massachusetts.

When a customer at a pancake house took the last child's booster seat, Bishop hit her in the head and declared, "I'm Dr. Amy Bishop." And there is the possibility she was involved in a plot to mail a pipe bomb to a Harvard doctor. Bishop was convicted and sentenced to life in prison without parole.[10]

May 2009: Scott Roeder shot and killed Dr. George Tiller, a performer of late-term abortions. Initially the case appeared to simply be a matter of an over-zealous antiabortion activist. However, according to his ex-wife, Roeder underwent a significant personality change a decade before the shooting.

He believed that the government put fluoride in the water to make people docile. He would not drink tap water as a result. The government also allegedly tracked money via the magnetic strip embedded in banknotes, which he developed a technique for removing. Described by family as being mentally ill, he did not see himself as such. Roeder was convicted and sentenced to life in prison without parole.[11]

June 2009: James von Brunn, an eighty-eight-year-old white supremacist, walked into the Holocaust Museum in Washington, DC, carrying a rifle he then used to kill a security guard before being wounded himself.

A denier of the Holocaust, he was steeped in the paranoia of conspiracies and secret cults. His online book *Kill the Best Gentiles* reads as an autobiography of paranoia. All the typical elements are there: the Illuminati, the Elders of Zion, the Trilateral Commission, plots against the white race, and so on. If there are conspiracies, there must be conspirators and it is the Jews and people of color that swell their ranks.

So what provoked his killing at the museum? He believed that his social security check had been reduced because someone in Washington saw his website. People's descriptions of him included familiar terms: "hothead," "loner," "filled with hatred." Brunn died awaiting trial.[12]

March 2007: David Garvin, a recently fired bartender, shot and killed three in New York's Greenwich Village. Despite no previous psychiatric history, family indicated that he believed the people were "out to get him." People who knew him described him as having a "wicked temper and a paranoid streak." Garvin was killed in a shootout with police.[13]

December 2007: On Christmas Eve Michele Anderson and her live-in boyfriend, Joseph McEnroe, left their trailer, walked a short distance to her parent's house, and proceeded to kill both parents with handguns. Knowing that her brother (with whom she was reportedly close), sister-in-law, and their young children would soon come home and become witnesses, the couple waited in ambush, then killed all of them, including a three-year-old. Anderson was found guilty of her crime.

The neighbors noted that the couple blackened the windows of their trailer. The reason? Because the neighbors reportedly spied on them. They feared their neighbors, who allegedly tried to break into their trailer and were "out to get them."[14]

September 2006: Douglas Pennington drove to Shepherd University where his two sons were students. He shot them both multiple times, killing them and then himself. The reason: he believed that someone was going to kidnap and torture his sons and wished to spare them that suffering.[15]

September 2006: Dail Brown Jr. shot his father twice in the face then decapitated and dismembered the body. The elder Brown had a month previously retired from the National Marine Fisheries Services, but the younger Brown believed his father was part of a syndicate and that his real job was not with the fisheries service but as a guardian of a research facility. According to Brown, the research facility removed female pages (essentially interns) from a government page program and waited until they "deteriorated," at which point he believed they became government property. Although Brown was described as having severe paranoid schizophrenia, the jury rejected this and found him guilty of first-degree murder.[16]

March 2004: Cynthia Lord killed her three sons with a single shotgun blast to their heads. She believed one of her sons was an FBI agent out to get her and that all three sons had become evil, soulless robot clones. Lord was found guilty but mentally ill.[17]

September 2004: Sergio Parra, a butcher both literally and figuratively, hacked his estranged wife to death with a knife on a Manhattan street. The reason: jealousy, as he believed she was cheating on him. Parra was convicted of second-degree murder.[18]

April 2003: Daniel Bondeson, a fifty-three-year-old potato farmer in Maine, laced his church's coffee with arsenic in retaliation against a person who had allegedly put something in his coffee, which resulted in a "tummy ache." One church member died, and Bondeson shot himself to death before more information could be gathered.[19]

February 2001: Robert Pickett arrived at the White House carrying a .38-caliber handgun and fired twice at police officers. He blamed the government for persecuting him by dismissing him first from West Point, then the IRS, where he worked. He made frequent use of lawsuits against a variety of organizations and individuals, including his own brother and his attorney. Pickett was convicted and sentenced to twenty-five years.[20]

January 1999: Andrew Goldstein approached Kendra Webdale on the platform of the New York City subway. He reportedly asked her for the time, then positioned himself behind her. At the last second he shoved her in front of the oncoming subway train, killing her.

He had been hospitalized numerous times and sought hospitalization on many other occasions. He had recently been discharged from a psychiatric facility despite being delusional at the time of discharge. In the aftermath the victim's family sued the hospital that discharged him. As a result, Kendra's Law was passed in New York allowing judges the authority to require psychotic individuals to take medications even while out of the hospital.

Goldstein was chronically paranoid, believing that others were out to get him with guns and poison. When questioned after the murder he talked about plots against him and someone talking through him. Goldstein was convicted of second-degree murder.[21]

July 1998: Russell Weston Jr. walked into the Capitol in Washington, DC, and killed two Capitol policemen, one at point-blank range.

He was observed by neighbors in his home state of Montana to yell at satellite dishes, which he believed were spying on him. He suspected that Navy Seals were in the cornfield behind his house, and in order to thwart the aim of sharpshooter assassins he would rock in a rocking chair. President Bill Clinton was one of those he believed was trying to kill him.

He accused an eighty-six-year-old woman of assault and battery (hitting him on the head with a cane). He lost the case and appealed to the state supreme court, lost again, and appealed that loss. For years, according to his parents, he believed the government and CIA were out to get him. Weston was found not competent to be tried. Charges are still pending, but until or unless competency can be restored (which isn't likely), he will not be tried.[22]

May 1998: Fifteen-year-old Kip Kinkle was suspended from school for having a gun in his locker. As a result his father reprimanded him, threatening to send him to a boarding school. Kip responded by shooting his father in the back of the head with a rifle. He then waited for his mother to return home and shot her six times in the head, face, and heart. The next day he returned to the school that suspended him armed with two knives, three pistols, and 1,127 rounds of ammunition. He fired off fifty rounds, killing two and injuring thirty-seven.

In his diary were classic paranoid statements: "I feel like everyone is against me," "My guns are the only things that haven't stabbed me in the back." Testimony at his trial, given by psychologist Dr. Orin Bolstad, indicated that Kip had major paranoid symptoms and saw the adults around him as being "unfair, arbitrary, and untrustworthy." Kip believed that the Chinese were poised to invade the United States, and that the US government had planted chips in his head. He was convicted and sentenced to 111 years in prison without the chance for parole.[23]

March 1996: Thomas Watt Hamilton walked into a primary school in Dunblane, Scotland, and in a three-minute rampage killed sixteen children and a teacher. He had written letters to various government agencies and to the press complaining that the police and schoolteachers were spreading lies about him. Hamilton was killed in the shootout.[24]

December 1994: Ralph Tortorici took thirty-five students hostage at the State University of New York, Albany. He believed that a computer chip, implanted in his brain and penis, gave him instructions via coded beeping sounds. A list of those conspiring against him included his family. Tortorici was convicted and sentenced to fifteen to forty years. He hung himself in prison.[25]

December 1993: Colin Ferguson, a Jamaican immigrant, boarded a Long Island–bound commuter train and killed six and wounded nineteen passengers. When he was apprehended, notes were found that included a list of reasons for the killings. Foremost was racism perpetrated against him by the New York City police, the New York State workers compensation board, the Equal Employment Opportunity Commission, New York governor Andrew Cuomo's staff, Adelphia University, and the New York City Transit Police.

He also included the "sloppy running of train #2" and a racist white female passenger on another train line. Diagnosed with delusional disorder, persecutory type, he was found competent not only to stand trial but also to defend himself. Needless to say, he lost the case. Ferguson was convicted and sentenced to 315 years and 8 months to life.[26]

August 1992: Dr. Valery Fabrikant entered the Engineering Department at Concordia University with three guns and proceeded to kill four faculty members.

He fired ten attorneys and defended himself, claiming that the deceased had plotted against him and attempted to give him a heart attack. He had previously filed a lawsuit against faculty in the department—which was dismissed as frivolous—and had a long history of paranoid behaviors. From his perspective, he was victimized by others who stole his research.

Even in prison he used the Internet to plead his case, claiming conspiracies against him. When not on the computer he occupied his time filing so many lawsuits that he was eventually declared a "vexatious litigant" and barred from filing further suits. Fabrikant was convicted and sentenced to life in prison.[27]

These reflect only a smattering of notable cases. Dr. Fuller Torrey, a leading expert in schizophrenia and psychosis, lists many more on his Treatment Advocacy Center's website.[28] Thousands of major and minor cases in which elements of paranoia are present occur daily. For example, at the time of this writing a gag order is in effect preventing disclosure of information about James Holmes, who allegedly murdered twelve people and wounded fifty-eight others in a Colorado movie theater. He may yet be found to have been paranoid at the time.

Anecdotes are helpful when trying to make a point, but they do not supplant good hard data. So, are there data indicating that paranoia leads to violence? The short answer is yes. There is a fairly substantial body of research that documents a significant positive relationship between paranoia and violence.[29] But the literature is sometimes misleading, because it is not paranoia or other delusions per se that result in violence directly. Rather, it is the development of anger and a perception of threat that results in violence.[30] As noted repeatedly, paranoid individuals perceive threats all around them and are often angered by the slights and abuses heaped on them by others.

Unfortunately, the manner in which the government collects crime data fails to capture such information. Typically it uses already established categories to report crime data. One would have to read the original police reports, transcripts from trials, or hospital case notes to gather all the relevant information. When such investigative research is done, occurrences of paranoia often emerge in fairly high percentages.

Much of the evidence in this regard comes from people who are seriously mentally ill, often suffering from schizophrenia. Research indicates that the percentage of those who are violent as a result of paranoid delusions range from between 10 to 50 percent, a substantial range reflecting vastly different methodologies and patient populations.[31] For example, when records were reviewed of people who had been arrested for suspicious activity near the White House—often on a mission to see the president—many who went on to later violence had paranoid delusions at the time of the incident.[32] Yet the mentally ill are far more likely to be the *victims* of violence rather than the *perpetrators*. As Dr. Edward Mulvey, an expert in violence and mental illness with the University of Pittsburgh, so eloquently put it: "Most mentally ill people are not violent, and most violence is not done by mentally ill individuals."[33]

Typically people who are psychotic and paranoid—for example, paranoid schizophrenics—commit crimes that are particularly grisly and that frequently involve knives. Often, the knives are employed postmortem for purposes of dismemberment based on the particular delusion involved. Evil spirits being freed via decapitation is a good example. But the fact is that while many psychotic individuals become violent, most of the violence is minor in nature. It is the truly bizarre and outrageous violence that catches the media's attention.

In most of the truly bizarre cases the paranoid individual typically develops a delusion that requires her to kill someone. Andrea Yates, a Houston, Texas, woman suffering from postpartum depression and postpartum psychosis, is a good example, although her delusions were of a religious nature. She believed her children were "defective" and were going to hell. In the twisted logic of her psychotic mind, and aided by interpretations of Bible passages, drowning her children was the solution to prevent their eternal damnation. And drown them she did—systematically, one at a time until all five were dead.[34]

An additional factor here is that individuals who are psychotic and paranoid often have a remarkable number of other deficits that ultimately contribute to violence. Chief among these are significant disturbances in thinking. That is not to say that non-psychotic paranoid individuals don't also have disturbances in thinking. As noted previously, paranoid individuals make a number of errors in the way they think and reason. Yet these errors are shades different from the way normal people think. Not so for those who are psychotic. Their disturbances in logical thought are orders of magnitude different from normal thinking. For example, believing there are spirits inside someone's head and cutting the head open in order to free them—and doing so with a Swiss Army knife reflects a substantial departure from reality.

A different picture emerges for the many cases of violence in which there is paranoia but no significant accompanying psychosis. As the opening example of the man who killed the women he thought were going to kill him illustrates, the basis for the violence is understandable.

If someone is coming to kill you, and you have the means to prevent that— by killing them first, for example—wouldn't you do it? Think about it for a minute. If you were *absolutely convinced* that the next person to walk into the room you are seated in had a gun and was coming to kill you, and you your- self had a gun, would you not seriously consider the option of killing them preemptively?

The problem is that the "absolutely convinced" part of all this is based on misjudgments, misinterpretations, and fallacious assumptions in the case of the paranoid individual. But to the person believing those judgments and assump- tions, the evidence is as valid as your belief that you are holding a book right now (or an electronic reading device, as the case might be). It is tangibly real, without question.

Now, many of us in this hypothetical situation described might think of alternative solutions—run to a neighbor's to hide or call the police, for example. Unfortunately for most paranoid individuals there is often a wide web of people involved in the conspiracies against them. Moreover, their basic stance is one of general distrust of others. They trust and rely on themselves exclusively.

Whether paranoia results in violence depends a bit on what the person is paranoid about. For example, someone whose paranoia is generally directed toward other specific individuals but not the government and justice system is more likely to use the courts as his method of dealing with problems. Frequent lawsuits over perceived injustices perpetrated at the hands of others, frequent calls to the police or elected officials, and so on are a common outcome. For other individuals, whose paranoia extends to or is focused on the government, taking justice into one's own hands becomes the solution. Convicted Oklahoma City bomber Timothy McVeigh and the militia movement are prime examples of this type of paranoia.

Violence is an obviously complex psychological phenomenon with many books, articles, and journals devoted to its study. There are different kinds of violence based on motives—sexual/mating violence is one example—and ultimately there are circuits in the brain that underlie the different aspects of violent behavior and intentions. The point is that one of the reasons animals, including the human variety, become violent is that they feel threatened. A paranoid individual feels threatened. Again, the basis for that may be invalid or nonexistent, but the feeling or perception of threat is very real to the paranoid individual.

To illustrate aspects of violence within the context of paranoia I will discuss several high-profile contemporary cases: the above-mentioned Seung-Hui Cho, Timothy McVeigh, John du Pont, Bruce Ivins, and Jiverly Wong. I did not personally interview or evaluate any of these individuals. They are included in this book because the information readily available about each demonstrates classic features of paranoia. In the case of John du Pont, he was diagnosed by an expert as suffering from paranoid schizophrenia. In most other cases the individual died at their own hands or by law enforcement before such determinations could be made.

SEUNG-HUI CHO: THE VIRGINIA TECH MASSACRE

The events of the Virginia Tech tragedy were seared into our minds that day on April 16, 2007. Like 9/11, the Sandy Hook Elementary School shootings, and the Kennedy assassination, many vividly recall where they were and what they were doing when they first heard about what happened. In this electronic age many of us witnessed it as the events unfolded. In the aftermath the portrait of a paranoid individual emerged.

On April 16, 2007, Cho began his day with a harbinger of violence to come, posting on the university's online forum the blunt statement "I'm going to kill people at Vtech today." Sometime around 7:00 a.m. Cho entered a dormitory on campus and killed two students. Then, after a seemingly inexplicable gap of about two hours, he entered Norris Hall, and, after chaining the doors shut to impede any rescue attempts, the killing continued.

Entering classrooms Cho methodically slaughtered the defenseless students and faculty, often reloading to ensure the deaths of the wounded. Each victim had at least three bullet wounds. (Among the dead was a Matthew LaPorte, no relation to the author.) Organized and cruelly efficient, Cho killed thirty-two people and wounded seventeen others. Survivors commented on the cold, emotionless expression he wore while killing. This was not a madman's rampage. This was not a frenzied psychotic yelling and cursing his alleged tormentors. This was a soulless killer. Then, with the dead all around and the police closing in, he shot and killed himself.

As is typical after such a rampage, the "why" questions immediately arose, with the general conclusion being a large question mark. No one knows why he did it. In the days following the event information about Cho emerged, painting a picture of a quiet, asocial individual. One of Cho's professors saw him as "very arrogant" and, ominously, with an "underlying tone of anger."[35] But nothing surfaced that addressed a motive. Then, from beyond the grave, Cho spoke. The two-hour-gap between the first and second round of shootings occurred because he took time to mail to NBC a videotape of compiled rants—his manifesto.

Postmortem diagnosis is a tricky business, and professionals are generally discouraged from embarking upon such an undertaking. Proper diagnosis requires a careful history in addition to an actual interview with the person. That being said, there was no lack of people willing to speculate about Cho's mental state, motives, and possible diagnosis in the days following the massacre. Watching and listening to his videotaped manifesto, the portrait of a paranoid individual emerged. This was an angry person. Angry about what? Well, as is typical for someone who is paranoid, angry about all the injustices and humiliations suffered at the hands of others. As he said:

> You just loved to crucify me. You loved inducing cancer in my head and terrorizing my heart and ripping my soul all the time. You have vandalized my heart, raped my soul and torched my conscious. Do you know what it feels like to be spit on your face and have trash shoved down your throat? Do you know what it feels like to dig your own grave? Do you know what it feels like to have your throat slashed from ear to ear? Do you know what it feels like to be torched alive? Do you know what it feels like to be humiliated and be impaled upon a cross and left to bleed to death for your amusement?

These are the words of an individual who has suffered innumerable slights, assaults, insults, and persecutions at the hands of others. Or at least that is what he perceived to be the case. And who were these tormentors? According to Cho, they were the "trust-fund," "vodka / cognac drinking" rich kids with "golden necklaces" that he saw all around him. As is typical of paranoid individuals, it is always others who are blamed: "You decided to spill my blood. You forced me into a corner and gave me only one option. The decision was yours. Now you have blood on your hands that will never wash off."

Cho saw himself as the victim in all of this. Rather than the coward he was, killing the innocent and defenseless, he was the martyr. "I die like Jesus Christ to inspire generations of the weak and the defenseless people."

In the years since the manifesto was made public, pundits continue to seek the answer to the elusive "why," as if like some holy grail it will make sense of the senselessness of Cho's actions. The sad fact is that the "why" is probably some insignificant reason, too inconsequential to show up on anybody's radar screen. Why did he go into a dorm and kill Emily Hilscher? Perhaps it was as simple as President George W. Bush said: she was "in the wrong place at the wrong time."[36] I suspect this was not the case. He probably saw her murder as settling a score—a score as trivial as Emily failing to hold a door open for him as he followed her into a building. The rest of us might interpret such a failure as a possible oversight or just a lack of politeness. To a paranoid individual such as Cho, it was an in-your-face insult designed to denigrate and demean him. It may have been the fifth or tenth or one hundredth such insult that day, and this paranoid camel was not about to forget this straw. He may have followed her and somehow managed to find out who she was or, more importantly, where she lived. She was a score to be settled, and he did so, making her the first of his victims. The door incident could have been weeks or months before the April rampage; paranoid individuals harbor grudges and seek to repay unkindness with unkindness.

TIMOTHY McVEIGH

On April 19, 1995, Timothy McVeigh exploded a homemade fertilizer bomb inside a rented truck in front of the Alfred P. Murrah Federal Building in Oklahoma City, killing 168, including many children in the building's daycare center. It was at that time the worst case of domestic terrorism on US soil, although it is doubtful McVeigh saw it as such. As detailed by reporter Brandon Stickney in his book *All-American Monster*, McVeigh had a long and strong paranoid streak.

From a young age, McVeigh was interested in guns, war, and survivalism and was rarely seen without two or three weapons. Joining the military he served in the first Gulf War, where those who knew him described him as "cold," "real different," and "like a robot." Unlike the other soldiers, he did not go to clubs, date, or drink. So negative and critical was his general attitude that others began calling him Timothy "Anti-McVeigh."

The first concrete clue regarding McVeigh's paranoia appeared after the war. He believed the US government had placed a computer chip in his buttocks while he slept in order to keep track of him. He became preoccupied with conspiracy theories—for example, the Kennedy assassinations—believing the government was responsible for them all. He began hiding guns in each room and believed a black car was following him. Those who knew him noted a marked deterioration into paranoia, especially as far as the government was concerned. He failed at jobs that put him in front of the public, as he was just "too intense."

If someone didn't do what he wanted, such lack of cooperation was met with intense rage. In the midst of all this, McVeigh became involved in the militia movement, a subject I will discuss briefly before returning to McVeigh.[37]

MILITIA AND CONSPIRACY THEORISTS:
COMMITTED OR COMMITTABLE

Militias came into existence in the American colonial period to provide protection for towns and their citizens.[38] They were like a large organized and armed citizen's watch. Over the course of time these groups have metamorphosed into antigovernment groups with all the earmarks of organized paranoia. (Such groups are not unique to the United States; they exist in countries all around the world and are similar to US groups in that they are nonprofessional soldiers who are prepared to defend the local citizenry.)

Historian and sociologist James William Gibson argues in his book *Warrior Dreams* that Vietnam left a vacuum that was filled by a *para*military attitude— as opposed to a military one—in males. The embodiment of this attitude is the film character Rambo, an angry and violent Vietnam vet suffering from the trauma he experienced as a prisoner of war. Indeed, many of those who go on some kind of killing rampage, such as Cho, dress in a Rambo-like uniform (black clothing and boots).[39]

The main concern of these militia groups is that we need to protect ourselves against those who seek to do us harm. What harm? First on the list is "their" desire to take away our guns. So we need to use violence, if necessary, outside the confines of the law to protect ourselves. And we may need to band together in order to stem the rising tide against us, hence the militias and other right-wing patriot groups. These groups include Posse Comitatus, Christian Identity, American Agriculture Movement, Aryan Nations, American Christian Patriots, Covenant Sword, White Patriot Party, Aryan Resistance, National Alliance, Liberty Lobby, Christian Patriots, Three Percenters, and the Silent Brotherhood.[40] They number among their constituents tax protestors, survivalists, militant farmers, neo-Nazis, white supremacists groups, skinheads, and so on. They all share distrust for the government and believe in a wide variety of conspiracies. That is not to say that there aren't militia members who adhere to the original spirit of what a militia is and who do not have a strong suspicion of the government.

Many of the paranoid rants of these groups involve the Jewish people, as they have throughout history when it comes to conspiracy theories. A cabal of Jewish bankers are seen as trying to take over the international banking system in order to destroy the white race. The process has been taking place since biblical times and is aided by changes in laws that allow interracial marriages. Supposedly the "Zionist Occupation Government," as conspiracy theorists call the secret group of Jews controlling various governments, is aided by "internationalists" such as the League of Nations, the United Nations, the Catholic Church, and Communists International. The ultimate goal is to merge all governments under one big evil empire—the New World Order.[41]

The US government is also thought to be part of this plot, and historic roots include ancient secrets passed down through time by groups such as the Gnostics, the Rosicrucians, and the Freemasons. The elite groups that received this information were the Illuminati. (The paranoia of these groups was decades ahead of the creative mind of Dan Brown, who wrote The Da Vinci Code). Since much of the battle for control will be pitched in the economic arena, it is not surprising that the IRS and Federal Reserve Board are part of the conspiracy.

The key to achieving the New World Order will be to disarm the citizenry. Who "they" come after first will, of course, be those who are armed. So banding together militia-style is the first line of defense against such a takeover. Legal recourse is fruitless since the court system has been infiltrated, so violent resistance is the only option.

But are these groups paranoid? Here are a smattering of claims made by militia members so you can judge for yourself:

- The security strips in $20 bills are tiny radio transmitters used to keep track of us.
- The markings/numbers on the back of highway signs are codes to be used by the UN when they take over the United States.
- When you join the military the government implants a computer chip in your buttocks.

- The Illuminati are in charge of the US Treasury, as evidenced by the eye in the pyramid on the back of a dollar bill.
- Fluoridation is a communist plot. (Read *The John Franklin Letters*, presumably written by Revilo Oliver, a fictional account of the rise of the United Nations, the take-over and destruction of the USA by Russia. Or see *Dr. Strangelove*, a Stanley Kubrick film in which fluoridation is used by the Russians to pollute Americans.)
- Gun control is designed to control people.
- Black helicopters fly overhead and will gather Americans and place them in concentration camps or carry UN troops that will round up Americans.[42]
- Russian troops are hidden in salt mines beneath Detroit to be used in the takeover of the United States.
- Street gangs are being trained by the government for use as troops.
- The government is using the weather to control people by creating hurricane, tornados, and other "natural" disasters.
- The Environmental Protection Agency monitors vehicles via remote control.
- The 1992 riots in LA were orchestrated to see how Americans would react to the imposition of martial law.
- The 1995 Oklahoma City bombing was perpetrated by the government in order to provoke martial law, eradicate the militias, and take away everyone's guns.[43]

What do you think? From a clinical standpoint, these are all examples of classic paranoid ideation. The problem with this type of thinking is the same problem we see in paranoid individuals: the tendency to find support for one's preconceived notions and ignore evidence to the contrary. This is the confirmatory bias discussed in chapter 8.

How did all this conspiracy stuff start? Kenneth Stern, in *A Force upon the Plain*, argues that Senator Joe McCarthy from Wisconsin was responsible for elevating a reasonable concern about communism during the 1950s into paranoia over communism. More importantly, he repeatedly referred to the "communist conspiracy." With the collapse of the Soviet Union in 1991 there is now paranoia in search of a target. While secrecy within the political realm is normal, it also provides the fodder for conspiracies. The paranoid individual takes those "conspiracies" and inflates them into vast movements in history so that any important event is connected to those vast conspiracies. Because of how vast they are, reasoned political solutions—such as elections—won't solve the problem.[44]

Morris Dees, cofounder of the Southern Poverty Law Center, notes that farmers who lost their farms became easy recruits to the militia movement. The message that "the government took your farm" resonated well with many of these individuals.[45]

These groups see the government as being illegitimate. If you don't subscribe to the same viewpoint, then obviously the government has "gotten" to you, and now you can't be trusted. Moreover, now that the government knows that you know the truth, it is coming after you to silence you. Here you have all the right ingredients to feel paranoid.

Fears that the government is "coming to get us" were stoked by two major events. The first was the standoff and subsequent massacre of the Branch Davidians in Waco, Texas in 1993.

The Davidians were a religious sect of sorts led by a self-proclaimed messiah figure, David Koresh. (The moral foundation of this group is highly suspect given that young teenage girls having sex with their leader was not only condoned but encouraged and required.) Wanted for firearm violations within the compound, Koresh and his followers were surrounded by a small army of ATF (Bureau of Alcohol, Tobacco, and Firearms and Explosives) agents on February 23. The agents tried a siege-like approach to smoke out the sect members by blaring strange music over loudspeakers and keeping bright lights constantly trained on the compound.

When this approach failed, the agents literally tried smoking them out with tear gas. However, something went terribly wrong and fires erupted almost immediately throughout the fortified compound. In the end only nine people survived, with eighty dead, including an estimated twenty children. Militia members saw this as a clear example of the government attempting to take away guns and control its citizens. Never mind that many of the sect members had self-inflicted bullet wounds in their heads or that evidence emerged indicating that the Davidians themselves had set the fires. The government was seen by many, even those outside the militia movement, as having acted in a heavy-handed manner.

The second galvanizing event was the assault on Ruby Ridge, Idaho, in August of 1992, where white separatist Randy Weaver engaged in a standoff with another small army of government agents. During this siege his fourteen-year-old son and wife were both killed. Again the government was portrayed as acting with undue force against an innocent family who simply wanted to be left alone . . . and not pay taxes and who had illegal firearms and who had killed a federal agent.[46]

Another good example of violence and paranoia is the case of Gordon Kahl in June of 1983 in Lawrence County, Arkansas. He believed that there was a communist satanic plot to destroy the country and that the IRS and its taxation system was part of that plot. As a result he refused to pay taxes. After Kahl failed to report to his probation officer, six US Marshals were dispatched to bring him in. Always in possession of a semiautomatic rifle, Kahl killed two of the six and wounded the rest. He escaped (albeit temporarily, as he was killed in a shootout in Alaska in 1983), and wrote a letter explaining that all US government law enforcement agencies, as well as all local police forces, were under the control of the Israeli secret police (the Mossad) and that they had "informants" in every town in America.[47]

TIMOTHY McVEIGH REDUX

So it is against the backdrop of fanatic militia beliefs and government conspiracies that we return to Timothy McVeigh, for he bought into the militia paranoia in a big way. So much so that he was asked to leave militia meetings because of his extreme militancy and advocacy for the use of violence. McVeigh viewed himself as a foot soldier in the fight against the government.

Unfortunately paranoia such as McVeigh's is fueled by disclosures regarding government cover-ups. When many Gulf War veterans complained of exposure to dangerous chemicals our government did what it routinely does—denied such exposure and assured all concerned that veterans have naught to worry about. Recall the government's reaction to claims about the effects of chemical

Agent Orange after the war in Vietnam, in which negative consequences were denied. Today the government acknowledges a variety of maladies associated with such exposure, ranging from multiple types of cancers, to diabetes, to heart disease.[48]

What do you think? Do you believe there is something called Gulf War Syndrome that will be found to have an identifiable cause? Well, the reality is that to date the best evidence does not support toxic exposure as a cause for this condition.[49] But research continues, and an identifiable cause may yet be discovered. The general and vague symptoms reported by Gulf War veterans are similar to those described by veterans of wars extending back to the Civil War. The list looks the same no matter the era. The symptoms are probably psychiatric in nature and related to the stress of combat. That is not to diminish the severity of the syndrome, as I do believe the symptoms are all too real. However, those real symptoms might not be caused by anything physical but rather by the experience of the horrors of war.

JOHN DU PONT

On January 26, 1996, John du Pont, heir to the chemical and manufacturing company, shot and killed Olympic gold medal–winning wrestler Dave Schultz. The background to this crime is a classic study in paranoia.

Born into a world of bluebloods and raised on the sprawling estate known as Foxcatcher Farm in southeastern Pennsylvania, John du Pont would over the course of his life develop classic features of paranoia, and probably schizophrenia. He acquired an intense interest in wrestling and for many years was the chief sponsor of the sport in the United States, going so far as to build a training center and Olympic-size swimming pool on the grounds of his estate. Wrestlers from around the world were housed and fed at his facility, including Olympic gold medalists Mark and Dave Schultz, brothers who hoped to recapture their form. Mark Schultz's initial encounter with du Pont was a memorable one, and he noted that "Du Pont's appearance and actions were, simply, odd. He seemed harmless but seriously, seriously off."[50]

John grew up essentially friendless and isolated on the eight-hundred-acre estate, and his paranoia may have been modeled for him by his mother, Jean. Described by John as "cold, cunning and conniving"[51] she kept the lightbulbs locked up for fear the help would steal them. Reportedly she also taught young John to be wary of the motives of the opposite sex, implying that women were only after his money. This is perhaps not an unreasonable lesson, given the vast amount of money at stake. She was also worried about possible kidnapping, which intensified when heiress Patty Hearst was kidnapped. Her influence led John to grow up with poor social skills and to become rather detached from normal social existence.

When John was in his thirties, clear evidence of paranoia emerged. It began with fears of being kidnapped. So preoccupied was John about possible kidnappers that he had two trained German shepherds accompany him on the grounds of the estate. Not stopping there, he installed a twelve-foot barbed wire–topped steel fence around the property, chained off side entrances, and had an electronic access system installed on the main gate. Steel blinds could be rolled down to seal windows. He instructed his wife to alter her times of departure and destinations to make it more difficult for would-be kidnappers to ambush them.

Vast sums were paid to individuals to search for electronic "bugs." Expensive ($77,000) equipment capable of peering seventy-five feet beneath the ground was employed to find the tunnels that allowed others to enter the mansion between the walls. He had the walls x-rayed to find the infiltrators. Du Pont installed trap doors and believed there were "goo" machines that supposedly made the house disappear. These machines reportedly stained the roof, and said stain took the form of his mother and father in a picture frame. The controls of the goo machine were invisible. In order to block space aliens from entering the mansion, expensive copper tiles were purchased.

Following the death of his mother, John began to deteriorate from a psychiatric standpoint. He became more reclusive, fired long-serving staff for no reason, and believed that he was infested with insects from outer space. At one point he gouged these bugs—and skin—out of his leg with a knife. Wrestlers from his training camp were sent to find the people crawling between the walls. They were also instructed to shoot at the Nazis in the trees on the estate.

Du Pont became convinced that the mansion was moving, and, using sophisticated time-lapsed photography, he filmed this migration, which he then showed to others to prove his claims. Unfortunately others could not see what he did. Wires were attached to barns to prevent them from shifting since he believed that such movements resulted in changes in the weather patterns in nearby Philadelphia. The same time-lapsed photography was used to capture the mist that was engulfing the house. Replaying of the videotape revealed nothing but a period of fuzziness when the autofocus lens adjusted.

The timers on exercise equipment were believed to take him back in time, and books on his bookshelf moved on their own accord. Water fowl on the estate's lake were hypnotizing him, and he eventually came to believe that he was the Dalai Lama of America. He developed an extreme fear of the color black, believing it portended death. This fear was so deep that he even had a black athlete removed from his estate. Despite his clear French roots, he believed that he was Bulgarian, often speaking broken English like someone from Eastern Europe might. (This belief had some important real-world consequences: he left the majority of his huge wealth to a Bulgarian wrestler.) He held even more bizarre beliefs. In addition to being the Dalai Lama, he was Jesus Christ, the last of the Romanovs, the devil, the president of Bulgaria, and the Führer.

Du Pont was particularly paranoid of the Russians, a fact that would figure prominently in his eventual murder of Dave Schultz. At one point during his brief marriage he put a gun to his wife's head and accused her of being a Russian spy, this in response to being asked to turn down the radio. Ironically, it was Dave Schultz who often helped quell du Pont's paranoia, reassuring him that he saw no aliens, heard no strange sounds, saw no buildings move, felt no insects crawling.[52]

Like many paranoid individuals du Pont was paranoid about a wide variety of things. People were trying to steal his money or were tunneling under the grounds of the estate, entering the mansion through the walls. There was, in fact, a four-hundred-foot tunnel that contained wires and telephone lines into the mansion. In order to counteract this threat he had razor wire, like that used in maximum-security prisons, installed *between* the walls of the house.

Trees contained Nazis and hidden pictures were seen in designs on dinner plates. Mechanical trees on the property were capable of movement and would position themselves beside the mansion, where their mechanical limbs would extend inside and steal valuables. Passed from limb to limb the booty would be spirited away to the hands of the waiting mastermind. The pool balls on the billiard table contained electronic transmitters, and his security detail searched the car each time before he entered it. He was convinced that some type of device within his mansion was capable of spraying an oil to make people disappear.[53]

Du Pont also carried grudges. For example, he attempted to make a large donation to the private school he attended in his youth in exchange for the firing of a teacher who many years before had failed him. The school refused.

It would be reasonable for anyone with such a huge estate to manage, and with so much money and heirlooms at stake (including a desk upon which the Declaration of Independence had been signed), to hire a security company. Du Pont did so, and for years this company provided security services. Many on the payroll were presumably able to send their kids to college using du Pont money. There were, in fact, concerns that this company may have played on John's paranoia in order to keep their lucrative contract. Many of the staff and wrestlers reported that du Pont appeared tense, anxious, and paranoid when security personnel were around and less so when they were not. They were seen occasionally firing warning shots out the window at would-be intruders. As is typical with paranoid individuals du Pont eventually came to distrust even those he hired to protect him and began carrying a gun. Instead of a briefcase, which du Pont felt could conceal a bomb, security staff carried clipboards.

There was a complicating factor in du Pont's paranoia: he was apparently a prodigious abuser of cocaine. As noted in chapter 7, paranoia is a common outcome of such abuse. However, it seems clear based on available accounts that his paranoia preceded his introduction to cocaine. Eventually, the wrestlers he had invited to live on his estate, and who were among the closest "friends" he probably ever had, became the target of his paranoia. As Dave Schultz was the de facto coach and mentor to the wrestlers, he naturally became the leader of the conspiracy against du Pont.

On that cold January day, du Pont arrived at Dave Schultz's house on the Foxcatcher estate accompanied by his security agent and a large handgun. As Schultz approached the car, du Pont fired, hitting Schultz while asking him, "You got a problem with me?" He fired two more shots, one as Schultz lay face-down dying in the snow.

He then returned to his mansion where police were eventually able to trick him into leaving the house, thereby capturing him without further bloodshed.

He was clearly psychotic, and his trial was delayed as he was found not compe-tent to stand trial.[54]

While imprisoned du Pont refused to provide his attorneys with useful information because he believed his jail cell was bugged. He even dismissed his attorneys as they became part of the vast conspiracies against him—along with the Olympic Committee, the CIA, the US government, and the district attorney. Further, there were vast international conspiracies against him. Held in the balance was the possible invasion of Newton Township, Pennsylvania, by the Russian army.

Once du Pont's competency was restored, due in large part to the admin-istration of antipsychotic medications, he stood trial for the murder and was found guilty but mentally ill of third-degree murder.

That verdict was a relatively new one as far as American jurisprudence was concerned. Following the acquittal of John Hinckley Jr. for the attempted assassination of President Ronald Reagan, many people, including govern-ment officials, were outraged. How could someone shoot the president of the United States and walk away? Never mind the fact that Hinckley and just about everyone else who is found not guilty by reason of insanity actually spend *more* time incarcerated in forensic psychiatric institutions than they would have spent in prison. Hinckley's acquittal somehow violated our sense of justice. So state governments, including Pennsylvania's, leapt into action and created a new verdict: guilty but mentally ill. This verdict allows us to concede on one hand that mental illness factors contributed to the crime and should therefore miti-gate against a harsher punishment. Yet on the other hand it still holds the person responsible for his or her actions. So it went for John du Pont. He was sentenced to thirteen to thirty years in prison, where he eventually died not far away from where this book was written.

The details of the killing of Dave Schultz are clear, but more important for the purposes of this book are the sequence of events leading up to it. Approximately ten days before the murder, du Pont had gone to California on a "secret mission." This was actually just a trip to purchase stamps, as he was an avid collector. Upon his return he confided to others that he discovered while in California that the person who posed a threat against him was on his estate, and he now knew the identity of that person. Moreover, he knew that his life was in jeopardy.[55]

Put yourself in du Pont's shoes and imagine that despite being surrounded by a small army of staff as well as the wrestlers on the property, there lurks an assassin. Moreover, you know who that assassin is. Living in such an environment would result in considerable anxiety and an ever-escalating vigilance. The mechanism whereby that information was revealed was referred to previously as sudden clarification—the paranoid individual's sudden realization about something important.[56] In the case that began this book (in which the paranoid person feared his life was in danger from the woman renting a room in his house and her drug-dealer cronies), the sudden clarification was a turned hairbrush on a dresser that signaled the imminent arrival of drug dealers to kill him. We will never know what the suddent clarification was in the case of du Pont.

BRUCE IVINS: ANTHRAX AND PARANOIA

The dust had not yet settled after 9/11, literally and figuratively, when selected members of the news media and lawmakers began receiving envelopes containing a brown granular substance. By the end of November five people had died and seventeen others were sickened by the brown substance: anthrax.

Experts had warned for years of possible biological and chemical terrorist attacks, and given the timing with 9/11 the anthrax letters were immediately suspected of being such an attack. The FBI began to suspect domestic terrorism, not Islamic radicals, and identified twenty to thirty scientists for closer scrutiny. Dr. Steven Hatfill was initially named as a "person of interest," which effectively ruined his career despite the fact that he was ultimately exonerated. Years later he would settle a lawsuit with the Justice Department for $5.8 million.[57]

The case appeared to disappear from media sight while the FBI conducted a careful investigation, which led them to an unlikely suspect—not an Islamic terrorist, but Dr. Bruce Ivins, a microbiologist and researcher with the US Army Medical Research Institute of Infectious Diseases. Just as the FBI closed in to make an arrest he committed suicide. In the aftermath coworkers, angered by his death, came to his posthumous aid, claiming the family-oriented, fun-loving, jolly-dispositioned, church-going Ivins was harassed and his reputation so smeared that he was driven to suicide.

The picture that has since emerged paints a very different and quite paranoid picture of the man.[58] Ivins's psychiatrist had reportedly referred to him as "homicidal" and "sociopathic." Jean Dudley, a social worker who treated Ivins and subsequently sought a restraining order against him, stated in a Maryland court that Ivins was a "revenge killer" and that he had made homicidal threats decades before while in college. "When he feels that he has been slighted, and especially towards women, he plots and actually tries to carry out revenge killings." He admitted to mixing poison and taking it to the soccer match of a young woman he was interested in with the intent of killing her if her team lost.[59]

In his counseling sessions Ivins admitted holding grudges against people from his past who he felt were deserving of punishment, and boasted of the ability to find out where they lived. When he became a suspect in the anthrax murders he bought a gun, hundreds of rounds of ammunition, and a bulletproof vest, then announced in his group therapy session he planned to kill his coworkers and others who had wronged him in what his therapist called "a blaze of glory."[60] He was subsequently admitted to a psychiatric institution as a result of this threat.

The FBI found three handguns; two stun guns; one Taser; electronic detection equipment; evidence that Ivins's basement had been used as a firing range; homemade reinforced body armor; smokeless handgun powder; and hundreds of rounds of ammunition in his home.

Even before 9/11 he had attempted to kill others and boasted that as a skilled scientist he'd accomplish the killings without detection. Moreover, he appeared to have a three-decades-old obsession with a sorority—Kappa Kappa Gamma—perhaps after his romantic overtures had been rejected by a member of that sorority decades before. He made contributions to Wikipedia's page on the sorority and posted to an online forum devoted to sororities and fraternities. He would drive three or more hours to a Kappa Kappa Gamma sorority house, look at it for ten minutes, then turn around and return home. Occasionally he broke into the house, stealing material on the sorority's secret rituals. The anthrax envelopes had been mailed from a mailbox near the Princeton Kappa Kappa Gamma sorority house. One letter in particular speaks directly to the issue of paranoia: "I like individual Kappas enormously, and love being around them. I never choose an enemy, but they've been after me since the

1960s, and REALLY after me since the late 1970s."[61] He believed that they were waging a "fatwa" against him.

It was perhaps the Kappa Kappa Gamma sorority preoccupation that led to Ivins's downfall. In the mid-1970s he was a postdoctoral fellow at the University of North Carolina. Studying microbiology at the same time was Nancy Haigwood, a Kappa Kappa Gamma sorority sister who Ivins became obsessed with. His "intrusive" questioning of her and obsession with her sorority put her off him. He retaliated by sneaking into her laboratory one night and stealing her lab notebooks.

Years later Haigwood moved to Maryland, not far from where Ivins lived and worked. One day she found her boyfriend's car vandalized and the letters "KKG" spray-painted on it and the fence behind her residence. Later someone, presumably Ivins, wrote a letter to the editor defending hazing by the Kappa Kappa Gamma sorority and signed Haigwood's name to it. As noted previously the FBI suspected a scientist insider as the anthrax culprit and contacted the American Society for Microbiology, asking its members for tips of likely suspects. Haigwood pegged Ivins.

E-mails from Ivins made available after his death provide a glimpse from inside his mental illness. "Even with the Celexa and the counseling, the depression episodes still come and go. That's unpleasant enough. What is REALLY scary is the paranoia."[62] "It's hard enough sometimes controlling my behavior. When I'm being eaten alive inside, I always try to put on a good front here at work and at home, so I don't spread the pestilence . . . I get incredibly paranoid, delusional thoughts at times, and there's nothing I can do until they go away, either by themselves or with drugs" (August 2000).[63]

That same year he wrote: "The thinking now by the psychiatrist and counselor is that my symptoms may not be those of a depression or bipolar disorder, they may be that of a paranoid personality disorder."[64] On one online posting he noted, "The skeletons are all out. I'm having a devil of a time rounding them back up. Let's see . . . how about mom who was an undiagnosed paranoid schizophrenic . . . Is that bones enough?"[65] Despite his illness he retained a sense of humor and insight, quipping in one e-mail that the *National Enquirer* headline would read "Paranoid Man Works with Deadly Anthrax" if they ever investigated his work. He also embedded within the messages attached to the anthrax spores the coded name of two female former colleagues he was allegedly obsessed with. More ominously he acknowledged in an e-mail to a former colleague, "I can hurt, kill and terrorize." Yet at the same time he tried to pin the blame on the two objects of his obsession. When confronted by one he claimed that it was another personality, "Crazy Bruce" who did it and this personality was "paranoid, severely depressed and ridden with incredible anxiety."[66]

He admitted to obsessions since childhood, and two of these clearly included at least two female colleagues. But in true paranoid fashion he then turned on them when he felt they were conspiring against him. In an e-mail to one of the two objects of his obsession he notes of the other: "I have come to learn, much to my surprise and disappointment, that [the other] has been saying some very negative things behind my back. It seems that whatever I say or do can get twisted, exaggerated or misconstrued by her, and now the bond of trust that I had with her is gone." He later acknowledged his paranoia and apologized to her.[67]

One of the big unanswered questions is why Ivins chose to poison members of the media and lawmakers. A hint is provided by his background and his own words. He had been involved in anthrax research for years with a specific aim to develop a vaccine in case of a terrorist attack. Like the rest of the country he appeared to have been deeply affected by the events of 9/11: "I am incredibly sad and angry at what happened, now that it has sunk in. Sad for all of the victims, their families, their friends. And angry. Very angry. Angry at those who did this, who support them, who coddle them, and who excuse them" (September 15, 2001).[68] Perhaps in his mind those "coddlers" were the media who did not expose radical Islam. The Department of Justice concluded that his research program was coming under increased scrutiny and criticism from within and outside the government. He allegedly saw the end of twenty-plus years of professional work looming ahead.

There is an ironic, paranoid twist to this story. Many believe that there was a conspiracy to frame Ivins. These conspiracy theorists believe that the government, lacking solid intelligence regarding Iraq's weapons of mass destruction, used a covert operation in which they willingly killed Americans in order to drum up support for the impending war. Then—as all good conspiracies require—they pinned the blame on an innocent (Ivins) and had him eliminated at the end, or drove him mad to the point of suicide in order to cover their tracks.

It is difficult to find much sympathy for someone who knowingly killed innocent individuals. Yet reading through Ivins's e-mails one gets a glimpse of the mental anguish that he and many paranoid individuals endure. "When I get these paranoid episodes; of course I regret them thoroughly when they are over, but when I'm going through them, it's as if I am a passenger on a ride. I don't want to become mean-spirited, hateful, angry, withdrawn and paranoid."[69] "When I see the terrible things that some paranoid schizophrenics have done, it honestly makes me want to cry. I don't want to be like that, and to think that I may be heading toward becoming that kind of person and that is the exact antithesis of who I want to be, I can't begin to tell you how much it hurts and scares me."[70] "I wish I could control the thoughts in my mind. They're things which come from the darkest recesses and which are both sad and scary to me." Perhaps Ivins summarized the situation the best when he said: "Go down low, low, low as you can go, then dig forever, and you'll find me, my psyche" and "I, in my right mind, wouldn't do it." The evidence would suggest that he *wasn't* in his right mind and that this was no fault of his own.[71]

ANTHRAX AND THE MAIL

The events of 9/11 and its aftermath aroused many a paranoiac's suspicions. The anthrax scare certainly affected paranoid and non-paranoid individuals alike. It affected Barbara more than most. Fearful and convinced that her mail was anthrax-infested she simply refused to empty her mailbox. Bills and letters alike piled up. Utility company employees passed by that very mailbox on their way to turn off her utilities.

JIVERLY WONG

On April 3, 2009, Jiverly Wong, a Vietnamese immigrant, walked into the American Civics Association in Binghamton, New York, where he had taken English language classes. There in a span of one minute he fired ninety-eight bullets from two handguns, killing thirteen and wounding four more before taking his own life. Among the victims were those who took classes with him and those who tried to teach him English. Like Seung-Hui Cho, Wong spoke from beyond the grave in the form of a letter sent to a television station. And like the other cases on the preceding pages, pieces of a paranoid puzzle fell in place.

Postmortem interviews with those who knew Wong revealed a "secretive" individual who was often angered by his poor command of the English language even as members of his own family mastered it. The *New York Times* reported a "growing paranoia with a fixation on law enforcement rooted in a few brief encounters that seemed to convince Mr. Wong that the police were out to get him."[72]

In the letter he wrote to a Syracuse television station he detailed—in very poor English—just what the police allegedly did to him. This includes, as best as can be determined based on his poor grammar, that undercover police: gave him "a lot of ass" during eight years; employed twenty-four-hour surveillance using "ultramodern" cameras; burned chemicals in his house that made him vomit because they sabotaged the switch on his fan; made him poor by causing him to lose his job; spread rumors about him both in California and New York; and were prejudiced against him.[73]

During 1994 the police allegedly followed Wong home and waited until he was asleep, at which point they broke into his house, sat on his bed, and touched him. This occurred thirteen times, and on at least one occasion they reportedly stole $20 from his wallet. He was shot in the back of the neck with an electric gun, and the police allegedly attempted to cause him to have a car accident by suddenly braking in front of him so that he would hit them from behind. This tactic was reportedly employed thirty-two times from 1990 to 1995. Exploiting Wong's poor command of English they would knock on his door and then harass and attempt to "dominate" him. They even went so far as calling his cell phone and leaving a voicemail message telling him to go back to Vietnam.

The letter was described by Dr. Park Dietz, a forensic psychiatrist who has testified as an expert witness in such high-profile cases as John Hinckley Jr. and Andrea Yates, as "coded for prosecutorial delusions." He noted that "every mass murderer we've studied has had a combination of paranoia, depression and suicidality" and that in paranoid individuals police and other government agencies are frequently ascribed as having malicious intent against them.[74]

In addition to the police in two states, the New York Department of Labor allegedly did not pay some of his unemployment benefits. At the end of the letter he places the blame for what he was about to do on the police, whom he saw as responsible for the situation he was in. And then, in what was perhaps his worst use of English—or a very purposeful ironic statement—he ended with "And you have a nice day."

So were any of these alleged events true? Well, what is known is that he was pulled over by the police for driving without having the car properly inspected. He had alleged that someone was trying to break into his house, but a police investigation found no evidence of a break-in.

He was also involved in a fender-bender and had at least five arrests, the most serious of which appeared to be for passing a bad check. Someone did apparently tip off the New York State Police that he was going to rob a bank to support his cocaine habit. Whether he had such a drug problem or whether there was any truth to the allegations is not known. He lived in a drug-infested neighborhood in California where undercover police were frequently seen watching the building where he lived. According to at least one neighbor in that building, men dressed in suits made inquiries about Wong on three or four occasions.

There were a number of factors in Wong's case that likely contributed to his paranoia. As noted in chapter 1, immigrants have higher rates of delusional paranoia than indigenous individuals do. His inability to understand what was said to him in English probably resulted in repeated instances in which those trying to communicate with him would lose patience or ridicule his poor language skills. Add to this occasional—largely negative—interactions with police and an overall marginal and stressful existence. Together these ingredients resulted in the powder keg of angry and resentful paranoia and the subsequent death of so many innocent victims.

CONCLUSIONS

The above cases should not simply be dismissed because of their high-profile nature. Paranoid individuals commit violent crimes as a result of their desire to exact vengeance, to preempt others from being violent toward them, or from misconstruing the actions of those around them. Such crimes are unfortunately not rare events. Most, of course, do not involve a large number of dead as many of the above cases did. Frequently there is nothing about paranoid individuals that would alert others to their potential for violence. Indeed, because violence is a statistically rare event, its prediction is a less-than-accurate endeavor.

The fact that many paranoid individuals are not manifestly bizarre or stigmatized by their disorder makes it likely that they are able to procure firearms in a society where obtaining them—and lots of them—is easy to do. Armed, the paranoid person who has been suffering for so long at the hands of their perceived tormentors is now in a position to exact their pound of flesh. All it takes is that final straw. Trouble is, it is impossible to determine what innocuous event constitutes that "final straw." Is it the fact that you grabbed the last parking space before they pulled into the lot? Is it that you said something that they could not fully or clearly hear? Was it your dog that barked at 7 a.m.? The cases above were selected for discussion here because of the large amount of available information. We will never know what was going through the mind of Adam Lanza that cold December day when he entered the Sandy Hook Elementary School killing twenty-six innocents. It could have been paranoia.

WHAT CAN BE DONE?

The prevention of violent crime at the societal level is in the domain of criminology. The detection and treatment of paranoia-related conditions was dealt with in chapter 10. But what about at the individual level? It is hoped that as a result of reading this book one would be able to better discern those who are likely paranoid. While terms like "cranky," "humorless," and "argumentative" are personality descriptors, they are also clinical features of many paranoid individuals. Since many paranoid persons will not voice outright paranoid concerns, such as "Why do you always persecute me?" the combination of personality characteristics should serve as warning signs or risk factors for paranoia. Once an individual is identified as possessing many characteristic features of paranoia, caution should be taken in dealing with him. Taunting him, getting into arguments, becoming petty in return all should obviously be avoided. Although it may be difficult to determine what event serves as the "final straw," a significant change in mood or demeanor should merit concern.

If it is a family member and the warning signs are not subtle but more direct in the sense that they are making paranoid comments, then finding and removing weapons should be considered. Rational discourse, logic, appeals to be understood—the usual methods we employ to defuse conflict situations—may prove to be ineffective. Yet the relationship one has with the individual does matter. A close family member or neighbor of many years will be heard, to some degree. Again, a frontal assault on their paranoia no matter what your relationship will typically not succeed.

The importance of identifying a paranoid family member and preventing them from engaging in acts of violence is highlighted by the case of Blaec Lammers. His mother expressed concerns about his mental health to police, who found him in possession (legally) of two assault rifles and four hundred rounds of ammunition. His plan was to enter a movie theater and open fire, then proceed to a nearby Walmart and begin shooting. When his supply of bullets was exhausted he planned on stealing more from the store in order to keep firing. His mother's actions saved an untold number of innocent lives. Lammers was found guilty of first-degree assault and sentenced to fifteen years.[75]

Chapter 12

IT'S A PARANOID WORLD WE LIVE IN

Do you feel safe and secure? Do you worry about people hacking into your computer? How many people do you really trust, and how many do you worry harbor ill will toward you? Do you worry that the government might be spying on you? Do you have virus-protection software on your computer? Do you worry that someone will root through your trash, collecting all those credit card offers you threw away and opening accounts in your name?

On the surface, a positive answer to these questions might suggest paranoia. At the same time, it's the rare individual who is not concerned about some of these issues. If the heir to the throne of England can have his cell phone conversations monitored and his embarrassing desire to be a feminine hygiene product in his paramour's knickers revealed to the world, what chance do the rest of us have to keep our business private?

Given the realities of modern life, there appear to be multiple reasons not to trust and to feel suspicious. Lose enough trust, feel enough suspiciousness, and you arrive on paranoia's doorstep. But are we really more paranoid than in times past? If so, what is it that is increasing our paranoia? This chapter will address these issues, starting with a bit of history.

RATES OF MENTAL ILLNESS

A straightforward question is whether the rate of paranoia is on the rise. Unfortunately, it is difficult to answer that question. Admission records to hospitals often list only broad diagnoses, such as schizophrenia, and then only those most likely to be reimbursed by insurance companies. Only with a careful reading of the narrative portion of a medical chart will a true sense of paranoia emerge. This has not been done to date. A further complication is that we often use the term *paranoia* rather loosely in everyday parlance. But does that term really translate into true clinical conditions of paranoia?

Dr. Fuller Torrey, mentioned in the previous chapter, argues that the rates of serious mental illnesses have been increasing steadily over time. In his book *The Invisible Plague*, he systematically reviews evidence that suggests that the rates of psychotic disorders—which would include many paranoid disorders—were not particularly high in the seventeenth century. So novel were the mentally ill that lunatic asylums were besieged by tourists who came to see patients talking and behaving bizarrely.[1] The saying "A penny for your thoughts" is thought to have emerged from such tourists giving money to the mentally ill, or their warders, to hear them talk gibberish.

By the eighteenth century rates began to climb rather significantly. The trend continued in the nineteenth and twentieth centuries. During those centuries the rates rose from a mere one or two cases per thousand people to three per thousand in the nineteenth century and up to five per thousand in the twentieth. As Torrey puts it: "At the end of the seventeenth century, insanity was of little significance and was little discussed. At the end of the eighteenth century, it was perceived as probably increasing and was of some concern. At the end of the nineteenth century, it was perceived as an epidemic and was a major concern. At the end of the twentieth century, insanity was simply accepted as part of the fabric of life."[2]

In England during the period of 1845–1855 there was a 73 percent increase in the number of insane individuals. Four years later (1859) the rates had increased another 16 percent. Statistics from the United States are not quite as high. Between 1840 and 1850 there was a 31 percent increase. The differences between the United States and England may reflect the fact that the original gene pool of settlers probably did not include a plethora of mentally ill individuals, given the rigors of transatlantic travel. Between 1880 and 1940 the rate of hospitalized psychiatric patients almost tripled (1.18 to 3.21 per thousand people in the population). A full 18 percent of males screened for the armed services during World War II were rejected due to mental illness.

There are those who dispute Torrey's findings, claiming a kind of "If you build it they will come" explanation. Actually, the explanation was first stated in the nineteenth century as a "lumber room" effect: if you build a lumber room, eventually you will fill it with pieces of lumber. Extending the analogy to mental illness, the building of lunatic asylums is what ostensibly caused the existing mentally ill to fill them. In other words, the number of mentally ill did not increase; rather, the number of asylums did. So those with mental illness now had a place to go, and once there they could be counted. This fails to explain why there were no decreases in the number of individuals in almshouses and jails during the same time period. The mentally ill were often kept in these institutions prior to the availability of asylums.

The very high rates of mental illness are no longer in dispute. A number of thorough epidemiologic studies highlight the large percentage of the population (over 50 percent) who will at one point in their lives suffer from a mental illness.[3] The evidence also suggests that rates are increasing. Rarely are paranoid disorders isolated in such studies, and, as discussed previously, paranoia is distributed across a variety of maladies. So it is a fairly safe assumption that rates of paranoia in general are also climbing. Unlike AIDS or a flu epidemic/pandemic, the substantial increases in mental illnesses has been slow and quiet but steady. Make no mistake, the rates are alarming yet no alarm is being rung. As Torrey says: "Living amid an ongoing epidemic that nobody notices is surreal. It is like viewing a mighty river that has been rising slowly over two centuries, imperceptibly claiming the surrounding land, millimeter by millimeter. The people who once lived on the land have either died or moved away, and few of their relatives are aware that the river was once much smaller."[4]

IS PARANOIA A CONSEQUENCE OF MODERN TIMES? THE CASE FOR URBANIZATION

Throughout history there have been attempts to articulate the factors believed to contribute to mental illness. Religious explanations such as sin and spirit possession predominated through much of human history. In the nineteenth century the list of contributing factors included steam engines, "tight lacing," and bee stings. However, for over a century there has been an awareness that the rigors of modern life may be contributing to mental illness. The increase in mental illness during the nineteenth century mirrored the increase in urbanization and industrialization. There is now a robust scientific literature documenting that with increased urbanization comes increased risk for paranoia and psychosis.[5]

Recall for a moment our previous discussion regarding the Paleolithic origins of paranoia during the Pleistocene epoch. We carry with us millions of years of living in small groups. Our brains are well equipped to live comfortably, happily, and in good mental health within a close-knit clan. It is possible that one of the prices of increased urbanization is increased mental illness in general, including paranoia. The growth of large cities in nineteenth- and twentieth-century England brought disproportionately greater levels of mental illness along with it. It is also possible that paranoid disorders *in particular* have increased significantly over time. Evidence for this comes from studies on psychosis and schizophrenia that have demonstrated that urban living is a risk factor for the development of both.[6] In fact, the risk for developing schizophrenia or psychosis, paranoia included, is roughly 2.4 times higher in dense urban areas than in rural settings.[7]

Think about your own situation. If you were to go out in your community and walk around for an hour, how many people would you encounter that you actually know by sight? How about by name? Finally, how many do you know well and trust to a considerable degree? Some of you reading this may live in small towns or communities, in which case you might just meet a few in each of the above categories. Those of you in large cities have a very high likelihood of meeting no one in any category.

I currently live in a small town of about fifteen thousand. I am a professor at the local university and a member of the medical staff at the local hospital. I do evaluations for the courts and provide clinical services to the larger community. I get around. As a result of this wide exposure I cannot go for more than an hour before running into someone I know. In this town there is often only one degree of separation between any two individuals. I still marvel over this phenomenon despite having lived here for close to twenty years. You are anonymous in a large city, whereas in a small one it seems everyone knows your business.

Having lived in large cities, there is no doubt in my mind that I feel more connected to those around me in a small town and more responsible to those individuals. Now think about our Paleolithic ancestors. In their case it was rare seeing someone they *didn't* know. In such small tight-knit bands, trust in most if not all members of your group was likely the norm based on extensive close personal interactions, which are the foundations for trust.

Is it just the large number of strangers that contributes to the (presumed) increase in paranoia? I would argue that there are a number of contributing factors. I believe one is the stress of modern life, which comes with urbanization. Over time those of us living in industrialized countries meet more people that we know less well and are under greater stress than in previous periods of human history. That stress comes in the form of greater noise levels, greater speeds of transportation, work schedules, financial woes, bad news reported nonstop by the media, and a myriad of other factors. Crowd too many rats together in a cage, and they start biting each other's tails off.

But there are other aspects of life today that I feel contribute to a diminished sense of security and, increasingly, paranoia: the technologies of modern life.

THE COMPUTER AGE

Computers and similar devices—cell phones, tablets, and so on—have become an integral part of everyday life. We are aware of their existence when, for example, we sit down in front of a computer, but how many of us are aware of those that are embedded in our cars? There they quietly collect data that can be revealed to others, say, after an accident. Your claims to have been traveling "only thirty-five miles per hour, Officer" might not jibe with the seventy-five-miles per hour that the computer clocked you at just prior to your losing control of the vehicle.

In what other ways are our lives being intruded upon and our sense of personal safety and security threatened? There are many. Let's start with the color laser printer hooked up to your computer. Did you know that the government can secretly track every document you print? Such documents contain a small area of tiny yellow dots that, when magnified under a blue light, will reveal a code identifying the type of printer and copier and the date and time the document was printed. The Secret Service admits to using such technology to deter those who create counterfeit documents. And this practice is perfectly legal, as there are no laws preventing such government intrusion in our private lives.[8]

Ours isn't the only country employing this technology; the Dutch have also used this technique to crack train ticket counterfeiting. Laser printers are capable of producing *very* realistic counterfeits, so the government, with the cooperation of laser printer manufacturers, can track down someone based on its knowledge of who bought the machine in question. So, if you decide to print some leaflets to hand out at an antigovernment rally, remember that your printer can reveal who you are.

NATIONAL SECURITY AGENCY

In the summer of 2013, Edward Snowden, a contractor working for the National Security Agency (NSA), leaked documents exposing the NSA's domestic and foreign surveillance programs. The disclosures started a firestorm that continues to burn today. The government defends its responsibility to keep its citizens safe. But many question whether this safety might come at too high a cost, considering the invasion of privacy of millions of innocent citizens.[9]

The government has been monitoring our electronic activity: cell phone calls, e-mails, web surfing, social media usage, photos, file transfers, videos, and text messages. It has even forced big-name corporations like Verizon, Google, YouTube, Apple, Facebook, Microsoft, Skype, and Yahoo! to turn over information. In the case of Verizon, information was turned over on a daily basis. This enabled government agents to listen to conversations, know the location from which text messages are sent, and monitor people in ways that are mind-boggling.[10]

It is not just electronic surveillance being used. In 2013, the US Postal Service reported receiving fifty thousand surveillance requests—requests to track or take note of mail to/from certain individuals. To put that number in perspective, the average number of such requests in the decade preceding that was eight thousand per year.[11]

The revelations contained in Snowden's leaked documents only confirm what has been suspected for a long time. Author and journalist James Bamford in his 2008 book *The Shadow Factory: The Ultra-Secret NSA from 9/11 to the Eavesdropping on America* described the variety of ways that the government's warrantless surveillance program has been intruding on the lives of ordinary Americans under the banner of homeland security.[12]

For example, so-called StingRay technology enables the government to obtain your cell phone serial number and locate where that phone is, even if it is within the confines of your home, since the technology is capable of penetrating walls.[13]

Was the NSA really interested in whether your wife told you to pick up a loaf of white or whole wheat bread on the way home from work? No; it is trawling through those vast amounts of data looking for patterns suggesting terrorist activities. Indications are they are gearing up to collect quite a lot of such data. A recently completed data warehouse in San Antonio, Texas, has 470,000 square feet to do just that. In Utah a facility is being built that will be able to store five *exabytes* of information. What's an exabyte, you might ask? As Bamford explains: "Five exabytes (5,000,000,000,000,000,000 bytes) represents enough information to fill thirty-seven thousand new Libraries of Congress and more than all the words ever printed. This is the annual equivalent of a thirty-foot stack of books for every man, woman, and child on the planet."[14] Currently, there are 7.2 billion of us on the planet. That amounts to *a lot* of data.

Not to be outdone, the US Department of Justice has also been snooping on us. It is employing surveillance aircraft that act like flying cell phone towers with the use of a device called a *dirtbox*. As with other organizations, DOJ agents are after criminals and terrorists and, again as with other agencies, data are collected on everyone. Every few minutes our cell phone makes known our location, even if we aren't actively using it. The signal not only can locate where we are—within ten feet of our actual location—but it also can identify uniquely which phone it is based on the phone registration number. And if the surveillers get bored with just knowing who and where we are, not to worry because they can amuse themselves by looking at the photos and text messages on our phones. All this bypasses the need to twist Verizon's and other carriers' corporate arms to supply such information.[15]

And now local police are getting in on the act. They are using license plate readers mounted on dashboards, security cameras, electronic toll pass, and other information-gathering strategies to collect detailed information on the movements of ordinary, noncriminal citizens.[16]

Such a degree of intrusion into our private lives has been feeding paranoid fears for decades. Back in 1990 if somebody complained that all of his or her activities—phone calls, credit card purchases, car trips, bank deposits, travel ticket purchases—were being routed to a secret room where the government monitors them, they would have been labeled "nuts"—or, more likely, *paranoid*. Today, such suspicions are correct. We now accept this as our new reality, not a paranoid individual's delusion.

Amazingly, all this surveillance appears to be within the bounds of the law. It is more than ironic that the underlying rationale for government surveillance is to keep Americans "safe and secure." It is quite possible that it is having the opposite effect.

WHO ELSE IS SPYING ON US—AND HOW?

Cell phones are capable of being tracked via the built-in GPS (global positioning system). Just ask Colombian cocaine kingpin Pablo Escobar, who was apprehended in 1993 using such technology.[17] So if you have a company cell phone and decide to call in sick while on your way to the beach, don't be surprised to find the contents of your desk waiting for you in a box when you get back.

Further, the Supreme Court recently ruled that employers have the right to examine how employees are using company-issued cell phones.[18] Yes, indeed, sending a suggestive "selfie" to your wife (or mistress) can now get you fired.

If you do manage to keep your job, be careful how you spend your time on the computer. The majority of employers track your web surfing. Let's face it, how many of us do a few online non-business chores, send a few (or a bunch) of non-business-related e-mails on company computer time?

The same technology employers might use to keep track of employees is also being used by retailers. A good example is Nordstrom, which tracks your movements while you're in their stores. If Nordstrom is doing it, you can be sure others are as well.

Returning to the topic of jealousy for a minute, it is worth noting that electronics have supplanted the age-old verbal confrontation. Placing small GPS devices in your partner's car will quickly confirm or challenge their explanation as to where they have been. Smaller than a deck of cards, these monitors record all sorts of information about where the car has been. That information can then be easily downloaded to your computer.

For under $50 you can buy stealth software programs that will record every keystroke made on a computer, including, presumably, those keystrokes meant to caress your illicit paramour. These programs will take an electronic snapshot of your partner's computer screen and e-mail it to you. Should they be sending any erotic photos of themselves, or receiving any from their lover, you'll know about it. You can receive in your e-mail box a report of all your partner's e-mails, websites they have visited, their instant messages and posts to Facebook. Deleted files can be recovered, making it difficult to erase your computer fingerprints from the scene of the crime.

As far as kids are concerned, in the old days our parents looked in our underwear drawer for drugs or sneaked a peek at our diaries to see if we were having sex. Now we read our kids' text messages and demand they send a photo of themselves and their whereabouts to prove they are at the library and not some drunken frat party.

So while some paranoid individuals worry about outsiders spying on them, it is sometimes those closest to us who are doing the most effective spying. But they are not alone: the company that connects us to the Internet collects information about when we use the net, which sites we visit, how often, and so on. Many of these companies sell this information to others. The sites themselves also gather such information and pass it on to others. The purpose? Marketing. The next time I visit Amazon.com, the site knows I prefer media from Tom Waits and Christopher Moore. The moment either artist produces a new CD (Waits) or book (Moore), my all-knowing friends at Amazon flash a note to me. Each time you use Google very specific information is gathered about you. Yet the vast majority of us (near 90 percent) do not think that such is the case.

Security researcher Brendan O'Connor demonstrated just how easy it is to electronically monitor computer users. For $57 he built a device out of off-the-shelf technology that allowed him to monitor the activities of a person's cell phone, including where they were. His conclusion, as reported by Somini

Sengupta in the *New York Times*, is "it's terrifyingly easy. It could be used for anything depending on how creepy you want to be."[19]Appropriately, he named the device "creepyDOL."

YOU'VE BEEN HACKED!

One of the problems of this digital age is that many of our computers are connected to the Internet almost all the time. This makes us vulnerable to computer programs used by people to essentially highjack our computers. Just ask Craig Matthew Feigin, who successfully installed such software on the computers of female college students, then took pictures of them in various states of undress and in various "positions" with their boyfriends. All twenty thousand of these pictures were then sent via the Internet overseas. Luis Mijangos took this a step further, blackmailing his victims by threatening to send the sexually explicit videos he had taken of them to family and friends if they did not provide him with sexually explicit videos. Jared Abrahams did the same, including catching Miss Teen USA exposed. All three men were convicted and sentenced to time in prison.[20]

The hackers engaged in these activities are not all lowlifes hoping to see you with your pants down. Members of the Harriton High School administration were using the webcams in students' laptops, provided by the school, to spy on the students and their families. No one was aware that the computers could be so used because—naturally—no one ever told them. The cost to the school to settle the lawsuit: $610,000![21]

Is it just your laptop or cell phone you need to worry about? Alas, no; your car may contain as many as four to seventy small computers, depending on how new it is. These computers can be hacked, disabling the ability to brake or steer. As developing technology enables cars to link to the Internet, the situation will get worse (or easier, if you happen to be a hacker), as more and more vehicles will be connected. Similarly, if you have a Wi-Fi–enabled lock on your front door that can be opened with a smartphone, this, too, can be hacked. No longer do thieves have to carry a rusty old crowbar around to gain entry to your home, your valuables, and your family.

If this wasn't enough even your refrigerator can be—and in over one hundred thousand cases was—hacked. These mutant fridges sent out more than 750,000 spam e-mails containing malware designed to steal passwords and other useful information.[22]

Unfortunately, even more nefarious deeds can be perpetrated via the invisible radio waves around us. Some smart toilets—yes, you read that correctly (if there can be smartphones, why not smart toilets?) can be controlled via an app on your smartphone. As such, they can also be hacked. So the pleasant bidet feature might be turned on at an inopportune time, or the soft music you were expecting to facilitate bodily functions could be changed to head-banging heavy metal.[23]

Mind you this is not just a domestic issue. Our hacker "friends" in Russia recently helped educate us about the dangers of weak passwords. Employing default login credentials, which can be freely obtained online, our Russian comrades hacked everything from security cameras to baby monitors. In the United Kingdom alone five hundred of these were hacked using passwords such as "1234."[24] The result was the world got a chance to view some dirty diapers being changed—or, for you UK readers, nappies—as well as some of us naked.

TRENDnet, a company that sells cameras connected to the Internet, had its system hacked. People who had placed such cameras in their homes, to monitor their babies, for example, found themselves exposed—in some cases quite literally—on the Internet for all to see.[25]

These intrusions are certainly annoying and sometimes embarrassing but are not as serious as surgically implanted medical devices such as cardiac pacemakers or nerve stimulators for the treatment of seizures. These, too, have the potential of being hacked, as they rely on information sent to them electronically to calibrate their functioning.[26]

COUNTERSURVEILLANCE FASHION

So what is someone to do to counteract all these electronic surveillance techniques? The answer may be Stealth Wear. Created by Adam Harvey, these garments and devices are manufactured with materials designed to keep the wearer from being detected by others, especially organizations of the government, such as the National Security Agency. As he states, it is "a way for us to protect ourselves from unwanted observations as well as protect what's important, privacy."

Included in the collection is the OFF Pocket, a cell phone cover that creates an electromagnetic barrier through which radio waves are incapable of penetrating. Also stylish is the Anti-Drone ensemble, designed to prevent drones from detecting your heat signature. The clothing ranges from a chest-high hoodie to a burka-like garment and scarf. The latter are inspired by Muslim dress and have the same underlying rationale. "The traditional hijab and burqa act as 'the veil which separates man or the world from God,' replacing God with drone."[27]

MICROCHIPS

Having read patient charts from various eras over the century past, I've seen the evolution of paranoid delusions, from the fear that radios were broadcasting one's thoughts, to cameras stealing one's soul, to telephones stealing one's thoughts, to radar, to x-rays, and most recently to computer chips. Each in their time was an implement used by those who were said to be torturing the paranoid individual.

Mid-1980s delusions often involved having computer chips implanted in the brain. Previously, this would have been a considered a delusion in the true sense of the word—something we generally believe cannot occur or does not exist. Ironically, progress is actually being made in creating computer chips that *can* be implanted in the brain. Previous barriers to success involving the flexibility of the chips and their ability to survive the brain's biological environment have been rapidly broken.

In fact, what was considered a delusion in 1983 is now a reality in the form of RFIDs (radio-frequency identification tags), those small devices attached to the more expensive items in stores. They are also embedded in library books, car tires, your passport, and the E-ZPass sticker that allows you to zip through the turnpike tollbooth.

As far back as the 1990s these little devices were placed in medical-grade glass and injected under the skin of livestock to keep track of them. They were also implanted in your family pet in case the animal was lost or stolen. When read by a scanner they reveal all the pertinent information you need, whether you are a vet or a USDA inspector. It was only a matter of time before humans became the target.

But why would anyone want to implant chips in humans other than—from the paranoid individual's viewpoint—to facilitate spying on them? Actually, one compelling reason is to help patients who suffer from Alzheimer's. These patients frequently wander and are unable to recall where they live, their phone number, or the names of family members. Many are unable to talk at all. Having a RFID under the skin that could be scanned to reveal pertinent identifying information could prove invaluable.

The same could be said for other medical conditions in which a patient might be unable to provide important information such as the type of medical problem they have or allergic reactions to medications. Indeed, would you rather wear one of those unstylish medical alert bracelets or have a RFID implanted?

There is one possibility that should make us all a bit uneasy and some of us paranoid; RIFD technology could lead to certain groups of individuals being targeted and forced to receive these implants. Many of us would probably agree that convicted sex offenders would seem a reasonable group to track, and perhaps those in government with high-security clearances. Soldiers with these implants would no longer need dog tags, which contain a limited amount of information and can be easily lost.

The danger is that the list of mandated groups will increase until virtually *everyone* has such an implant. How many of us carry badges read by a device that allows us to enter areas that are off-limits to those without such a badge? The RFIDs would replace these badges, as well as retinal scanners or other security devices.

Then other "paranoid" dangers begin to creep in. What about installing a GPS in individuals to monitor where they are? Scanners can be bought relatively cheaply, making it possible for someone to hack into *you*, not your computer (this is called "spoofing"). The device is so small—toothpick thickness and rice sized—that you could be injected with it if rendered unconscious and not even know it's there upon awakening.

The materials to implant and read the chip are relatively cheap and can last for many years. There are also devices now that monitor what you drink;

at least in the case of alcohol. Called SCRAM (Secure Continuous Remote Alcohol Monitor), they are used much like the GPS ankle bracelet that Martha Stewart so fashionably wore following her release from prison.[28] These gadgets monitor those who are court-ordered to abstain from alcohol. Just ask Lindsay Lohan, who was court-ordered to wear one as the result of numerous run-ins with the law. Employed in lieu of housing alcohol offenders in expensive jails for their crimes, the devices are able to monitor at least one aspect of your biological functions from a distance. When equipped with a GPS, a SCRAM (for more information, see http://www.scramsystems.com/) can reveal not only *that* you are drinking, but where you are doing it at. Just ask Lindsay Lohan.

EYE SPY IN THE SKY

For most of human history spies had to physically follow us around to see what their targets were doing. Technological advances allowed them to follow us from above, in dirigibles, which gave way to airplanes, helicopters (in basic black, thank you), jets, and eventually satellites, up to today's drones. The satellites that provide the picture of my house on Google Earth reveal very detailed information. Imagine what the government's spy satellites are capable of seeing.

Frankly, I consider it unlikely that the government will target me no matter what I say in this book, since its satellites are extremely big, expensive hunks of technology. So I'm less worried about the bigger ones than the *microsatellites* now being launched. These are lower tech than the big satellites, and dozens of them are being launched by private companies. Ostensibly to be used for variety of useful purposes, such as monitoring crop growth, there are downsides. They are capable of taking pictures regularly, as opposed to the Google camera, whose picture of my house is probably a few years old.[29] These microsatellites can't see my face, but they could regularly see if my car is parked out front or not. Just the fact that I could walk out into what I thought was a private backyard and have my picture taken from above without my awareness or permission is kind of creepy. Poor Taylor Swift, the superstar singer discussed in chapter 6, probably has a fleet of these hovering above her in the ether.

A recent addition over the skies of America are aerial drone planes—yes, the very same that are so effective in identifying Islamic extremists in the Middle East and blowing them up from distant locations. These are being used for a variety of legitimate purposes such as searching for missing persons in remote locations, tracking wildfires, and tracking illegal aliens crossing the Mexico–US border.[30]

Until recently it was only governments or corporations that were able to afford such technology. The cost of small drones is now such that for under $1,000 you can get a camera-equipped drone. So now I can effectively spy on my neighbors across the field . . . or they can spy on me.

Like any technology, what starts out for one purpose can easily be used for other purposes, including tracking us from above. But not to worry if you live in Deer Trail, Colorado, because folks there are considering issuing gun permits to hunt drones. Although the permit may cost you $25, you could make it back by receiving a bounty of $100 for each one you shoot down. The project is the brainchild of Phillip Steel, who was concerned about the United States becoming a "surveillance society."[31] The good folks of Deer Trail are not alone. A recent nationwide poll revealed that 86 percent of Americans are concerned that commercial drones could be used in ways that violate their privacy.[32]

I (THEY) SEE YOU

Look around any city, and you'll find, right out in the open, "security" cameras and lots of them. The British Security Industry Authority estimated that there are close to six million such cameras in Britain alone, with 1.5 million in public places like town centers, airports, and shopping malls.[33] That is one camera for every eleven people. If you want to go unnoticed, don't go to London, for it is estimated that you will be captured on tape around two hundred to three hundred times a day![34]

Cheap cameras these are not. They are perfectly capable of reading the brand on a pack of cigarettes one hundred yards away. The way these cameras are used is also unsettling. Some international borders and many airports now use face-recognition software. But this software not only identifies who we are but how we act and react under certain circumstances. Cameras placed on bill-boards are being used to gauge our responses to particular ads. Once these electronic billboards "see" that we are of a particular age and gender, they display ads specifically targeted for us.

This Big Brother–type of technology is also being used in your place of work. HyperActive Technologies in Pittsburgh, Pennsylvania, has a program, HyperActive Bob, which monitors employees in the fast-food industry. Among the information gathered is how long an employee takes to prepare a burger or how much time is spent in the bathroom.[35]

Sociometric Solutions does it one step better. Embedded in their employee ID badges is a location sensor, microphones, and an accelerometer. Together they can monitor conversations between employees, examine body posture and language, detect voice tone (for more information, see http://www.sociometricsolutions.com/). Ironically, some research has demonstrated that when you provide workers with a small measure of privacy—such as a curtain—their productivity increases.[36]

The technology behind the traffic cameras that nab drivers exceeding the speed limit has been around for a while, so we shouldn't be surprised to learn that these cameras can read the license plate on a particular car and determine if it appropriately belongs on that make of car or was stolen from another vehicle.

At some level many of these surveillance devices will benefit the law-abiding citizens among us. If my car is stolen, these license plate–reading cameras will hopefully locate it. But they are a bit unnerving. While in England once I rented a car but unknowingly failed to pay the London driving tax or, as it is more properly known, the "congestion charge." One of the multitude of cameras took a picture of my car, sending the image to a computer that checked to see if the congestion fee had been paid. Finding it had not, it then checked the registration to find the owner (the rental company), which then checked who the renter was on that particular day. Two months later that renter—yours truly—received a fine that was many times the amount of the congestion fee. And it is very possible that I was the only human being involved in the whole process.

These cameras are apparently quite the moneymaker for British municipalities. The borough of Camden in London makes a good deal of money each year using these cameras to catch moving vehicle violations. I might have contributed to this sum, as I have no idea where I was caught on film.

One final note just to beat this motorized horse to death: Britain is now experimenting with a camera system linked to orbiting satellites—a favorite among the paranoiac's fears—to catch speeders. The system can determine how fast you are driving using the satellite to monitor the distance and speed between two points. The system even works in the United Kingdom's dismal weather.[37]

The ground-based camera then snaps a picture of your license plate, and you receive a ticket in the mail, perhaps without human involvement.

Lest you smirk at the poor Brits who have to endure this on a regular basis, we Americans are having our license plates scanned and the information stored more than we might realize. High-tech automatic license plate–readers can be found on bridges, mounted on patrol cars, and elsewhere. In fact, there is a phone app for police so they can do it just strolling by your car! These readers are indiscriminately capturing our license plates and, in some states, storing that information.[38]

Obviously this is being done to catch criminals, which most of us aren't, but because this information is apparently shared among law enforcement agencies, they can piece together a moving history of any of us.

Just ask the mayor of Minneapolis, R. T. Rybak. The *Star Tribune* used a public-records request to publicize a map of the forty-one times Rybak's car was photographed by automatic readers throughout the city.[39]

The potential abuse of this technology is that it will single out specific individuals or groups. During my day the government might have followed on foot those attending an antiwar protest and, more rarely, tapped attendees' phones. Now, license plate–readers have already targeted attendees at local mosques in New York City, members of the Tea Party, and anti-abortion protesters. Over a five-year period the Department of Homeland Security provided $50 million in grant money for agencies to purchase these readers.[40]

SMILE, YOU ARE ON CAMERA, AND WE RECOGNIZE WHO YOU ARE

We are quickly reaching a point where, one day soon, a bio-digital composite of each of us may be commonplace. Face prints, along with your fingerprints, a sample of your DNA, and retinal scans when combined can result in a nice inventory of biometric data.

Attendees at the 2001 Super Bowl in Tampa had their faces scanned as they entered the stadium, without their knowledge or permission. Although not yet ready for prime time, the Department of Homeland Security has been developing BOSS (Biometric Optical Surveillance System). When perfected, this system will employ two towers containing cameras, infrared and distance sensors that will create a three-dimensional image. These would be linked to a computer, where a database would quickly identify persons captured by the cameras.[41]

While all these technological developments are ultimately designed to make us more safe from terrorists and criminals, to date there is no unequivocal evidence demonstrating they are doing so. This is rather remarkable, as communities throughout the United States are spending huge sums of money on surveillance cameras and systems without clear evidence that they reduce crime.

Although police use video cameras to apprehend criminals, the tables were turned on April 1, 2009, during the annual meeting of the G20 (Group of Twenty) in the United Kingdom. Captured on video was a policeman striking a man, Ian Tomlinson, as he walked hands in pockets *away* from police. He subsequently died as a result of his injuries, and the officer in charge was dismissed from the force—but not convicted.[42]

The Electronic Privacy Information Center (EPIC), a nonprofit research center in Washington, DC, that monitors privacy and civil liberty issues, reports that the government is capable of searching your house without ever setting foot inside.[43] If you grow marijuana in your home, beware—thermal imaging can detect the telltale signs of indoor grow-lights, and police can subsequently obtain a search warrant to confirm their suspicions. The Supreme Court ruled that this was a violation of the Fourth Amendment, indicating that it constituted an unreasonable search.

As noted above, the government can monitor your cell phone and know where you are at any moment. Yet all this technology is soooo twentieth century compared with what lies ahead: *nanotechnology*. These devices are measured in the billionth of a meter scale. They are very, very small devices; one to two million of them are needed to fill the space occupied by the head of a pin. The technology holds great promise to develop stronger and better materials to build things, such as computers or implantable medical devices.

Computers of the future will be much smaller than present-day computers and will be much more powerful as a result of nanotechnology. Further, new methods for delivering drugs to treat conditions such as brain tumors are close to being a reality. Yet embedded in this is the ability to spy on people in ways that border on science fiction. So all the devices already being used to spy on us will become better and much, much smaller.

Now, one can argue that all these technologies will only make life better, safer, and healthier. So, while a nano-device implanted to monitor the activity of my father suffering from Alzheimer's seems like a good thing, what if you are suspected of being a terrorist, drug dealer, or critic of the government? That's the flip side of this conundrum: what can be used for good can also be misused for all the wrong reasons.

KODAK FIENDS OF TODAY

When the Kodak camera was introduced in 1888 it became a huge sensation, and an equally huge problem. The problem was that it invaded the privacy of the people being photographed. The photographers, mostly women, were labeled "Kodak fiends" as a result, and it was clearly not a complimentary term. It implied that these camera fiends were invading the privacy of others.[44]

Not surprisingly men got their hands on the camera too and headed for the beach. For that is where women without much clothing on—by the standards of the day—were to be found. Some beaches and landmarks, like the Washington Monument, posted signs forbidding the taking of pictures.

The *Hartford Courant* noted that "the sedate citizen can't indulge in any hilariousness without the risk of being caught in the act and having his photograph passed around among his Sunday School children."[45]

Such words presaged the viral videos of today. Programs like *Tosh.0* and *America's Funniest Home Videos* revel in displaying the sometimes incomprehensibly stupid behavior of our fellow humans. YouTube has provided a forum as well for such idiocy, as well as a worldwide stage for it to be played on.

Cameras are ubiquitous today and capture much of our behavior. In 2012 an estimated one billion were shipped in cell phones and computer tablets. Google has marketed Google Glass, a pair of computer glasses with a built-in camera.

Small, helicopter-like drones are being used by paparazzi to capture pictures of celebrities in places otherwise inaccessible. So-called *creep shots*—pictures of women's breasts and butts taken in public—are a sad reality. Coupled with the face-recognition software noted earlier, the creep behind the creep shot is now in a position to potentially identify the person he "creeped."

Although cameras are extremely useful in many situations, the fact remains that they can invade our privacy. As noted in the *Economist*, "Freedom has to include some right to privacy: if every move you make is being chronicled, liberty is curtailed."[46] Think about your behavior when you know you are being watched versus when you know you aren't. How much more relaxed do you feel when no one is watching you? Most of us are acutely aware of when eyes are upon us, and the feeling we get is one all too familiar to those who are paranoid.

PARANOIA IN CYBERSPACE

One of the latest trends in the Internet age is *cyber-stalking*, whereby malicious individuals impersonate others and post incorrect information, usually suggesting that sex will be the outcome if contacted. As Tom Zeller of the *New York Times* put it, "It is the online equivalent of scrawling 'for a good time, call Jane Doe' on the bathroom wall."[47]

These cyber-stalkers—men lusting for sex—arrive at the doorsteps of their victims literally looking for love . . . or at least sex. The effects on the victim appear to be the same as occurs in real-world stalking: fear, depression, and some degree of paranoia. Although laws have been passed against such activities, just as they were a decade before for more conventional stalking, there is no overwhelming evidence that they've had a noticeable impact. Cases such as the cyberbullying of Megan Meier, a thirteen-year-old who hung herself after being "befriended" on the social media site Myspace by a boy named Josh, is a sad example of this. "Josh" turned out to be Lori Drew, the mother of a friend of Megan, who gained Megan's confidence then maliciously rejected the vulnerable teen. Drew confessed and was indicted in 2008 but acquitted a year later.

The increased use of wireless networks has introduced another level of hacker threat. These networks, which allow us to use our laptops by the pool and throughout the house without the inconvenience of being tethered to a cable or phone line, are easily detected by others and if not secure allow others to access the Internet using our accounts, whereby they can then download pornography, among other activities.

Private investigators have traditionally plied their trade by hitting the streets. The term *gumshoe*, used to refer to these investigators, derives from the rubber soft-soled shoes used by early detectives to sneak around quietly. Current gumshoes never need to leave the comfy confines of their office, given the information readily available in cyberspace. Through perfectly legal means investigators can access databases and find out your phone records: who you called, when, and how often; financial records; real estate holdings including any secret apartment you might be renting for trysts with your lover; where you've ever lived; who your kids are; what you drive; and a host of other things. You can find a wide variety of publicly available information online. Now imagine what you could get your hands on if you were willing to pay or subscribe to the really good databases, which the numerous private investigative firms do.

Just for kicks I started a search on someone I lost touch with many years ago and within minutes found several potential leads to that person. If I'd been willing to shell out $50 I could have received the following information: statewide criminal check; sex offender check; bankruptcies and liens; address history; small claims and judgments; value of their home; information about their neighborhood; and a lot more. Of course once I find the address I can easily use one of the available (free) software packages to zoom in on their house via satellite imagery.

As it was, I probably had enough to contact them or, if I were of the type, to begin stalking them. There are numerous sources explaining how to find personal information on the Internet. Now this may sound like a paranoid's nightmare, but there are useful aspects to having this kind of information. If I am about to hire someone to watch my child, knowing a bit about them, beyond what they tell me about themselves, would be quite useful. Knowing what a philandering husband is doing with his money is useful during a divorce or custody dispute.

One effective way to find out more about what that philanderer is up to is to look at his (or her) e-mails. Of course one immediately runs into the problem of the password. This is but a minor inconvenience that $100 can solve with the help of such sites as YourHackerz.com (http://yourhackerzsite.blogspot. com/), Piratecracker.com (https://piratecrackers.wordpress.com/about/), or SlickHackers.com. As their names hint at, these sites will get you the perp's password and the password of the floozy he is philandering with. Armed with the password, you can do some real damage. Mind you, it is a crime to use others' accounts, but it is only a misdemeanor and one rarely prosecuted and difficult to prove. This is unfortunate, given the damage that hackers can cause. Apparently it is relatively easy to hack into someone's account; just ask Sarah Palin, who as a vice-presidential candidate had her e-mail account hacked.[48]

The information gathered through such means is often used not for purposes of harassment, although they certainly can be, but for more nefarious reasons: identity theft. In 2012 one out of twenty Americans were victims, 7 percent of which were smartphone users.[49] With great frequency news stories report on computers stolen, lost, or hacked and confidential information obtained with millions of records compromised. As I was putting the finishing touches on this book I received a call from a credit card company to confirm my application. The caller had all the pertinent information: date of birth, Social Security number, address, mother's maiden name, and so on. Problem is I never applied for the card. Someone stole my information.

LET ME READ YOUR MIND

But all of these invasive techniques pale in the face of what is to come: mind reading. Currently scientists are using sophisticated technology to probe the mechanisms that underlie thought. Put my head in a MRI scanner, give me a math problem to solve, and you'll be able to see the math region of my brain hard at work, or hardly working, depending on the difficulty of the calculation. Such research has helped identify a wide variety of cognitive functions as well as human emotions.

If scientists can view the math-processing part of our brains, what about lying? Can they detect when someone is not telling the truth? Not reliably, is the short answer. Even lie detector machines (polygraphs), which look at physiological changes such as increased respiration, heart rate, and sweating can't reliably tell if someone is being deceptive. That is why results of such tests are not admissible as evidence in a court of law. However, as our sophistication in this area progresses we will be able to tell if someone is lying, or in love with us, or going to kill us or blow themselves and everyone else around them up with a bomb, based on particular brain activity the person cannot inhibit or alter. Currently, getting on a plane involves enduring a scanner and the occasional "stink eye" from security personnel. In the future the scanner will focus on your brain only, and a single question may identify your intentions. Again, techniques such as this will help keep us safe but can be used unwisely as well. The current stuff of paranoid delusions—mind reading—will be tomorrow's reality.

And tomorrow may already be here in the form of *interpersonal assessment technology*. This technology, in the form of a smartphone app, can not only recognize faces but also determine the emotions on the face it recognizes.[50] So when your boyfriend shows up late for a date, all you need to do is pull out your cell phone while he tells you his lame excuse and let the phone decide whether or not he is lying. The implications of such technology are far-reaching. Poker games of the future will likely be played by individuals wearing Halloween masks. Indeed, the term *poker face* may disappear from our lexicon. Being able to detect whether someone is lying when they say, "So nice to see you again" is getting closer to one of paranoia's core fears: mind reading.[51]

FOOTBALL AND PARANOIA

One of the most common delusions of paranoid individuals is that they are being spied on, often with the aid of electronic devices. So when the New York Jets accused the New England Patriots of spying on them during a game, many thought the Jets were being a bit, well, paranoid. Turns out it was true (the spying, that is). The Patriots were secretly videotaping opposing coaches in violation of league regulations.[52] According to sports reporter Greg Bishop of the *New York Times*, paranoia is common in football and with good reason. As Bishop puts it, "Coaches in the National Football League may rank among the most paranoid people on the planet, along with counter-intelligence agents and U.F.O. conspiracy theorists. They shred game plans. They sweep the offices for bugs. They surround team head-quarters with security."[53]

In order to ensure that the New York Giants were adequately protected from spies in preparation for their appearance in the Super Bowl XLII, the Tempe, Arizona, police department was assisted by security officials from the Giants organization and the National Football League, private security guards, as well as the FBI and Bureau of Alcohol, Tobacco, Firearms, and Explosives.[54] (It must have been the concerns about performance-enhancing drugs that brought the latter group into the picture.) Not exclusively an American phenomenon, similar acts of spying have been alleged in rugby, soccer, and car racing.

SO WHAT?

One can easily argue that all these security cameras, drones, face-recognition cameras, and the rest are actually making us feel *safer*, since they can be used to capture criminals and terrorists. Further, does it really matter that someone knows whether I spend ten minutes in the menswear department in a clothing store? Do we have any data that these devices make us feel less safe, and perhaps paranoid?

Perhaps a good place to start in order to answer the above question is to look at the former East Germany, where the government regularly snooped on its people. It is estimated that one out of every three people was an informant who snitched on coworkers, friends, and even family. It is also estimated that up to ninety thousand letters per day were being opened by security personnel.[55] Although there are no official studies supporting this, for obvious reasons, there are personal accounts from people who lived through this intrusive regime. Take, for example, Anna Funder, who lived in East Berlin. In her book *Stasiland*, she describes how government surveillance shaped the very nature of social relations. "Relations between people were conditioned by the fact that one or the other of you could be one of them. Everyone suspected everyone else and the mistrust this bred was the foundation of social existence."[56]

Another area where this issue can be examined is the workplace. Most big companies monitor their employees' activities, including the use of security cameras and the monitoring of e-mail, Internet usage, and phone calls. Studies looking at the effects of such surveillance often focus on productivity, physical health, absenteeism, and job satisfaction. But some studies have noted ill effects on self-esteem and other psychological variables, although trust and paranoia are not among them.[57]

Rather than looking for scientific studies, which rarely address the specific question you want an answer to, why not go directly to the source? In other words, ask the person on the street if they trust others. That was done in an Associated Press/GfK poll conducted at the end of 2013.[58] When asked how they felt about people who prepared their food when eating out, or about those swiping their credit card when making a purchase—only about a third of those surveyed reported that people could be trusted. That number is down from the 50 percent of Americans who felt that way in 1972. Nearly two-thirds of the people polled reported that when dealing with people, "You can't be too careful."[59]

It is even more revealing to look at those who grew up with all this technology: millennials—people who reached adulthood around the year 2000. In 2014 only 19 percent of this group felt that people could be trusted! This is compared to 31 percent of Gen Xers and 40 percent of Boomers. However, both Gen Xers and Boomers have experienced a decrease in trust since 1987, when they were asked the same question.[60]

All this mistrust would be understandable if crime rates were on the rise. Instead, crime throughout the majority of the United States is at all-time lows.[61]

If it isn't crime causing our mistrust then a reasonable explanation is the highly surveilled world we now live in. But there is at least one other factor that has likely contributed to our levels of distrust: the events of 9/11.

LIFE IN AMERICA POST-9/11

There is no doubt that the events of 9/11 had a profound impact on the American psyche. Even Pearl Harbor did not affect our collective sense of safety as much as 9/11. The attack on Pearl Harbor was made by Japanese military planes striking US troops. The 9/11 terrorist attacks, made on US soil, were not perpetrated during wartime and targeted innocent civilians. In the wake of these attacks, it was not surprising, from a psychiatric standpoint, to see an increase in the number of cases of posttraumatic stress disorder (PTSD). This disorder often occurs following a life-threatening or horrific event and is characterized by emotional numbing, hypervigilance, avoidance of situations that remind the person of the event, and reexperiencing of the event through flashbacks or nightmares. Typically the individual also becomes depressed. Such was the fate of many Americans in the immediate aftermath of 9/11, especially those in the New York City area. Moreover, many continued to suffer from PTSD years after the event.

But what of paranoia? A fair number of studies of varying levels of sophistication examined depression, anxiety disorders—of which PTSD is one—and substance abuse. The closer you were to New York City at the time of the attacks, the more likely you were to suffer from one of these problems. Surprisingly not a single study asked the question of whether there were increases in rates of paranoid disorders following 9/11.

In talking with colleagues at conferences many told me that they noted a sharp spike in the number of patients presenting with 9/11-related paranoid delusions, such as believing that they were being followed by Osama bin Laden, founder of al-Qaeda, the terrorist group that claimed responsibility for the attacks. Even patients in other countries had such delusions.

As time went on fewer of these individuals were seen. When I looked through professional journals I found an occasional case report of someone who developed terrorist-related delusions after 9/11 where none had existed beforehand. But was there a greater impact of 9/11 in terms of paranoia?

There is good reason to wonder if paranoia did increase, since previous research has demonstrated that following traumatic events of any sort, the rate of delusions in those exposed to that traumatic event increases. It is reasonable to expect that paranoid delusions may therefore have increased post-9/11.

I asked a couple of my graduate students to investigate. They called 363 psychiatric facilities across the country to find out whether the rates of paranoid-related disorders have increased since 9/11. Because we kept the phone calls brief, we received answers from over 90 percent of respondents: a very high rate for this kind of study. Overall we found that 11 percent of facilities said they had seen such an increase. This was seven years after the attacks. Many said they saw far more such patients initially, but that since that time they still see increased numbers of these patients. When we looked at the data, we found an expected regional difference: 17 percent of facilities in the northeastern United States, which includes New York, reported increases, compared to about 7 percent in the Midwest and South and 12 percent in the West.

When we asked these facilities to estimate the percent increase, the numbers were all over the place. The average was an 8 percent increase, and most reported less than a 10 percent increase. Some reported as much as a 30 percent increase! We then asked if they saw a change in the content of the delusions; specifically, were more people experiencing terrorism-related paranoid delusions? Overall about 15 percent of facilities reported such increases, with the Northeast again having the highest rates (21 percent) relative to the rest of the country.

So what does all this mean? Well, there is probably no epidemic of paranoia as a result of 9/11. Fully 73 percent of the facilities we contacted who reported no increases in paranoia said they had not seen even a single case of terrorism-related paranoia. In contrast, one facility stated that at that very moment there were three patients on their unit with terrorism-related paranoia.

These findings are not so surprising, and my professional opinion is that they would be little different if the disorder in question was posttraumatic stress disorder. It is unlikely that folks living in Nebraska or New Mexico experienced the same level of traumatization as those living closer to the sites on the East Coast where the events unfolded.

The findings do suggest that those events probably did affect rates of paranoia. Employing our paranoia rheostat metaphor again, 9/11 dialed our suspiciousness system up a few notches, more so those of us living in the Northeast. For some, those increases were sufficient to reach clinical levels of paranoia.

It must be kept in mind that the survey was of psychiatric inpatient institutions; the sickest of the sick. For every patient who is hospitalized for a psychiatric disorder there are untold numbers who are ill but are not hospitalized. If posttraumatic stress disorder was the focus of our little study we would have found similar results, albeit with higher percentages, no doubt. If we extended the study to include outpatient facilities, individual psychotherapists, counselors, clergy, and so on, we would most likely have seen the submerged part of the iceberg: more people with posttraumatic stress disorder as a result of 9/11 that were *not* hospitalized than those who were.

I suspect that the same findings would apply for paranoia. The difference, of course, is that, as noted repeatedly in this book, many with paranoid disorders do not seek treatment. The total number of people who experienced significant elevations in paranoia as a result of 9/11 cannot even be guessed at given the lack of attention to the issue. I suspect that it is not insignificant.

One of the more pernicious legacies of 9/11 is the effect it had on our sense of safety. Poll after poll documents that we Americans feel less safe, are less trusting, and are more worried about and fearful of more terrorism to come. A *New York Times* poll in 2006 found that 69 percent of New York City residents reported feeling "very concerned" about another terrorist attack.[62] A month after 9/11 that number was 74 percent, showing that in the intervening five years there had been only a slight reduction.

At the same time 60 percent of those same individuals claimed that they don't trust the government to tell them the truth about the danger associated with another terrorist attack.[63] Indeed, the multiple times security levels are raised to their highest level without an apparent reason results in the jaded feeling that the government is crying wolf. It certainly helps to sell a particular piece of legislation if there are threats all around that require more money to thwart. It also helps to justify the use of surveillance by the NSA.

A TREASURE TROVE OF CONSPIRACIES

For those of you with a *lot* of time on your hands, and an interest in all things conspiratorial, I suggest you order a copy of *Matrix III: The Psycho-Social, Chemical, Biological, and Electronic Manipulation of Human Consciousness* by Valdamar Valerian.[64] This page-turning sequel to *Matrix II: The Abduction and Manipulation of Humans Using Advanced Technology* goes well beyond the normal fodder of conspiracy theories. Details regarding the Philadelphia Project, or Project Rainbow; Phoenix Projects 1–3; origins of the radiosonde and connections with the work of Wilhelm Reich; government weather-control programs and hidden agendas; the Montauk mind-control projects; the deliberate murder of thousands of American children in mind-control research and time-tunnel experiments; government time-tunnel projects and operational procedures—how inventor Nikola Tesla and mathematician John von Neumann contributed to these projects—the "martyrdom clause"; mind control by individual signature; technical ways to produce planetary holograms; Maitreya effects; the explanation behind closed time loops; government rationale and plans for the confinement camps and slave labor; Project Dreamscan; Project Moonscan; the Airborne Instrument Labs; Project Mindwrecker; the alien groups known as the Kondrashkin and their interaction with US government mind-control programs; the Kamogol II and Giza Groups; the negative Sirians; Soviet scalar weaponry; Orion Group manipulations; 6th root race incarnations; telepathy-producing drugs and their use and suppression; the FAA and zero-time generators; technical spin-offs from the Philadelphia Project; the International Aerospace Alliance; cross-section of implant devices; Wilhelm Reich and mind control; Reichian Orgastictype programming and its use by the US government and Sirians; the Psi Corps; alien soul trading, Montauk, and the aliens from the Antares system; the Leverons; the Elohim Group; the US Navy and time-tunnel projects; the US government and the Greys; electronic life support; systems of the Reptilian Humanoids; new life-form masses over the poles and their relation to yearly outbreaks of flu-like disease; AIDS and Fort Detrick (NSA); Maglev trains and the US underground-tunnel network; the missing human genes; buried spacecraft and alien technical archives under the Giza pyramid; the coming new money; the "Black Nobility"; Nordic and human copper-based blood systems and physiology; the technology of cloning and the development of synthetic humans and political replacement programs; the Middle East situation; congressional awareness of drug and alien agenda; the MIB; the US Army and the black helicopter forces; government mobile mind-disruption technology; nature and purposes and the Orion Group; fourth-density transmutation of the human race; geological changes; Sirian Mind Control technology; and more![65]

When you actually dig into the details of any of the above, you find a rich source of paranoid plots. For example, the World Health Organization developed the AIDS virus as part of a program of population reduction. It got out of hand, although the government has a way to cure it. The infamous black helicopters are capable of mind control and can control the weather. Time travel is being used by the government. If your interests are in alternate versions of history—or reality, for that matter—this is the book for you.

CONSPIRACY THEORIES

In the old days, defined as when I was growing up, conspiracy theories took a while to get around. Thanks to the Internet they spread quickly. How long did it take for conspiracy theories regarding Princess Diana's death or the government's role in 9/11 to get out?

Why is it that events like the Kennedy assassinations or 9/11 immediately, and seemingly predictably, beget a host of conspiracy theories? Perhaps it is the mere fact that we cannot comprehend how such colossal events could be entirely perpetrated by such small individuals. It can't simply be that one insignificant person can buy a cheap mail-order rifle and kill the president of the United States. Therefore, it is "somewhat likely" that some federal officials were "directly responsible for the assassination of President Kennedy." At least that is what 50 percent of us believe, according to a Scripps Howard newspaper survey.[66]

The Twin Towers could not possibly have been felled by box cutters, no matter who wielded them. The pollsters at Scripps Howard found that 36 percent of Americans believe that it was "very likely" or "somewhat likely" that federal government officials either participated directly in the 9/11 attacks or took no action to stop them "because they wanted the United States to go to war in the Middle East."[67] The same poll also found 16 percent of Americans believe that the destruction of the World Trade Center was the result of explosives planted there by the government and not because of the two jets that plowed into them. Similarly, many believe that US cruise missiles and not terrorist-flown jets hit the Pentagon, despite videotapes that clearly show a jet hitting the building at a very high rate of speed. In true paranoid fashion many believe the tapes to have been doctored by the government.[68]

About 40 percent of us also believe that President Franklin Roosevelt knew that Pearl Harbor attacks were coming but didn't try to stop them because he wanted war with Japan; that TWA Flight 800 was shot down "on purpose" off the coast of Long Island by the US Navy; and that the federal government is withholding proof of the existence of intelligent life on other planets.[69]

In many respects the government can't really blame the public for its lack of respect. Revelations regarding the monitoring of our electronic activities without our awareness in the name of "homeland security" help undermine our trust in the government. Recent exposure of the NSA's (National Security Agency) surveillance program has had a dual effect. On the one hand it tells us we can't trust our government. It sneaks around and gathers information on us in intrusive ways. But the second effect is that it tells us there is a hidden danger out there: terrorists. They exist somewhere, plotting our destruction. Both of these effects result in increases in our suspiciousness systems.

But it is not just the NSA that is intruding on our privacy; the US Postal Service is also in on the act. Following the 2001 anthrax mailings, described in chapter 11, the Postal Service initiated the Mail Isolation Control and Tracking program that basically photographs everything mailed in the United States. That's about 160 billion pieces of mail a year! From those images government agencies are able to get a pretty good idea of who you are in contact with. Fortunately a court order is required to actually open your mail.

The revelations about the so-called intelligence information regarding weapons of mass destruction as a pretext for war in Iraq also undermines the government's credibility. The media have mined our distrust of the government and fueled it with realistic fiction: movies like *The Third Man* and *Conspiracy Theory*, and TV programs such as *The X-Files*. Videos made by both amateur and professional filmmakers, available on such sites as YouTube, create the same effect. Take a look at *Loose Change*, a documentary series that challenges the conventional explanations of the events on September 11, 2001 (https://www.youtube.com/watch?v=CDx1GLqvBO8). Polls suggest that those who consume these non-mainstream media offerings are most likely to ascribe to a conspiracy theory.[70] Websites like *911truth.org* are devoted to following events that promulgate conspiracy theories. These sites receives thousands of hits every day.

Yet one can distrust the government, even to a large degree, and not be considered paranoid. The use of the term *paranoid* when referring to people who believe in conspiracy theories stretches the meaning of the word as a pathological psychological state.

As noted previously, suspiciousness exists on a continuum, and some of us have more than others. In the midst of our unreasonable suspicions are some valid ones. In the absence of evidence we cannot simply label people who believe in outlandish theories as "paranoid." Several years ago if you had said the government is monitoring everybody's cell phone calls and text messages you might have been labeled as paranoid. Along comes Edward Snowden and the "paranoid" become "prescient."

When the conspiracies are toward a particular person or the group to which that person belongs, then perhaps we are closer to a true paranoid condition. The line between "the government is trying to take our guns" and "the government is trying to take *my* guns" can be a thin one indeed.

CONSPIRACY UK STYLE

As with many major news stories involving suspicious circumstances, the tragic deaths of Princess Diana and her paramour, Dodi Fayed, immediately resulted in conspiracy theories. The most vocal and long-lasting proponent of these is the father of Dodi, Mohamed Al-Fayed, owner of Harrods department store in London.

The facts of the case are that on August 31, 1997, Diana and Dodi, along with their driver, Henri Paul, were killed in Paris when their Mercedes-Benz hit the wall of a tunnel at a high rate of speed. Paul was found to have alcohol in his system. These were the findings of all three commissions and investigations that have examined the case over the years, including the most recent one in February 2008.

However, according to Al-Fayed, there was a vast conspiracy at play. At the top was the Duke of Edinburgh, Prince Philip, whose motive was to prevent a dark, curly-haired Muslim from marrying British royalty. With the approval of the prime minister, Tony Blair, the duke instructed the British Secret Intelligence Service, M16, to do the deed. Enlisted to carry out the plot was a photographer, James Andanson, since deceased—or, according to Al-Fayed, gotten rid of. It was Andanson who blinded Henri Paul with strobe lights while he was driving the Benz. Then, using his small Fiat, he pushed the much larger and heavier car into the wall.

Andanson was probably aided in this endeavor by Paul himself, who was duped by M16 into participating in the whole thing. Next came the French ambulance drivers who took their time getting to the hospital, supposedly so the three accident victims had time to bleed to death in the ambulance.

Then the French pathologists took over, switching Henri Paul's blood with someone else's to make it appear that he was drunk at the time. Among others included in this vast plot were Diana's brother-in-law, Robert Fellowes (also the queen's secretary); her former husband Prince Charles; the English ambassador to France; the American and French secret services; newspaper editors, France's judiciary; police commissioners; one of Diana's sisters; and her attorney.

Mr. Al-Fayed alleges that hours before their death he received a phone call from the couple, who were to announce their engagement and Diana's pregnancy after they had told her two sons. Investigators asked individuals in-the-know about Diana's menstrual cycle and methods of contraception and concluded that she was not pregnant. To this Mr. Fayed responded: "All these witnesses saying this are part of the cover up and have been told what to say."[71]

Now, it would be easy to conclude at this point that Mr. Al-Fayed sounds rather paranoid. But like a good crime novel there are a few twists in the plot. There is apparently a letter written by Diana's divorce attorney in which he documents—years before—Diana's worry that there was a plot to kill her. There is also a wooden box, the contents of which Diana allegedly instructed Al-Fayed to make public in the event of her untimely death. He attempted to secure this box, only to find access to it barred by Diana's family. Both the letter and the box apparently do exist.

Face it, a mundane explanation like a drunk driver going too fast is not as interesting as the plot and cast of characters described above. There are plenty of books and websites on Princess Di, with much more speculation about what "really happened" for the conspiratorially inclined. Lest we be too harsh on Mr. Al-Fayed, keep in mind that he lost a son under tragic circumstances. As noted in chapter 8, there is a relationship between traumatic experiences and the development of paranoia.

MISTRUST CONTAGION

The current climate of America, according to the pollsters at the Pew Research Center, appears to be one ripe for paranoia to develop at the individual level. Less than a quarter of Americans claim that we can trust the government, and this extends to state and local governments, for which we hold increasingly more negative views.[72]

In the late 1960s into the 1970s Americans said they trusted the government close to 80 percent of the time. In 2013 that number was 26 percent. More than half of us (53 percent) now report that the government threatens our personal rights and freedoms, while in 2001 only 30 percent felt this way. More Republicans (70 percent) feel this way than do Democrats (38 percent). And 31 percent of us view the government as a "major threat."[73]

More ominously, since 2000, the number of us who are *angry* with the federal government has doubled and now stands at 19 percent, although it is down from its high point in 2011, when 26 percent of us were angry with the government. In terms of paranoia, 35 percent of us in 2010 felt that the government was doing a poor job at keeping our nation safe from foreign and domestic threats. This compares to 29 percent in 2008. Fully 37 percent of Americans feel the government is not doing very well at making us feel safe and secure. This is up 5 percent over two years.[74]

Compared to 1997, more of us today feel the government is negatively impacting our daily lives (43 percent versus 31 percent), and fewer feel it is having a positive impact (50 percent in 1997 versus 38 percent today). Mind you, these statistics are from surveys taken before revelations about the NSA gathering the e-mails and phone calls of Americans. Surveys since reveal that 74 percent feel the NSA is infringing on the privacy rights of Americans, and 55 percent feel such intrusions are not justified. Close to 50 percent feel it is infringing on their own individual rights.[75]

Both the administration and Congress are viewed negatively, although the ratings for Congress aren't even half as bad as those for the administration. Other government institutions received poor ratings. A notable exception is the postal system, which 70 percent of us view favorably.[76]

But our discontent, distrust, and anger are not reserved for government exclusively. Ratings as low or lower are also bestowed on banks and financial institutions, large corporations, the entertainment industry, labor unions, and the national news media. Fortunately for me, as a professor, 61 percent have favorable ratings of colleges and universities.

PUTTING IT ALL TOGETHER

There are two points to be made about all the issues raised above: hacking, surveillance, security cameras, and so on. One relates to those who are paranoid; the other to the rest of us who—presumably—are not, at least not yet. All the technology and changes discussed in this chapter have been the stuff of paranoid delusions for decades. Paranoid individuals have always been concerned about people spying on them, with a variety of devices. Belief in these devices—miniature microphones and cameras, x-ray technology—was once considered a delusion, such as the ability to "read" someone's mind. Yet today such beliefs are either true—as in the possibility that one is being watched from above by a drone or from outer space by a satellite—or soon to be true, as in the ability to detect what someone is thinking by looking at her brain activity.

This is the worst of times for paranoid individuals, and it looks like it is only going to keep getting worse. With an increased emphasis on homeland security comes increased government spending on ways of catching would-be terrorists. And the government rarely does things in small doses. So a *lot* of money is being spent on these technologies, the end result of which, ostensibly, is to catch terrorists and make the USA a safer place to live. The downside is that such technologies will be used non-judiciously on those of us who aren't terrorists. This is what paranoid people fear. Again, we all have a suspiciousness circuit, so the same fears will also likely arise in those of us who are not paranoid. Keep in mind our earlier discussion in chapter 1 of the rates of paranoid experiences in the general population; they are quite high. Whether all this technology will subsequently lead to increased clinical cases of paranoia, as opposed to just increased suspiciousness, is an empirical question.

But think about the nature of your behavior when you know you are being watched. Go to a public park somewhere and just sit and enjoy the day. Now go to a similar one where four video surveillance cameras are perched, recording what you are doing. See what effect being watched has on you emotionally.

It is ironic that the Supreme Court upholds our right to make public comments anonymously when this right is in danger of being taken away by technology. We will be identifiable if proposed changes—such as national identification cards and face-detection software—come to pass. Based on this, paranoid individuals are correct. The government *is* watching them and *can* identify who they are. The same applies to all of us. The poor ratings we give the government perhaps reflect this.

Increasingly these video-monitoring systems are being accessed via the internet. Although the process is legal, for example, for law-enforcement purposes, there is the potential for information to be hacked and used for other, nefarious purposes. The ability to hack such wireless networks, even those that are encrypted, appears to be relatively easy.

Interestingly, because these video networks are employed by municipalities, it isn't even necessary to hack into the network to view the video they capture. Freedom of information laws can be used to legally obtain this information by making a formal request. So if you are trying to spy on your philandering spouse, you can just watch the video footage from the area where you believe they are philandering. Don't be surprised if you *don't* see them on tape. It appears that, at least in the United States and Britain, members of minority groups and women are most likely to be caught on tape.[77]

Any guess as to the gender of the police officer behind the controls that position the cameras?

CONSPIRACY UK STYLE: PART 2

Pity poor Jenny Paton of Poole, England. Local officials began a surveillance operation that rivals a cold-war spy novel. They looked at who she called and followed where she went, all in attempt to catch her red-handed. Plotting a terrorist attack? No. Illegally enrolling her kids in a neighborhood school where officials thought she did not reside.

Unfortunately for Paton, it was all perfectly legal, as ordinary citizens in Britain can be, and often are, put under surveillance by their local governments. These local governments, which do not need judicial approval, are able to engage in these behaviors under the Regulation of Investigatory Powers Act, which some have dubbed the "snooper's charter." This act "legislates for using methods of surveillance and information gathering to help the prevention of crime, including terrorism." But in addition to terrorism the act is apparently used by officials to catch high-profile criminals engaged in such activities as failing to recycle, letting their dog bark, putting their trash out prematurely, or illegally selling fireworks.[78]

Officials are permitted to make use of the ubiquitous surveillance cameras, undercover agents, and electronic searches of phone calls and websites visited. According to a report issued by the House of Lords: "The development of electronic surveillance and the collection and processing of personal information have become pervasive, routine and almost taken for granted."[79]

Included among these important pieces of electronic information is the weight of your trash can. Reportedly radio frequency identification chips attached to your rubbish bin automatically send this vital information to a database. One can only imagine the consequences of an overweight bin. The consequences for Jenny? Well, once she found out that she had been under surveillance she was "gobsmacked."[80] (I'm not sure exactly what that means, but it doesn't sound good).

The second point relates to us non-paranoid individuals. While I want this book to sell, I don't want to do so at the expense of the truth, by making claims that are not justified. Are we more paranoid now than in the past? I believe that we are, although the same may be said for rates of depression and anxiety disorders. But there are some unique circumstances that conspire to create increases in our suspiciousness system at this point in history.

Electronic devices continue to intrude on our lives in ways not foreseen even a generation ago. Surveillance cameras are cheap and, in many places, omnipresent. Although these devices are looking for *them*—robbers, terrorists, thieves—they are seeing/monitoring *us*. In the old days, perhaps thirty years ago, you needed a camera with a zoom lens and actual footwork to surveil someone. Today, if there is no surveillance camera, then there is someone—actually many someones—with cell phone cameras ready to capture a person's image and send it long distances. I can't even walk across campus without being seen by the webcam positioned at the heart of the university. Anyone in the world with Internet access can watch me walk, trip, or run into a tree like a classic absentminded professor.

These are admittedly relatively minor things that, for most of us, don't even register. I would argue that, like advertising, it is the pervasive nature and cumulative effect of these devices that increase the tones of our suspiciousness system. You take money out at an ATM and don't think twice about the camera watching you. But you and your brain do note it is there. Every store you enter has a camera watching you. Your phone calls to various service centers are often recorded "for training purposes." Your computer is infected with viruses and pop-up screens. Your inbox is littered with spam unless you pay for protection. Authentic-looking e-mails ask you to confirm information regarding your account while actually soliciting information that can be used for identity theft.

Then there is the government: drones, satellite pictures, NSA surveillance, and screening at airports with "backscatter" x-ray machines that reveal *everything*. Were this not bad enough the backscatter technology has now hit the road. Mounted in vans and sold by American Scientific & Engineering of Massachusetts, these mobile devices have been generally used in the Middle East theaters of war and on the US border. They are capable of seeing into oncoming trucks to determine whether they contain militants or illegal aliens. But the same technology could be directed at you and me. There would be nothing to prevent someone from watching your x-ray image having sex with your wife, or the neighbor's wife, as the case might be.

There is a significant move afoot to have a national identification card that will contain all the usual information, such as name and address, but also picture, fingerprints, and microchips, where a significant amount of other information can be stored. In the future this information may also include bio-information, such as your DNA. This is nothing new, and perhaps we should look back in history at previous civilizations that have employed identification systems for its peoples. The Romans had *tesserae*, small tablets used to identify slaves. South Africa used the *passbook* to facilitate apartheid practices. These identification devices are now so sophisticated they can even track the individual holding them.

CONSPIRACY UK STYLE: PART 3

So you are walking down the street in London, and suddenly the trash bin you are approaching starts to display an ad, and as you pass by, it wishes you a good day—by name. Such an event is not so far off, for some streets in London contain high-tech "spy" trash bins that track people via their smartphone signals. Installed during the 2012 Olympic Games, two hundred of these high-tech bins collected cell phone data—for example, serial numbers—on over four million cell phones in just one week. The company that made the bins, Renew, boasted that they would "cookie the streets." Just as Internet "cookie" files track what you do on the computer, so, too, these spy bins would track you in your tracks, so to speak.[81]

The data were to be used for commercial purposes. If you were tracked routinely walking down the same street at the same time on the way to a fish-and-chip shop, an advertisement for a rival shop would display itself as you passed by. However, the uproar over these snooping bins resulted in the plug being pulled, literally and figuratively, on the project. I guess Londoners were gobsmacked by the idea. (I still don't know what that means, but I bet the word fits here).

IS AN EPIDEMIC ON THE HORIZON?

Any one of the issues noted above is likely to have little impact on us. But it is the *cumulative* effect that should concern us. Back in 1960 if a woman was five feet five inches, weighed about one hundred and twenty pounds, and had thirty-six-inch hips, she was pretty happy with the way she looked, because these are the measurements of arguably the most beautiful woman of that day—Marilyn Monroe.

A mere fifteen years later women with the same body size were dissatisfied with the way they looked. Why? Because our conception of feminine beauty changed during that time period. But how did it change? Well, those women whom we have traditionally viewed as beautiful—models and actresses—were becoming increasingly thinner. Even Playboy centerfolds were becoming thinner and thinner, although no less bustier (so I am told), as were Miss America contestants. The images of these slender women were, and still are, ubiquitous. They are in magazines, TV commercials and programs, movies, billboards, bus ads, online pop-up ads, and hundreds of other places. Research indicates that we don't generally stop and study these ads, but we do notice them, thousands and thousands of times each year.

As we moved from the 1960s Marilyn Monroe ideal figure to the 1980s Jamie Lee Curtis body, to the 1990s Kate Moss physique, women became less satisfied with their bodies and unhappy as a result. From the general soup of body dissatisfaction emerged a group of vulnerable individuals who developed actual eating disorders. It was an epidemic and continues to this day.

Twenty years ago you didn't have a shredder in your home, or virus-protection software, or security cameras omnipresent, nor did drones fly overhead. You certainly didn't worry when boarding a plane. Your conversations and mail were not being monitored. Today is different, and I worry that the result may be increased rates of paranoia. Women didn't pay attention to advertisements back in the 1970s, but mere exposure affected them negatively, often in the form of eating disorders. We don't "pay attention" to security cameras, shredders, and the like, but they affect us as well: sometimes in the form of paranoia.

Just as seeing a security camera here or there is not likely to influence people, seeing one advertisement of a thin model also likely has little effect. Even though we do notice them, no one advertisement makes a woman desire to be thinner, for example. But being bombarded with tens of thousands of pictures and moving images of thin females can significantly affect how women perceive and feel about themselves.

I believe the same phenomenon is affecting our sense of security, safety, and trust. Just as increasing dissatisfaction with one's body led to anorexia nervosa and bulimia nervosa in some vulnerable individuals, so, too, do increased intrusions in our lives by electronics and the government result in a diminished sense of safety and security. At the same time there are increased levels of distrust and anger.

The result of these decreases and increases (safety and distrust, respectively) are probably increased levels of suspiciousness among the general population, as well as increases in actual paranoia in the clinical sense. Being more aware of the size of one's body or concerns about one's safety are not clinical conditions. But they are the rich soil from which the clinical eating disorders and clinical paranoid disorders emerge, especially for genetically and psychologically vulnerable individuals. This incipient process has not raised alarms because paranoid individuals generally do not draw attention to themselves, except when violence occurs. On that suspiciousness continuum the current climate today increases levels so that the "circumspect" now become "cautious," the "concerned" become "wary," the "guarded" become "mistrustful," and the "suspicious" become "paranoid."

Now the observant reader will no doubt recall that genetics play a major role in determining who develops a paranoid disorder or any mental disorder, for that matter. While this is true, genes only load the gun; the environment pulls the trigger. The world we live in is a risk factor for paranoia just as exposure to the sun, cigarette smoke, and red meat are risk factors for cancer. Whether paranoia or cancer, many of us are at risk, especially the genetically predisposed.

CONSPIRACY: AMERICAN STYLE

Within weeks of singer Michael Jackson's untimely death, a conspiracy theory emerged courtesy of none other than his sister, LaToya Jackson. She alleged but provided no proof that there was a conspiracy to kill her brother, ostensibly to obtain his song catalog, reported to be worth over a billion dollars. Using drugs to control him, "they" even talked him into performing again despite his desire not to. He reportedly told his sister that he was going to be killed by others, the identities of whom LaToya apparently knows.[82] For those of you who have doubts, especially about how vast this conspiracy is, LaToya will put it in perspective for you: "Wait until you see how everything unfolds. It's going to be the biggest conspiracy of all times."

Chapter 13

WHAT CAN BE DONE ABOUT THE PARANOIA PROBLEM?

On September 16, 2013, Aaron Alexis entered the Washington Navy Yard, America's oldest military station, using his government-issued security clearance card. There he methodically hunted down and killed twelve innocent civilian workers and wounded three others before being killed by police.[1]

Immediately and predictably law enforcement and journalists started piecing together the puzzle that was Alexis. The picture that emerged is a now all too familiar one: paranoia. Nine years previously he had stared at passing construction workers for thirty days without saying a word to any of them. With no provocation or exchange of words Alexis shot the car of one of the workers because he believed he had mocked him earlier that day. He was never prosecuted. Coworkers reported that he carried grudges over minor events for weeks.

Six weeks before the carnage Alexis called police complaining that he was the victim of an "ultralow frequency attack" for the past three months. Changing hotels three times failed to thwart these attacks. Three tormentors had been dispatched by an individual with whom Alexis had had an altercation at an airport. Using a microwave machine they sent vibrations into his body to harm him.

In the weeks leading up to his killing rampage Alexis twice sought mental health treatment at Veterans Health Administration hospitals for paranoia. At neither visit did he demonstrate any of the features that would have resulted in alarm, let alone immediate hospitalization.

Two days before the killings he legally purchased a pump-action shotgun. The staff member at the store where he purchased the gun in Virginia noted that Alexis was "as normal as you or me."

Sawing off the shotgun, he wrote "my elf weapon" on the side. According to the FBI's assistant director of the Washington Field Office, Valerie Parlave,

"ELF" (extreme low frequencies) is known among conspiracy theorists as the "weaponization of remote neurofrequencies for government monitoring and manipulation of unsuspecting citizens."

Alexis received his secret security clearance because there were no red flags that would trigger disqualification: illegal drug use, felony crimes, adultery, or financial problems. Sadly, paranoia was not on that list. Aaron Alexis's epitaphs were etched into the side of his sawed-off shotgun: "end to the torment" and "better off this way."[2]

BAFFLED

It has puzzled me for years why paranoia and paranoid disorders have not received more attention with the professional community and the popular press. From a clinical standpoint paranoia is found in so many different conditions, and not just those that mental health professionals treat. In fact, it is probably the case that more primary-care physicians come in contact with paranoid individuals than do mental health professionals. Yet rarely does one see professional articles on the topic.

Outside the clinical realm there has been scant attention to paranoia, although it is mentioned occasionally, like in the case of Seung-Hui Cho (chapter 11). Yet no one has connected the dots.

More people are killed each year in our country by paranoid individuals than by terrorists. As has been argued in the preceding pages, the number of such events will likely only increase as the number of cases of paranoia increases. Although there is little solid research to explain this increase, I believe the cause for it includes general trends in psychiatric illnesses that have been on the upswing for centuries, traumatizing events such as 9/11, and the current environment. That environment is "polluted" with threats to our personal security. We, the non-paranoid, may not dwell on such threats, but we are aware of them on some level. How many of you have home-security systems or a paper shredder in your home or office? How many of you had them even ten years ago? Does that mean you are paranoid? Probably not. Does it mean you no longer trust that your garbage will not be picked through? Probably yes, which is why you shred things.

Part of the problem is the Paleolithic brain we all carry around with us. Developments in science, technology, culture, and a multitude of other factors have changed more rapidly than our brains have. We are built to function best in a close-knit group of individuals who are well-known to us, for it was within such an environment that our brains evolved. That is not to say that we are completely incapable of dealing with situations that do not resemble that hunter-gatherer environment in which our species evolved. We are a pretty adaptable species, and our brain is an amazingly adaptable organ. But it does mean that things may not work as well outside of that environment.

I'll use an example provided by Drs. Leda Cosmides and John Tooby, two preeminent evolutionary psychologists, to illustrate that point. Take a banana, which to us looks yellow under a variety of conditions: daylight, overcast skies, moonlight, rainy conditions, at dusk, and again at dawn. From the standpoint of physics, the actual wavelengths of light reflected off the banana under those different environmental conditions makes the color of the banana change as those conditions change. The reason we see the same color is that our brain evolved to continue to be able to see the yellow banana as yellow for the purposes of identification. There is a built-in (evolved) compensation for the changes in wavelength.[3]

Put that same banana under the kinds of lights that illuminate a parking lot at night, and the banana appears a different color to us. Why? Because such light was not part of the environment in which our brains evolved during the Pleistocene epoch. Those sodium vapor lights are a new arrival, and our brains have not yet adapted to them by keeping the colors we perceive constant.

Now let's extend this idea to paranoia. We have not yet adapted fully to being in such large groups and having our privacy invaded in so many different ways. It doesn't mean we are disabled in this regard. You can still tell it is a banana in the sodium vapor lit–parking lot even if you are not seeing the color of the banana like you would if it were under natural lighting conditions. At worst you may perceive it, under the artificial lighting conditions, as being more ripe than it really is, in which case you probably have a rather unpleasant-tasting banana in your mouth.

Similarly, we can deal with being around large groups of people. But increased levels of the suspiciousness system are likely to be the consequence. Put that increased level together with the other factors discussed in this book, such as traumatic events, invasions of our privacy, individual biology, and so on, and you have the makings for increased levels of paranoia and paranoid disorders.

PARANOIA MAGAZINE

There is a magazine for just about everything these days, and the topic of paranoia is no exception. As one might expect, contained in each issue of *Paranoia* are conspiracy stories galore. Of course you'll find the standard conspiracy fare: a programmed assassin killed John Lennon; all the moon landings were in fact staged in a warehouse in Mercury, Nevada; George (the Elder) Bush and John Kerry, distantly related, are descendants of Vlad the Impaler, better known as Dracula; and a heavy seasoning of Knights Templar, UFOs, 9/11 theories, Elders of Zion, and the Illuminati. But there are new revelations to be found as well, including stories on the ancient race of Scythians, who eventually became the elves, vampires, witches, and pixies we know so well today.

Most of the articles and blurbs found in the magazine probably fall more into the category of alternative history or outright fantasy. As noted previously, just because you believe more than one person shot Kennedy (either of them) doesn't make you paranoid. If those assassins are coming after *you*, then we might be talking paranoia. So perhaps a better title for this periodical would be *Skeptical* or *Fanciful* magazine.

PUBLIC HEALTH

It would be nice to end this book on a cheery note. I think the good news in all this is the fact that paranoid disorders in many cases can be effectively treated. The bad news comes in two forms: first, many who could be effectively treated do not recognize their problem and, as a result, will not seek or accept treatment. Second, the underlying risk factors for the development of paranoia are not things that can be readily changed. We can't evolve our brains any faster. We can use virus-protection software to guard against hackers breaking into our computers, but that only buys us a little comfort, just like the person with obsessive-compulsive disorder gets temporary relief by washing his hands. Ultimately, the concerns regarding safety (or germs) will be resurrected.

My hope is that this book will help spark an interest in paranoia. Everybody who sits down to write a book of nonfiction hopes for the same: that those reading the book will find the topic of such interest that they will pass it on to friends, who in turn will pass it on to others. (Actually, we authors hope that what you pass on is the *title* of the book, not the book itself. Let them buy their own copy.)

As noted previously it would be the rare person who has not been affected by paranoia in terms of having a family member or friend or coworker so afflicted. So hopefully there is fertile ground for interest in the topic. But making paranoia the focus of media attention, much like autism or obsessive-compulsive disorder or anorexia nervosa has been in the past, is going to require a major event to jump-start it. Someday, a paranoid individual will kill a large number of innocent people or will attempt to kill the president. Then perhaps we will see the word *Paranoia* splashed across the cover of *Time* magazine.

But what will be the effect of that headline? Well, here is where I have a great deal of hope. Raising the overall level of awareness about paranoia and paranoid disorders, the professional community, including the National Institutes of Health, the World Health Organization, and Centers for Disease Control and Prevention will pay more attention as well. This could translate into increased funding targeting paranoia.

Look what happened when the specter of a flu pandemic first arose. That was a model of public health at its best. Physicians were warned and armed with information, much of it printed, to pass on to their patients. Public buildings put out hand sterilizers and signs extolling the virtues of covering one's mouth when sneezing. (Some of us missed that lecture back in kindergarten.) We were taught what to look for and what to do when we found what we were looking for. Such measures have been taken with the flu, substance-abuse, depression, eating disorders, and a host of other problems. Saliently missing from that list is paranoia and paranoid disorders.

Primary care physicians (PCPs) are likely to be on the first line of intervention. While paranoid individuals are mistrustful, that does not mean they are completely devoid of trust. Most of us, paranoid individuals included, trust our PCP. Thus, the education these doctors receive regarding these disorders is crucial and will result in a fundamental change in their perspective. When a PCP encounters a patient with a mental health problem, the typical response is to refer him or her to a mental health professional. Let's say a doctor is seeing a patient who complains of a sore throat as a result of bulimia nervosa. He might prescribe something to treat the throat problem but will probably feel a bit out of his league—and rightly so—as far as treating the underlying eating disorder. Even PCPs qualified to tackle the problem simply don't have the time based on the practice of medicine these days.

With paranoia and paranoid disorders this model of referring patients to other professionals simply won't work. The primary issue here is trust, and the extent to which patients trust their PCP becomes extremely important. The PCP is in a position to guide the patient in the direction of help, perhaps by prescribing medications or encouraging them to see someone the PCP trusts, and who the patient by extension might be more inclined to trust as well.

It is usually family members raising the issue, not the paranoid individual. As such, it is also the family that can be in the best position to help persuade the afflicted to accept help. Working together with PCPs, members of the clergy, or others whom the patient might trust, there remains hope for treatment engagement and a significant improvement in their condition.

A final point is that I hope this book increases understanding of paranoia and paranoid disorders, for with increased understanding comes increased compassion for these individuals. Their often querulous and contentious nature makes them a relatively unsympathetic lot. However, their behaviors are simply the manifestations of the underlying pathology rooted in their brains. Sitting next to someone who is coughing is annoying. But you don't tell them to shut up or make rude comments to them because you understand that the cough is just a symptom of an underlying problem in the respiratory system, such as pneumonia or an upper respiratory infection. Similarly, the edgy defensiveness, lack of trust, and rigid nature of the paranoid patient is the outward manifestation of an underlying problem in the brain that they are no better able to stifle than is the patient with an upper respiratory infection. Treatment, not scorn; patience, not abuse is what is needed for these human beings.

Appendix 1

LIST OF COMMON PARANOID FEATURES

Keep in mind that depending on the person, these features will combine in a variety of ways such that no two paranoid individuals look the same. Thus, some features may be more prominent or nonexistent in one person compared to another.

mistrust or suspicion of others' motives

aloof; doesn't get deeply emotionally involved

anxious, fearful, worrisome

bears grudges and seeks revenge

belief in malevolent others, known or unknown, who abuse, torment, harass, threaten, wrong, vilify, accuse, disparage, mistreat, persecute, and taunt them

belief that one is being talked about, followed, stared at, or watched

belief that others will harm, injure, or kill them

belief in a conspiracy involving one or more persons or organizations (e.g., Mafia, CIA)

belief that they are being intentionally bumped or jostled when in crowds

black-and-white way of viewing things

constant mobilization and vigilance for perceived threats

constantly calling the police to complain about things

conviction that someone will do them harm

defensive

often dwelling on these issues in their imagination

edgy, irritable, quarrelsome, and querulous demeanor

emotionally cold and detached

evasiveness; moves away from people

everything "means" something; no chance occurrences

excessive sense of self-importance

feeling "wronged" by others

flaring up when certain "touchy" subjects are brought up or even alluded to

frequent references to listening, looking, and monitoring devices including by x-rays, radio waves, microwaves, computers, and computer chips that have been implanted

grandiosity

guarded

high levels of anger

hostility

hostility occasionally erupts into verbal or physically violent outbursts

humorlessness

hypersensitivity, which results in self-references even when no reference is actually made (ideas of reference)

hypervigilance

inference of maliciousness based on specious reasoning

inferential leaps based on insignificant details

jealousy

lack of trust

litigiousness

looking for threats

making mountains out of molehills

often "hard" people in the sense that it is a "dog-eat-dog" world, so they don't expect breaks and don't cut any either

overly concerned with "evidence"

persecutory delusions

rigid and fixed beliefs that are not modified by evidence to the contrary

rigidity

secretiveness

susceptibility to slights (intended or unintended) by others

Appendix 2

CONDITIONS AND SUBSTANCES CAUSING OR CONTRIBUTING TO PARANOIA

SUBSTANCES

ACTH
Actifed
Albuterol
alcohol intoxication
alcohol withdrawal
alcohol hallucinosis
alpha-Methyldopa
amphetamines
anticholinergic drugs
antimalarial drugs
antitubercular drugs
arsenic
atropine toxicity
barbiturates
bromide intoxication
Bromocriptine
Bupropion
carbon monoxide
    poisoning

Cimetidine
cocaine
Contac
cortisone
DDAVP
Diphenylhydantoin
disulfiram (Antabuse)
ephedrine
ibuprofen
imipramine
indomethacin
levodopa
lidocaine
LSD
manganese
marijuana
mephentermine
Methylphenidate
    (Ritalin)

mercury
mescaline
methyltestosterone
nasal decongestants
nitrous oxide
pentazocine
pervitin
phencyclidine (PCP)
phenylpropanolamine
prednisone
procaine penicillin
propylhexedrine
propranolol
salbutamol
thallium

Conditions

acute intermittent
   porphyria
Addison's disease
AIDS
Alzheimer's type
   dementia
bipolar disorder
cerebrovascular disease
Creutzfeldt-Jakob
   disease
Cushing's syndrome
delirium
encephalitis lethargica
epilepsy (temporal lobe
   origin)
Fahr's disease
fat embolism

folate deficiency
hearing loss
hemodialysis
hepatic encephalopathy
herpes simplex
   encephalitis
HIV infection
Huntington's chorea
hydrocephalus
hypercalcemia
hypertensive
   encephalopathy
hyperthyroidism
hypoglycemia
hyponatremia
hypoparathyroidism
hypopituitarism

hypothyroidism
Klinefelter's syndrome
leukoencephalopathy
liver failure
malaria
malnutrition
Marchiafava-Bignami
   disease
Menzel-type ataxia
metabolic
   encephalopathy
metachromatic
   leukodystrophy

TYPES OF DEMENTIAS

Alzheimer's disease

Lewy body dementia

Pick's disease

frontotemporal dementia

dementia associated with Parkinson's disease

vascular dementia

primary progressive aphasia

semantic dementia

AIDS Dementia Complex

dementia associated with tertiary syphilis

dementia associated with Huntington's disease

Amyotrophic lateral sclerosis

Creutzfeldt-Jakob disease

normal pressure hydrocephalus

Binswanger's disease

Wernicke-Korsakoff syndrome

dementia due to repeated traumatic brain injury

herpes encephalitis

corticobasal degeneration

Fatal Familial Insomnia

NOTES

INTRODUCTION

1. Most professional mental health organizations discourage their members from making diagnoses about individuals they have not personally evaluated. I will refrain from offering diagnoses except in cases where either I have personally evaluated the patient or a mental health professional has and rendered a diagnosis. More frequently I will instead refer to "paranoid features" or words to that effect.

CHAPTER 1: MEET PARANOIA

1. John Haslam, *Illustrations of Madness* (London: Routledge, 1810), p. 20.
Not only was he Matthews's keeper; he was also largely responsible for maintaining his status as a dangerous lunatic despite efforts from others to have Matthews set free.

2. Ibid., p. 43.

3. Michael Jay, *The Air Loom Gang* (New York: Four Walls Eight Windows, 2003).

4. Ibid.

5. D. Freeman et al., "Psychological Investigation of the Structure of Paranoia in a Non-Clinical Population," *British Journal of Psychiatry* 186 (2005): 427–35.

6. R. Freedman and P. J. Schwab, "Paranoid Symptoms in Patients on a General Hospital Psychiatric Unit," *Archives of General Psychiatry* 35 (1978): 387–90.

7. W. Eaton et al., "Screening for Psychosis in the General Population with a Self-Report Interview," *Journal of Nervous and Mental Disease*, no. 179 (1991): 689–93.

8. D. Freeman et al., "Concomitants of Paranoia in the General Population," *Psychological Medicine* 41, no. 5 (May 2011): 1–14.

9. L. Ellett, B. Lopes, P. Chadwick, "Paranoia in a Nonclinical Population of College Students," *Journal of Nervous and Mental Diseases* 191, no. 7 (July 2003): 425–30.

10. M. Olfson et al., "Psychotic Symptoms in an Urban General Medicine Practice," *American Journal of Psychiatry* 159, no. 8 (August 2002): 1412–19.

11. H. Verdoux et al., "A Survey of Delusional Ideation in Primary-Care Patients," *Psychological Medicine* 28, no. 1 (January 1998): 127–34.

12. Freeman et al., "Psychological Investigation of the Structure of Paranoia in a Non-Clinical Population."

13. Freeman et al., "Concomitants of Paranoia in the General Population."

14. W. Rössler et al., "Psychotic Experiences in the General Population: A Twenty-Year Prospective Community Study," *Schizophrenia Research* 92 (2007): 1–14.

15. K. R. Laurens et al., "Community Screening for Psychotic-Like Experiences and Other Putative Antecedents of Schizophrenia in Children Aged 9–12 Years," *Schizophrenia Research* 90 (2007): 130–46.

16. Richard Shaver, *Reality of the Inner Earth* (New Brunswick, NJ: Global Communications/Inner Light Publications, 2005).

CHAPTER 2: INSIDE THE MIND OF PARANOIA

1. A delusion in the clinical sense of the term implies a false belief that is maintained despite evidence to the contrary that contradicts our culturally defined sense of reality.

2. Chidanand Rajghatta, "NRI Shooter Was a Loner, Misfit," *Times of India*, May 11, 2003, accessed on May 14, 2015, http://timesofindia.indiatimes.com/world/us/NRI-shooter-was-a-loner-misfit/articleshow/46087188.cms.

3. David Shapiro, *Neurotic Styles* (New York: Basic Books, 1965).

4. Structured Clinical Interview for DSM-IV Axis II Disorders and the Psychosis Screening Questionnaire.

CHAPTER 3: KINDS OF PARANOIA

1. The interested reader can find out more about these disorders by reading the following books: P. A. Garety and D. R. Hemsley, *Delusions: Investigations into the Psychology of Delusional Reasoning* (Oxford: Oxford University Press, 1994), A. Munro, *Delusional Disorder: Paranoia and Related Illnesses* (New York: Cambridge University Press, 1999), M. J. Sedler, ed., *The Psychiatric Clinics of North America* (Philadelphia: W. B. Saunders Company, 1995).

2. B. Ordine and R. Vigoda, *Fatal Match* (New York: Avon Books, 1998).

3. According to the manual used to diagnosis mental disorders, *Diagnostic and Statistical Manual of Mental Disorder, 4th Edition, Text Revision* (*DSM-IV-TR*), the definition of a delusion is

A false belief based on incorrect inference about external reality that is firmly sustained despite what almost everyone else believes and despite what constitutes incontrovertible and obvious proof or evidence to the contrary. The belief is not one ordinarily accepted by other members of the person's culture or subculture (e.g., it is not an article of religious faith). When a false belief involves a value judgment, it is regarded as a delusion only when the judgment is so extreme as to defy credibility. Delusional conviction occurs on a continuum and can sometimes be inferred from an individual's behavior. It is often difficult to distinguish between a delusion and an overvalued idea (in which case the individual has an unreasonable belief or idea but does not hold it as firmly as is the case with a delusion).

American Psychiatric Association, *Diagnostic and Statistical Manual of Mental Disorder, 4th Edition* (Washington, DC: American Psychiatric Association Press, 2000), p. 821.

4. Linda Lyons, "One-Third of Americans Believe Dearly May Not Have Departed," Gallup, July 12, 2005, accessed April 3, 2015, http://www.gallup.com/poll/17275/onethird-americans-believe-dearly-may-departed.aspx.

5. This is referred to as an *illusory correlation*.

6. A. Buchanan, "Acting on Delusion: A Review," *Psychological Medicine* 23, no. 1 (February 1993): 123–34; A. Buchanan et al., "Acting on Delusions II: The Phenomenological Correlates of Acting on Delusions," *British Journal of Psychiatry* 163 (1993): 77–81.

7. Ian Freckelton "Querulent Paranoia and the Vexatious Complainant," *International Journal of Law and Psychiatry* 11 (1988): 130.

8. CourtTV, March 24, 2006.

9. Ibid.

10. Kate Shatzkin, "Judge Commits Man, 28, Who Admits Killing Woman". *Baltimore Sun*, April 25, 1995.

11. Simon Winchester, *The Professor and the Madman* (New York: HarperCollins Publishers, 1998).

12. Ibid., p. 124; original hospital records.

13. There is a lively debate within the psychology community over the relative importance of *situational factors* versus *stable personality factors* in determining behavior, with most of the evidence supporting stabile personality factors.

14. B. F. Grant et al., "Prevalence, Correlates, and Disability of Personality Disorders in the United States: Results from the National Epidemiologic Survey on Alcohol and Related Conditions," *Journal of Clinical Psychiatry* 65, no. 7 (July 2004): 948–58.

15. There is a lot of conflicting evidence on this issue with many studies finding a significant relationship between sensory deficits and paranoia, others none at all.

16. M. R. Eastwood et al., "Acquired Hearing Loss and Psychiatric Illness: an Estimate of Prevalence and Co-Morbidity in a Geriatric Setting," *British Journal of Psychiatry* 147 (1985): 552–56.

17. B. Kalayam et al., "Patterns of Hearing Loss and Psychiatric Morbidity in Elderly Patients Attending a Hearing Clinic," *International Journal of Geriatric Psychiatry* 6 (1991): 131–36.

18. P. G. Zimbardo et al., "Induced Hearing Deficit Generates Experimental Paranoia," *Science* 212 (June 1981).

19. A. F. Cooper et al., "A Comparison of Deaf and Non-Deaf Patients with Paranoid and Affective Psychoses," *British Journal of Psychiatry* 129 (1976): 532–38; S. L. Corbin and M. R. Eastwood, "Sensory Deficits and Mental Disorders of Old Age: Causal or Coincidental Associations?," *Psychological Medicine* 16 (1986): 251–56; Kalayam et al., "Patterns of Hearing Loss and Psychiatric Morbidity in Elderly Patients Attending a Hearing Clinic."

20. Solitary confinement is certainly not a new phenomenon. In the eighteenth century the *Philadelphia system* was the predominant rehabilitation model. In it prisoners were kept in solitary confinement with little human interaction or sensory distractions. In such a quiet environment they were able to reflect on their sins away from the evil influences of society. The end result: a rehabilitated prisoner, at least in theory.

21. Sharon Shalev, "Solitary Confinement and Supermax Prisons: A Human Rights and Ethical Analysis," *Journal of Forensic Psychology Practice* 11, no. 2-3 (2011): 151–83; Bruce A. Arrigo and Jennifer L. Bullock, "The Psychological Effects of Solitary Confinement on Prisoners in Supermax Units: Reviewing What We Know and Recommending What Should Change," *International Journal of Offender Therapy and Comparative Criminology* 52 (2008): 622–40.

22. Stuart Grassian, "Psychiatric Effects of Solitary Confinement," *Washington University Journal of Law and Policy* 22 (2006): 327–80.

CHAPTER 4: WHERE ELSE DO WE FIND PARANOIA?

1. S. K. Inouye, "Delirium in Older Persons," *New England Journal of Medicine* 354 (2006): 1157–165.

2. Pam Belluck, "Hallucinations in Hospital Pose Risk to Elderly," *New York Times*, June 20, 2010.

3. I've taken the liberty of listing some of them in Appendix 3.

4. S. Page and T. Fletcher, "Auguste D: One Hundred Years On," *Dementia* 5 (2006): 571–83.

5. M. M. Bassiony and C. G. Lyketsos, "Delusions and Hallucinations in Alzheimer's Disease," *Psychosomatics* 44 (2003): 388–401; R. Migliorelli et al., "Neuropsychiatric and Neuropsychological Correlates of Delusions in Alzheimer's Disease," *Psychological Medicine* 25 (1995): 505–13.

6. R. C. Hamdy, "Paranoid Delusions?," *Southern Medical Journal* 96 (2003): 635–36.

7. S. Östling and I. Skoog, "Psychotic Symptoms and Paranoid Ideation in a Nondemented Population-Based Sample of the Very Old," *Archives of General Psychiatry* 59 (2002): 53–59.

CHAPTER 5: WHERE DOES PARANOIA COME FROM?

1. R. B. Lee and I. Devore, *Man the Hunter* (Hawthorne, NY: Aldine de Gruyter, 1968).

2. Ibid.

3. Jena McGregor, "The Average Work Week Is Now 47 Hours," *Washington Post*, September 2, 2014.

4. This was important in a literal sense since with the move to stereoscopic vision, in order to accurately grab swaying branches as we climbed through trees, we lost the ability to see behind us.

5. S. Mithen, *After the Ice Age: A Global Human History 20,000–5,000 BC* (Cambridge, MA: Harvard University Press, 2004) p. 107.

6. There is a lively debate among anthropologists about this issue; see, for example, Lee and Devore, *Man the Hunter*.

7. Michael Balter, "Human Language May Have Evolved to Help Our Ancestors Make Tools," *Science Magazine*, January 13, 2015.

8. L. C. Aiello and R. I. Dunbar, "Neocortex Size, Group Size, and the Evolution of Language," *Current Anthropology* 34, no. 2 (1993): 184–93.

9. L. Weiskrantz, "The Origins of Consciousness," in *Origins of the Human Brain*, ed. J. Changeux and J. Chavaillon (Oxford: Oxford University Press, 1996), p. 241.

10. Mithen, *After the Ice Age* p. 106.

11. Ibid., p. 107.

12. Sandy Eldredge and Bob Biek, "Ice Ages—What Are They and What Causes Them?," *Utah Geological Survey* 42, no. 3 (September 2010).

13. David M. Buss, "Evolutionary Psychology," *Psychological Inquiry* 6, no. 1 (1995): 1–30.

14. "Health, United States, 2014"; US Department of Health and Human Services, accessed on May 14, 2015, http://www.cdc.gov/nchs/data/hus/hus14.pdf#059.

15. Francis Galton, *Memories of My Life* (London: Methuen, 1908), p. 276.

16. For a nice critique of evolutionary psychology I recommend an excellent article written by Sharon Begley titled "Why Do We Rape, Kill and Sleep Around?," which appeared in the June 29, 2009, issue of *Newsweek*.

CHAPTER 6: THE ENGINE OF PARANOIA: THE SUSPICIOUSNESS SYSTEM

1. Michael Linden et al., "The Psychopathology of Posttraumatic Embitterment Disorder," *Psychopathology* 40 (2007); Michael Linden et al., "Diagnostic Criteria and the Standardized Diagnostic Interview for Posttraumatic Embitterment Disorder," *International Journal of Psychiatry in Clinical Practice* 12, no. 2 (2008): 93–96.

2. B. Angrist et al., "Early Pharmacokinetics and Clinical Effects of Oral D-amphetamine in Normal Subjects," *Biological Psychiatry* 22 (1987): 1357–68.

3. I believe that my good ratings on evaluations at the end of the semester by students are not the result of mood elevating drugs used by the students . . . although one can never be sure.

4. Ironically, both Ms. Swift and I hail from Reading, Pennsylvania. I have a vague recollection of her sitting behind me in second period biology class, although the age difference between us suggests my memory may be inaccurate.

5. Melissa Block, "Anything That Connects: A Conversation with Taylor Swift," National Public Radio, October 31, 2014.

6. Josh Eells, "The Reinvention of Taylor Swift," *Rolling Stone*, September 8, 2014. p. 40.

7. Ibid.

8. Nancy Jo Sales, "Taylor Swift's Telltale Heart," *Vanity Fair*, April 2013.

9. Ibid.

10. Eells, "The Reinvention of Taylor Swift."

11. Ibid., p. 72.

12. "Taylor Swift Swim Stalker: Chicago Man Arrested after Swimming to Star's Swanky Beach Front Pad," *Huffington Post*, May 16, 2013.

CHAPTER 7: DRUGS AND PARANOIA

1. W. R. Bett, "Benzedrine Sulphate in Clinical Medicine: A Survey of the Literature," *Postgraduate Medical Journal* 22 (1946): 205–18.

2. Ibid., p. 205.

3. D. Young and W. B. Scoville, "Paranoid Psychosis in Narcolepsy and the Possible Danger of Benzedrine Treatment," *Medical Clinics of North America* (1938): 637–46.

4. Bett, "Benzedrine Sulphate in Clinical Medicine," p. 215.

5. Akihiko Sato, "Methamphetamine Use in Japan after the Second World War," *Contemporary Drug Problems* 35, no. 4 (2008).

6. Drug Enforcement Administration, Office of Diversion Control (2007).

7. "DrugFacts: Drug-Related Hospital Emergency Room Visits," National Institute of Drug Abuse, May 2011.

8. Drug Abuse Warning Network, 2011: National Estimates of Drug-Related Emergency Department Visits, US Department of Health and Human Services, 2011.

9. Drug Abuse Warning Network, "Amphetamine and Methamphetamine Emergency Department Visits, 1995–2002," July 2004.

10. John Nova Lomax, "Doug Supernaw," *Houston Press*, May 10, 2007.

11. B. Angrist, "Psychoses Induced by Central Nervous System Stimulants and Related Drugs," in *Stimulants: Neurochemical, Behavioral, and Clinical Perspectives*, ed. I. Creese (New York: Raven Press, 1983).

12. B. Angrist et al., "Early Pharmacokinetics and Clinical Effects of Oral D-Amphetamine in Normal Subjects," *Biological Psychiatry* 22 (1987): 1357–68.

13. S. L. Satel and W. S. Edell, "Cocaine-Induced Paranoia and Psychosis Proneness," *American Journal of Psychiatry* 148 (1991): 1708–711.

14. D. Janowsky and C. Risch, "Amphetamine Psychosis and Psychotic Symptoms," *Psychopharmacology* 65 (1979): 73–77.

15. M. Sato et al., "Acute Exacerbation of Paranoid Psychotic State after Long-Term Abstinence in Patients with Previous Methamphetamine Psychosis," *Biological Psychiatry* 18 (1983): 429–40.

16. Angrist et al., "Early Pharmacokinetics and Clinical Effects of Oral D-Amphetamine in Normal Subjects."

17. Philip K. Dick, *Clans of the Alphane Moon* (Ace, 1964).

18. Sato et al., "Acute Exacerbation of Paranoid Psychotic State after Long-Term Abstinence in Patients with Previous Methamphetamine Psychosis"; M. Sato et al., "Relapse of Paranoid Psychotic State in Methamphetamine Model of Schizophrenia," *Schizophrenia Bulletin* 18 (1992): 115–22.

19. G. W. Kraemer et al., "Amphetamine Challenge: Effects in Previously Isolated Rhesus Monkeys and Implications for Animal Models of Schizophrenia," in *Ethopharmacology: Primate Models of Neuropsychiatric Disorders*, ed. K. A. Miczek (New York: Alan Liss, Inc., 1983).

20. Deborah Buckhalter, "Police Say Drug-Addled Trio Imagined Attacker," *Jackson County Floridan*, August 25, 2014.

21. Anita Slomski, "A Trip on 'Bath Salts' Is Cheaper Than Meth or Cocaine but Much More Dangerous," *Journal of the American Medical Association* 308 (2012), doi:10.1001/jama.2012.34423.

22. DrugFacts: High School and Youth Trends," National Institute on Drug Abuse (December 2014).

23. Not to mention the tax revenues reaped by states that legalize it, the money from which can be spent targeting more serious drugs of abuse, such as heroin.

24. Deborah Brauser, "Cannabis-Related ED Visits Rise in States with Legalized Use," *Medscape*, December 16, 2014.

25. D. M. Semple et al., "Cannabis as a Risk Factor for Psychosis: Systematic Review," *Journal of Psychopharmacology* 19 (2005): 187–94.

26. THC is short for Δ^9–Tetrahydrocannabinol and is the active ingredient in cannabis.

27. D. Freeman et al., "How Cannabis Causes Paranoia: Using Intravenous Administration of Δ^9–Tetrahydrocannabinol (THC) to Identify Key Cognitive Mechanisms Leading to Paranoia," *Schizophrenia Bulletin* (July 15, 2014).

CHAPTER 8: OTHER WAYS TO TURN ON PARANOIA

1. H. M. Sweeney, *The Professional Paranoid* (Venice, CA: Feral House, 1998).

2. Ibid., p. 7.

3. Ibid., p. 4.

4. One worries that when the I-Pod Generation starts to age and the cumulative damage to their hearing from listening to loud music occurs, they will be developing paranoia in record numbers. I hope my daughter reads this book and takes note of this fact.

5. H. Bonner, "The Problem of Diagnosis in Paranoid Disorder," *American Journal of Psychiatry* 107 (1951): 677–83.

6. M. Kaffman, "Paranoid Disorders: Family Sources of the Delusional System," *Journal of Family Therapy* 5, no. 2 (1983): 107–16.

7. H. M. Hitson and D. H. Funkenstein, "Family Patterns and Paranoidal Personality Structure in Boston and Burma," *International Journal of Social Psychiatry* 5, no. 3 (1959): 182–90.

8. Rianne Stam, "Posttraumatic Stress Disorder and Stress Sensitization," *Neuroscience & Biobehavioral Reviews* 31, no. 4 (2007): 558–84; D. Collip et al., "Does the Concept of 'Sensitization' Provide a Plausible Mechanism for the Putative Link between the Environment and Schizophrenia?," *Schizophrenia Bulletin* 34, no. 2 (2008): 220–25.

9. J. Scott et al., "Psychotic-Like Experiences in the General Community," *Psychological Medicine* 36 (2006): 231–38.

10. D. Freeman and D. Fowler, "Routes to Psychotic Symptoms," *Psychiatry Research* 169 (2009): 107–12.

11. *Wikipedia*, s.v. "Steve Rocco" (politician), last modified June 2, 2014, accessed on May 14, 2015, http://en.wikipedia.org/wiki/Steve_Rocco (politician).

12. Brendan A. Maher, "Anomalous Experience and Delusional Thinking: The Logic of Explanations," in *Delusional Beliefs*, ed. T. F. Oltmanns and B. A. Maher (New York: John Wiley, 1988); B. A. Maher, "Delusions: Contemporary Etiological Hypotheses," *Psychiatric Annals* 22 (1992): 260–68.

13. R. P. Bentall, "Cognitive Biases and Abnormal Beliefs: Towards a Model of Persecutory Delusions," in *The Neuropsychology of Schizophrenia*, ed. Anthony David and John Cutting (Hillsdale, NJ: Lawrence Erlbaum Associates, 1994); P. A. Garety and D. R. Hemsley, *Delusions: Investigations into the Psychology of Delusional Reasoning* (Oxford: Oxford University Press, 1994).

14. C. C. Hernton, "Between History and Me: Persecution Paranoia and the Police," in *Even Paranoids Have Enemies*, ed. J. H. Berke et al. (London: Routledge 1998).

15. Doyle Murphy, "Officer Slager Laughed About 'Pumping' Adrenaline after Killing Walter Scott: Recording," *Daily News*, April 12, 2015, accessed on May 14, 2015, http://www.nydailynews.com/news/national/michael-slager-recorded-laughing-walter-scott-kill-article-1.2182848.

16. "Michael Brown Shooting," NBC News, accessed May 14, 2015, http://www.nbcnews.com/storyline/michael-brown-shooting.

CHAPTER 9: THE MONSTER WITH THE GREEN EYES: JEALOUSY

1. Shepherd presents the etymology of the word *jealousy*, which appears to derive from the French word *jalousie*, a noun meaning "shutter" or "blind." It then became used to refer to untrusting men who spy on their presumably unfaithful spouse from behind the *jalousie*. M. Shepherd, "Morbid Jealousy: Some Clinical and Social Aspects of a Psychiatric Symptom," *Journal of Mental Science* 107 (1961): 687–753.

2. Thomas Arnold, *Observations on the Nature, Kinds, Causes, and Prevention of Insanity*, vol. 2 (London: G. Ireland, 1786), p. 424.

3. David M. Buss, *The Dangerous Passion* (New York: Free Press, 2000).

4. Paul Mullen and J. Martin, "Jealousy: A Community Study," *British Journal of Psychiatry* 164 (1994): 35–43.

5. David Buss has argued convincingly that these individuals may have good reason to be jealous. Among married couples perhaps a third of women and up to half of men report having at least one extramarital affair. Buss, *The Dangerous Passion*.

6. Paul Mullen, "The Clinical Management of Jealousy," *Directions in Psychiatry* 15 (1995): 1–7.

7. G. L. White and P. E. Mullen, *Jealousy* (New York: Guilford Press, 1989); Mullen and Martin, "Jealousy: A Community Study."

8. Paul E. Mullen and L. H. Maack, "Jealousy, Pathological Jealousy, and Aggression," in *Aggression and Dangerousness*, ed. D. P. Farrington and J. Grunn (New York: John Wiley & Sons, 1985), pp. 103–126.

9. Buss, *The Dangerous Passion*.

10. Ibid.

11. E. D. Richardson et al., "Othello Syndrome Secondary to Right Cerebrovascular Infarction," *Journal of Geriatric Psychiatry and Neurology* 4 (1991): 160–65.

12. Alistair Munro, *Delusional Disorder* (New York: Cambridge University Press, 1999).

13. B. C. Breitner and D. N. Anderson, "The Organic and Psychological Antecedents of Delusional Jealousy in Old Age," *International Journal of Geriatric Psychiatry* 9 (1994): 703–707; K. S. Shaji

and C. Mathew, "Delusional Jealousy in Paranoid Disorders," *British Journal of Psychiatry* 159 (1991): 442.

14. D. Enoch, "Delusional Jealousy and Awareness of Reality," *British Journal of Psychiatry* 159 (1991): 52–56.

15. Breitner and Anderson, "The Organic and Psychological Antecedents of Delusional Jealousy in Old Age."

16. M. Soyka et al., "Prevalence of Delusional Jealousy in Different Psychiatric Disorders," *British Journal of Psychiatry* 158 (1991): 549–553.

17. K. Shrestha et al., "Sexual Jealousy in Alcoholics," *Acta Psychiatrica Scandinavica* 72 (1995): 283–90.

18. Paul E. Mullen, "Editorial: Jealousy and the Emergence of Violent and Intimidating Behaviours," *Criminal Behaviour and Mental Health* 6, no. 3 (1996): 199–205; Paul E. Mullen and L. H. Maack, "Jealousy, Pathological Jealousy, and Aggression," in *Aggression and Dangerousness*, ed. D. P. Farrington and J. Gunn (New York: John Wiley & Sons, 1985); Mullen and Martin, "Jealousy: A Community Study."

19. O. W. Barnett et al., "Jealousy and Romantic Attachment in Violent and Nonviolent Men," *Journal of Interpersonal Violence* 10 (1995): 473–86; Mullen, "Editorial: Jealousy and the Emergence of Violent and Intimidating Behaviours"; Mullen and Maack, "Jealousy, Pathological Jealousy, and Aggression."

20. Mullen, "Editorial: Jealousy and the Emergence of Violent and Intimidating Behaviours"; Mullen and Maack, "Jealousy, Pathological Jealousy, and Aggression," pp. 199–205.

21. A. R. Delgado and R. A. Bond, "Attenuating the Attribution of Responsibility: The Lay Perception of Jealousy as a Motive for Wife Battery," *Journal of Applied Social Psychology* 23, no. 16 (1993): 1337–56.

22. R. R. Mowat, *Morbid Jealousy and Murder* (London: Tavistock Publications, 1966).

23. Barnett et al., "Jealousy and Romantic Attachment in Violent and Nonviolent Men."

24. B. Morenz and R. D. Lane, "Morbid Jealousy and Criminal Conduct," in *Explorations in Criminal Psychopathology*, ed. L. B. Schlesinger (Springfield, IL: Charles C. Thomas Publisher Ltd., 1996).

25. G. B. Palermo et al., "Murder-Suicide of the Jealous Paranoia Type," *American Journal of Forensic Medicine and Pathology* 18 (1997): 374–83.

26. Morenz and Lane, "Morbid Jealousy and Criminal Conduct."

27. Mowat, *Morbid Jealousy and Murder*.

28. Ibid.

29. E. W. Mathes and C. Verstraete, "Jealous Aggression: Who Is the Target, the Beloved or the Rival?," *Psychological Reports* 72 (1993).

30. Paula Reed Ward, "The Ferrante Trial: A Look Inside the Cyanide Poisoning Case," *Pittsburgh Post Gazette*, October 19, 2014.

31. K. K. Kienlen et al., "A Comparative Study of Psychotic and Nonpsychotic Stalking," *Journal of the American Academy of Psychiatry and the Law* 25 (1997): 317–34.

32. Mark Armstrong and Kwala Mandel, "Steven Spielberg Curbs Alleged Stalker," *People.com*, October 18, 2002.

33. Kienlen et al., "A Comparative Study of Psychotic and Nonpsychotic Stalking," pp. 317–34.

34. W. J. Fremouw et al., "Stalking on Campus: The Prevalence and Strategies for Coping with Stalking," *Journal of Forensic Sciences* 42 (1997): 666–69.

35. Kienlen et al., "A Comparative Study of Psychotic and Nonpsychotic Stalking."

36. John R. Hall, *A New Breed: Satellite Terrorism in America* (New York: Strategic Book Publishing, 2009).

37. Ibid., p. 36.

38. Deborah Dupre, "Human Targets: KENS 5 Reports on Texan Tis Tortured in Houses of Horror," examiner.com, February, 19, 2010, accessed on May 15, 2015, http://www.examiner.com/article/human-targets-kens-5-reports-on-texan-tis-tortured-houses-of-horrors.

39. Texas Medical Board Meeting Minutes, October 9–10, 2008, https://www.tmb.state.tx.us/dl/62726860-C596-770B-C013-36D4FA88680B.

40. *Love and Death* script—Dialogue Transcript, Drew's Script-o-Rama, accessed on May 15, 2015, http://www.script-o-rama.com/movie_scripts/l/love-and-death-script-transcript.html.

41. D. A. DeSteno and P. Salovey, "Evolutionary Origins of Sex Differences in Jealousy?," *Psychological Science* 7 (1996): 367–72; C. R. Harris and N. Christenfeld, "Jealousy and Rational Responses to Infidelity across Gender and Culture," *Psychological Science* 7 (1996): 378–79.

42. Social learning theory would argue that these differences between males and females reflect different socialization processes rather than some evolutionary adaptation.

43. *Love Actually* quotes, IMDb. com, accessed on May 15, 2015, http://www.imdb.com/title/tt0314331/trivia?tab=qt&ref_=tt_trv_qu.

44. B. Buunk and R. B. Hupka, "Cross-Cultural Differences in the Elicitation of Sexual Jealousy," *Journal of Sex Research* (1987): 12–22.

45. Ibid.

CHAPTER 10: TREATING PARANOIA

1. Today, it is a judge or jury that determines insanity, with clinicians simply providing expert information for the trier of fact to use in making the decision.

2. Ironically, in the week during which I was writing this section an air-quality alert was issued warning people not to go out and exercise due to poor air quality. This particular therapeutic goal may be difficult to achieve in many parts of the world these days.

3. "Expedia.com Survey Reveals Vacation Deprivation among American Workers Is at an All Time High," expedia.com, accessed May 15, 2015, http://mediaroom.expedia.com/travel-news/expediacom-survey-reveals-vacation-deprivation-among-american-workers-all-time-high-1351.

4. It is noteworthy that trepanning has made a bit of a comeback of late. There are those who extol the beneficial effects of having a hole drilled in your head. You can find all you need to know, including the cut-rate surgery available in Mexico, at: http://www.trepan.com/.

5. R. Neugebauer, "Treatment of the Mentally Ill in Medieval and Early Modern England," *Journal of the History of the Behavioral Sciences* 14 (1978): 158–69.

6. R. Whitaker, *Mad in America* (New York: Basic Books, 2002).

7. "Benjamin Rush (1746–1813)," Penn Biographies, UPenn.edu, accessed May 15, 2015, http://www.archives.upenn.edu/people/1700s/rush_benj.html.

8. A. Brigham, "The Medical Treatment of Insanity," *American Journal of Insanity* 3 (1847): 353–58. (This journal later became the *American Journal of Psychiatry*, which it remains to this day.)

9. M. Kosfeld et al., "Oxytocin Increases Trust in Humans," *Nature* 485 (2005): 673–76.

10. This condition was previously referred to erroneously as *general paresis*, reflecting the fact that in some patients tertiary syphilis resulted in paralysis if it invaded the spinal cord.

11. C. Tsay, "Julius Wagner-Jauregg and the Legacy of Malarial Therapy for the Treatment of General Paresis of the Insane," Yale Journal of Biology 13, no. 86 (June 13, 2013): 245–54, accessed May 15, 2015, http://www.ncbi.nlm.nih.gov/pubmed/23766744; E. Shorter, *The History of Psychiatry: From the Era of the Asylum to the Age of Prozac* (New York: John Wiley & Sons, 1997).

12. Tsay, "Julius Wagner-Jauregg and the Legacy of Malarial Therapy."

13. Ibid.

14. Andrew Scull, *Madhouse: A Tragic Tale of Megalomania and Modern Medicine* (New Haven, CT: Yale University Press, 2005).

15. This one just won't die. To this day a lively debate persists regarding the existence and legitimacy of PMS, or, as it is called currently, *premenstrual dysphoric disorder*. Alas, there are no such debates regarding testicular-related disorders.

16. R. Porter, *Madness: A Brief History* (Oxford: Oxford University Press, 2002); Shorter, *The History of Psychiatry*.

17. Actually it was his colleague, Almeida Lima, who did the surgery, as Moniz suffered from gout.

18. Jack El-Hai, *The Lobotomist: A Maverick Medical Genius and His Tragic Quest to Rid the World of Mental Illness* (Wiley, 2007); Elliot S. Valenstein, *Great and Desperate Cures* (New York: Basic Books, 1986).

19. Valenstein, *Great and Desperate Cures*, p. 231.

20. That doesn't mean that patients were always conscious during the procedure. ECT was employed to render patients unconscious. Freeman administered the ECT as well as doing the "surgery."

21. El-Hai, *The Lobotomist*; Valenstein, *Great and Desperate Cures*.

22. There is a great deal of controversy about antipsychotic medications. A fuller, if somewhat polemic, discussion of this issue can be found in Whitaker, *Mad in America*.

23. C. Foster et al., "A Randomized Controlled Trial of Worry Intervention for Individuals with Persistent Persecutory Delusions," *Journal of Behavior Therapy and Experimental Psychiatry* 41 (2010): 45–51.

24. D. Freeman et al., *Overcoming Paranoid and Suspicious Thoughts* (New York: Basic Books, 2008).

CHAPTER 11: PARANOIA AND VIOLENCE

1. H. R. Rollin, "McNaughton's Madness," in *Daniel McNaughton*, ed. D. J. West and A. Walk (Ashford: Gaskell, 1977), p. 92.

2. Wills Robinson and Chris Spargo, "Florida State University Shooter Told Former Friend He Was Sending Her Mystery Package and Ex That Government Was Watching Him as He Showed Increasingly Erratic Behavior," *Daily Mail*, November 20, 2014, accessed May 18, 2015, http://www. dailymail.co.uk/news/article-2842011/Gunman-opens-fire-Florida-State-University-library-shooting-two-captured-authorities.html.

3. Victoria St. Martin and Keith L. Alexander, "White House Jumper Dominic Adesanya Ordered by Judge to Mental Health Facility," *Washington Post*, October 27, 2014, accessed May 18, 2015, http://www.washingtonpost.com/local/crime/white-house-jumper-dominic-adesanya-ordered-by-judge-to-mental-health-facility-for-evaluation-and-treatment/2014/10/27/3127e16e-5e0e-11e4-9f3a-7e28799e0549_story.html.

4. David Montgomery and Manny Fernandez, "Omar J. Gonzalez, Accused of White House Intrusion, Is Recalled as Good but Troubled Neighbor," *New York Times*, September 23, 2014, accessed May 18, 2015, http://www.nytimes.com/2014/09/24/us/omar-gonzalez-veteran-white-house-fence.html.

5. Crimesider Staff, "Paul Kevin Curtis, Miss Man Arrested in Ricin-Tainted Letter Case," Crimesider, CBS News, April 18, 2013, accessed May 17, 2015, http://www.cbsnews.com/news/paul-kevin-curtis-miss-man-arrested-in-ricin-tainted-letter-case/.

6. Michael Daly, "Alabama Hostage Standoff: Jimmy Lee Dykes Seized Boy to Gain Attention," *Daily Beast*, February 6, 2013, accessed May 18, 2015, http://www.thedailybeast.com/articles/2013/02/06/alabama-hostage-standoff-jimmy-lee-dykes-seized-boy-to-gain-attention.html.

7. Connie Rice, "Christopher Dorner's Web of Lies about the PAPD," Los Angeles Times, June 26, 2013.

8. "Tucson Gunman before Rampage: I'll See You on National TV," CBS News, April 11, 2014, accessed May 18, 2015, http://www.cbsnews.com/news/jared-loughner-who-shot-gabrielle-giffords-in-tucson-ranted-online/.

9. Zack McMillin and Marc Perrusquia, "Police Killers Identified as Activists on Mission to Spread Anti-Government Message," *Commercial Appeal*, May 21, 2010, accessed May 18, 2015, http://www.commercialappeal.com/news/local-news/relatives-id-west-memphis-suspects.

10. *Wikipedia*, s.v. "2010 University of Alabama in Huntsville Shooting," last modified May 1, 2015, accessed on May 18, 2015, http://en.wikipedia.org/wiki/2010_University_of_Alabama_in_Huntsville_shooting.

11. Stephanie Simon, "Roeder Guilty of Murdering Abortion Provider," *WSJ Business*, January 29, 2010, accessed May 18, 2015, http://www.wsj.com/articles/SB10001424052748703389004575033052416975506.

12. Del Quentin Wilber, "Von Brunn, White Supremacist Holocaust Museum Shooter, Dies," Washington Post, January 7, 2010, accessed May 18, 2015, http://www.washingtonpost.com/wp-dyn/content/article/2010/01/06/AR2010010604095.html.

13. Adam Nichols et al., "Garvin Was a Shooter? No Surprise, Some Day," *Daily News*, March 16, 2007, accessed May 18, 2015, http://www.nydailynews.com/news/garvin -shooter-no-surprise-article-1.217802.

14. Natalie Singer, "Court Papers Tell of Victims' Terrifying Last Moments," *Seattle Times*, December 28, 2007, accessed May 18, 2015, http://www.seattletimes.com/seattle-news/ court-papers-tell-of-victims-terrifying-last-moments/.

15. Michael Laris and Robert Samuels, "Man Kills 2 Sons, Himself at University in W.Va.," *Washington Post*, September 3, 2006, accessed May 18, 2015, http://www.washingtonpost.com/ wp-dyn/content/article/2006/09/02/AR2006090201223.html.

16. Tom Jackman, "Man Found Guilty of Killing and Dismembering His Father," *Washington Post*, July 22, 2009, accessed May 18, 2015, http://www.washingtonpost.com/wp-dyn/content/ article/2009/07/21/AR2009072103116.html.

17. "Alaska Mom Goes on Trial in Killings of 3 Sons," *USA Today*, April 24, 2007, accessed May 18, 2015, http://usatoday30.usatoday.com/news/nation/2007-04-24-alaska-mom-trial_N.htm.

18. "Butcher Sentenced for Killing Wife," *New York Times*, April 10, 2007, accessed May 18, 2015, http://query.nytimes.com/gst/fullpage.html?res=9C02E7D9153FF933A25757C0A9619C8B63.

19. Pam Belluck, "Poisonings at Church Are Termed Retaliation," *New York Times*, April 19, 2006, accessed May 18, 2015, http://www.nytimes.com/2006/04/19/us/19maine.html.

20. Brian Knowlton, "Secret Service Shoots Armed Man near White House," *New York Times*, February 8, 2001, accessed May 18, 2015, http://www.nytimes.com/2001/02/08/news/ 08iht-shoot.2.t.html.

21. Jennifer Bain, "Kendra Webdale's Infamous Subway-Push Killer Says Mental-Health Law Needs to Be Restructured," *New York Post*, December 29, 2012, accessed May 18, 2015, http://nypost. com/2012/12/29/kendra-webdales-infamous-subway-push-killer-says-mental-health-law-needs- to-be-restructured/.

22. CBSNEWS.com staff, "Who Is Russell Weston, Jr.?" CBS News, July 25, 1998, accessed May 18, 2015, http://www.cbsnews.com/news/who-is-russell-weston-jr/.

23. "Who Is Kip Kinkel?," *Frontline*, accessed May 18, 2015, http://www.pbs.org/wgbh/ pages/frontline/shows/kinkel/kip/writings.html.

24. Nick Cohen, "The Life and Death of Thomas Watt Hamilton," *Independent*, May 18, 2015, accessed May 18, 2015, http://www.independent.co.uk/news/uk/home-news/the-life-and-death- of-thomas-watt-hamilton-1672323.html.

25. "The Story of Ralph Tortorici," *Frontline*, accessed May 18, 2015, http://www.pbs.org/ wgbh/pages/frontline/shows/crime/ralph/summary.html.

26. James Barron, "Death on the L.I.R.R.: The Overview; Portrait of Suspect Emerges in Shooting on L.I. Train," *New York Times*, December 9, 1993, accessed May 18, 2015, http://www. nytimes.com/1993/12/09/nyregion/death-lirr-overview-portrait-suspect-emerges-shooting-li- train.html.

27. Mara Bovsun, "Crazy Professor Valery Fabrikant Kills 4 in Concordia University Rampage," *Daily News*, April 21, 2013, accessed May 18, 2015, http://www.nydailynews.com/news/ justice-story/justice-story-college-prof-kills-4-article-1.1320928.

28. E. Fuller Torrey, *The Insanity Offense: How America's Failure to Treat the Seriously Mentally Ill Endangers Its Citizens* (New York: W. W. Norton & Company, 2012).

29. M. S. Humphreys et al., "Dangerous Behavior Preceding First Admissions for Schizophrenia," *British Journal of Psychiatry* 161 (1992): 501–505; J. Lanzkron, "Murder as a Reaction to Paranoid Delusions in Involutional Psychosis and Its Prevention," *American Journal of Psychiatry* 118 (1961): 426–27; M. G. Link and A. Stueve, "Psychotic Symptoms and the Violent/Illegal Behavior of Mental Patients Compared to Community Controls," in *Violence and Mental Disorder*, ed. J. Monahan and H. Steadman (Chicago: University of Chicago Press, 1994); H. Petursson and G. H. Gudionsson, "Psychiatric Aspects of Homicide," *Acta Psychiatrica Scandinavica* 64 (1981): 363–72; J. W. Swanson et al., "Violence and Psychiatric Disorder in the Community: Evidence from the Epidemiologic Catchment Area Surveys," *Hospital & Community Psychiatry* 41 (1990): 761–70; P. J. Taylor et al., "Delusions and Violence," in *Violence and Mental Disorder*, ed. J. Monahan and H. Steadman (Chicago: University of Chicago Press, 1994); A. Buchanan, "Acting on Delusion," *Psychological Medicine* 23 (1993): 123–34; A. Buchanan et al., "Acting on Delusions II: The Phenomenological Correlates of Acting on Delusions," *British Journal of Psychiatry* 163 (1993): 77–81; Jeremy Coid et al., "The Relationship between Delusions and Violence," *Journal of the American Medical Association Psychiatry* 70 (2013): 465–71.

30. Coid et al., "The Relationship between Delusions and Violence."

31. P. Mullen et al., "Psychosis, Violence and Crime," in *Forensic Psychiatry*, ed. J. Gunn and P. J. Taylor (Oxford: Butterworth-Heinemann, 1993), pp. 329–72; R. Novaco, "Anger as a Risk Factor for Violence among the Mentally Disordered," in *Violence and Mental Disorder*, ed. J. Monahan and H. Steadman (Chicago: University of Chicago Press), pp. 21–59; P. Taylor et al., "Delusions and Violence," in *Violence and Mental Disorder*, ed. Monahan and Steadman, pp. 161–83.

32. David C. Shore et al., "Murder and Assault Arrests of White House Cases: Clinical and Demographic Correlates of Violence Subsequent to Civil Commitment," *American Journal of Psychiatry* 146, no. 5 (1989): 645–51.

33. "Mental Disorder and Violence," talk given at 31st Annual Pittsburgh Schizophrenia Conference, December 12, 2014.

34. *Wikipedia*, s.v. "Andrea Yates," last modified April 18, 2015, accessed May 18, 2015, http://en.wikipedia.org/wiki/Andrea_Yates.

35. Shaila Dewan and Marc Santora, "Troubled State of Virginia Tech Killer Was Known in '05," *New York Times*, April 18, 2007.

36. "President Bush Offers Condolences at Virginia Tech Memorial Convocation," Cassell Coliseum, April 17, 2007.

37. B. M. Stickney, *All-American Monster: The Unauthorized Biography of Timothy McVeigh* (Amherst, NY: Prometheus Books, 1996).

38. T. Andryszewski, *The Militia Movement in America* (Brookfield, CT: Brookfield Press, 1997).

39. William Gibson, *Warrior Dreams* (New York: Hill and Wang, 1994).

40. Southern Poverty Law Center, http://www.splcenter.org.

41. K. S. Stern, *A Force upon the Plain* (New York: Simon & Schuster, 1996); Morris Dees and J. Corcoran, Gathering Storm: America's Militia Threat (New York: HarperCollins, 1996).

42. The belief that black helicopters silently follow the innocent is a favorite delusion among

paranoid individuals. This is clearly not possible given the loud noise a standard helicopter generates. However, the situation for paranoid individuals just got worse. The global helicopter manufacturer Eurocopter has apparently developed blades that will reduce the sounds of the helicopter to a paltry three to four decibels . . . a mere whisper.

43. "The Militia Movement," ADL.org, accessed May 18, 2015, http://archive.adl.org/learn/ext_us/militia_m.html?LEARN_Cat=Extremism&LEARN_SubCat=Extremism_in_America&xpicked=4&item=mm; Gibson, *Warrior Dreams*; Dees and Corcoran, *Gathering Storm*, Stern, *A Force upon the Plain*.

44. Stern, *A Force upon the Plain*.

45. Dees and Corcoran, *Gathering Storm*.

46. Clyde Haberman, "An Idaho Family, and Federal Tactics, Under Siege," *New York Times*, October 26, 2014.

47. *Wikipedia*, "Gordon Kahl," last modified May 18, 2015, accessed May 18, 2015, http://en.wikipedia.org/wiki/Gordon_Kahl.

48. "Veterans' Diseases Associated with Agent Orange," US Department of Veterans Affairs, accessed May 18, 2015, http://www.publichealth.va.gov/exposures/agentorange/conditions.

49. Kurt Kroenke et al., "Symptoms in 18,495 Persian Gulf War Veterans: Latency of Onset and Lack of Association with Self-Reported Exposures," Journal of Occupational and Environmental Medicine 40 (6): 520–28.

50. Mark Schultz, *Foxcatcher* (New York: Penguin Group, 2014), p. 170.

51. B. Ordine and R. Vigoda, *Fatal Match* (New York: Avon Books, 1998).

52. C. A. Turkington, *No Holds Barred* (Atlanta: Turner Publishing, 1996).

53. Schultz, *Foxcatcher*, p. 250.

54. In order to be found competent to stand trial defendants must understand the nature of the charges against them and effectively assist in their own defense.

55. Ordine and Vigoda, *Fatal Match*.

56. Attributed to Dr. William Carpenter Jr., professor of psychiatry and pharmacology, School of Medicine, University of Maryland (and author of the foreword to this book).

57. Scott Shane and Eric Lichtblau: "Scientist Is Paid Millions by US in Anthrax Suit," *New York Times*, June 28, 2008.

58. The US Department of Justice's full report *Amerithrax Investigative Summary* (June 2000) is available online on its website, http://www.justice.gov/archive/amerithrax/docs/amx-investigative-summary.pdf, and contains extensive material on Dr. Ivins's mental state.

59. "Anthrax Suspect 'Homicidal,'" CBS News, accessed May 18, 2015, http://www.cbsnews.com/news/anthrax-suspect-homicidal/.

60. Scott Shane, "Panel on Anthrax Inquiry Finds Case against Ivins Persuasive," *New York Times*, March 23, 2011.

61. Madeleine Brand and Laura Sullivan, "Documents: Bruce Ivins Sent False Samples," August 6, 2008, NPR, accessed May 18, 2015, http://www.npr.org/templates/story/story.php?storyId=93341386.

62. *Amerithrax Investigative Summary*, p. 44.

63. Ibid.

64. Ibid., p. 45.

65. Ibid.

66. Ibid.

67. Ibid.

68. FBI "Affidavit in Support of Search Warrant," October 31, 2007, p. 13.

69. *Amerithrax Investigative Summary*, p. 44.

70. Ibid., p. 45.

71. Ibid.

72. M. Fernandez and N. Schweber, "Binghamton Killer Kept His Fury Quiet," *New York Times*, April 12, 2009.

73. Ibid.

74. William Kates, "I Am Jiverly Wong Shooting the People," *NBC Washingtonian*, accessed May 18, 2015, http://www.nbcwashington.com/news/archive/Letter-Binghamton-Killer.html.

75. Heather Hollingsworth, "Blaec Lammers, Alleged 'Twilight' Shooting Plotter Was 'Born Different,' Mom Says," *Huffington Post*, November 21, 2012.

CHAPTER 12: IT'S A PARANOID WORLD WE LIVE IN

1. E. Fuller Torrey and Judy Miller, *The Invisible Plague* (New Brunswick, NJ: Rutgers University Press, 2001).

2. Ibid., p. 5.

3. R. C. Kessler et al., "Lifetime Prevalence and Age-of-Onset Distributions of DSM-IV Disorders in the National Comorbidity Survey Replication," *Archives of General Psychiatry* 62 (2005): 593–602.

4. Torrey and Miller, *The Invisible Plague*, p. 300.

5. See, for example, Jim Van Os et al., "Prevalence of Psychotic Disorder and Community Level of Psychotic Symptoms," *Archives of General Psychiatry* 58 (2001): 660–68.

6. J. Van Os et al., "Do Urbanicity and Familial Liability Coparticipate in Causing Psychosis?," *American Journal of Psychiatry* 160 (2003): 477–82; Dana March et al., "Psychosis and Place," *Epidemiologic Reviews* 30 (2008): 84–100.

7. Evangelos Vassos et al., "Meta-Analysis of the Association of Urbanicity with Schizophrenia," *Schizophrenia Bulletin* 38 (2012): 1118–23.

8. Jason Tuohey, "Government Uses Color Laser Printer Technology to Track Documents," *PCWorld*, November 22, 2004.

9. Jeffrey Toobin, "Edward Snowden's Real Impact," *New Yorker*, August 19, 2013.

10. "NSA Spying on Americans," Electronic Frontier Foundation, accessed May 16, 2015, https://www.eff.org/nsa-spying.

11. Ron Nixon, "Report Reveals Wider Tracking of Mail in U.S.," *New York Times*, October 27, 2014.

12. James Bamford, *The Shadow Factory* (New York: Anchor, 2009).

13. Hanni Fakhoury, "Stingrays: The Biggest Technological Threat to Cell Phone Privacy You Don't Know About," Electronic Frontier Foundation, October 22, 2012, accessed May 15, 2015, https://www.eff.org/deeplinks/2012/10/stingrays-biggest-unknown-technological-threat-cell-phone-privacy.

14. Bamford, *The Shadow Factory*.

15. Aaron Mamiit, "US Using Planes Equipped with 'Dirtbox' to Spy on Your Phone Calls," *Tech Times*, November 16, 2014.

16. "You Are Being Tracked: How License Plate Readers Are Being Used to Record Americans' Movements," ACLU, accessed May 16, 2015, https://www.aclu.org/feature/you-are-being-tracked.

17. David Minsky and Tim Elfrink, "Cell-Phone Tracking: Miami Cops Know Where You Are," *Miami New Times*, February 16, 2012.

18. Courtney Rubin, "If You Own the Phone, You Can Read the Text Message," Inc., June 21, 2010.

19. Somini Sengupta, "A Cheap Spying Tool with a High Creepy Factor," *New York Times*, August 2, 2013.

20. "Individual Sentenced after Guilty Plea to Unauthorized Access of a Computer," FBI.gov, accessed May 16, 2015, http://www.fbi.gov/jacksonville/press-releases/2009/ja040209.htm; Larry McShane, "Luis Mijangos Gets 6 Years for Hacking Women's Computers, Blackmailing Them for Explicit Photos," *New York Daily News*, September 1, 2011; Sasha Goldstein, "California Teen, Guilty in Miss Teen USA 'Sextortion' Plot, Sentenced to 18 Months in Prison," *New York Daily News*, March 17, 2014.

21. "Lower Merion School District Settles Webcam Spying Lawsuits for $610,000," *Huff Post Tech*, December 11, 2010.

22. "Spam in the Fridge," *Economist*, January 25, 2014.

23. Kashmir Hill, "Here's What It Looks Like When a 'Smart Toilet' Gets Hacked," *Forbes*, August 15, 2013.

24. Amber Hunt, "Data Breach Shows Dangers of Weak Passwords," Cincinnati.com, August 10, 2014; "How 'Home Hackers' Spy on You and Your Children . . . with YOUR Webcam," *Daily Mail.com*, accessed May 16, 2015, http://www.dailymail.co.uk/news/article-2763664/How-home-hackers-spy-children-YOUR-webcam-The-shocking-evidence-shows-private-lives-snooped-streamed-live-web.html#ixzz3a89z2KRC.

25. Dara Kerr, "FTC and TrendNet Settle Claim over Hacked Security Cameras," CNET, September 4, 2013.

26. Eric Basu, "Hacking Insulin Pumps and Other Medical Devices from Black Hat," *Forbes*, August 3, 2013.

27. Tim Maly, "Anti-Drone Camouflage," *Wired*, January 17, 2013.

28. Emma Anderson, "The Evolution of Electronic Monitoring Devices," NPR, May 24, 2014.

29. Anne Eisenberg, "Microsatellites: What Big Eyes They Have," *New York Times*, August 10, 2013, accessed May 16, 2015, http://www.nytimes.com/2013/08/11/business/microsatellites-what-big-eyes-they-have.html.

30. Mark Hachman and Chloe Albanesius, "Beyond Warfare: 12 Non-Lethal Uses for

Drones," *PC* online, August 22, 2013, accessed May 16, 2015, http://www.pcmag.com/slideshow/story/307900/beyond-warfare-12-non-lethal-uses-for-drones.

31. Matt Ferner, "Drone Hunting Practice Begins in Colorado Town," *Huffington Post*, January 23, 2014.

32. Associated Press-GfK Poll, December 2014, accessed May 15, 2015, http://ap-gfkpoll.com/main/wp-content/uploads/2015/01/AP-GfK_Poll_December_2014_GMOs.pdf.

33. David Barrett, "One Surveillance Camera for Every 11 People in Britain, Says CCTV Survey," *Telegraph*, July 10, 2013.

34. These and other chilling statistics can be found in *Under the Watchful Eye* by Mark Schlosberg and Nicole Ozer, accessed May 9, 2015, http://www.aclunc.org/docs/criminal_justice/police_practices/under_the_watchful_eye_the_proliferation_of_video_surveillance_systems_in_california.pdf.

35. Corilyn Shropshire, "Fast-Food Assistant 'Hyperactive Bob' Example of Robots' Growing Role," *Pittsburgh Post-Gazette*, June 16, 2006.

36. Maria Konnikova, "The Open-Office Trap," *New Yorker*, January 7, 2014.

37. Richard Savill, "New Speed Cameras Trap Motorists from Space," *Telegraph*, April 20, 2010.

38. "You Are Being Tracked."

39. Eric Roper, "City Cameras Track Anyone, Even Minneapolis Mayor Rybak," *Minneapolis Star Tribune*, September 19, 2014.

40. Kade Crockford, "State Secrecy and Opaque Funding Programs Cloud Public's Understanding of Federal Grants for Surveillance Gear," ACLU, July 18, 2013.

41. Charlie Savage, "Facial Scanning Is Making Gaines in Surveillance," *New York Times*, August 21, 2013.

42. Jules Carey, "The Ian Tomlinson Case Shows Why the Police Cannot Investigate Themselves," *Guardian*, August 12, 2013.

43. Epic.org, accessed May 16, 2015, https://www.epic.org/.

44. Kashmir Hill, "The Technologies Are New; The Privacy Fears Aren't," *Forbes*, January 10, 2012.

45. Elizabeth Brayer, *George Eastman: A Biography* (Rochester, NY: University of Rochester Press, 2006).

46. *Economist*, November 16, 2013, p. 13.

47. Tom Zeller, "A Sinister Web Entraps Victims of Cyberstalkers," *New York Times*, April 17, 2006.

48. Danny Shea, "Sarah Palin's E-Mail Hacked: How It Was Done," *Huffington Post*, October 19, 2008.

49. Dave Thier, "Study: 1 in 20 Americans Have Been Victims of Identity Theft," *Forbes*, February 24, 2012.

50. Gary Shapiro, "What Happens When Your Friend's Smartphone Can Tell That You're Lying," *Washington Post*, October 31, 2014.

51. To be fair, Mr. Shapiro also points out obvious benefits to society as a result of such technology. For example, the ability to tell if a politician is being truthful or not. Or the ability to bring up information about someone we don't recognize as a result of developing Alzheimer's.

52. Greg Bishop, "Paranoia as Prevalent as Special Teams in American Football," *New York Times*, November 13, 2007.

53. Ibid.

54. Ibid.

55. Margaret Evans, "Berlin Wall: East Germans Lived in Fear under Stasi Surveillance," CBC News, November 9, 2014.

56. Anna Funder, *Stasiland: Stories from behind the Berlin Wall* (New York: Harper Perennial, 2011).

57. Carl Botan, "Communication Work and Electronic Surveillance: A Model for Predicting Panoptic Effects," *Communications Monographs* 63, no. 4 (1996): 293–313.

58. Associated Press-GfK Poll, October 2013, accessed May 15, 2015, http://surveys.ap.org/data%5CGfK%5CAP-GfK%20October%202013%20Poll%20Topline%20Final_TRUST.pdf.

59. Ibid.

60. "Millennials in Adulthood: Detached from Institutions, Networked with Friends," Pew Research Center, March 2014, accessed May 9, 2015, http://www.pewsocialtrends.org/2014/03/07/millennials-in-adulthood/.

61. Justin Wolfers, "Perceptions Haven't Caught Up to Decline in Crime," *New York Times*, September 16, 2014.

62. Robin Toner and Marjorie Connelly, "9/11 Polls Find Lingering Fears in New York," *New York Times*, September 7, 2006.

63. Ibid.

64. Valdamar Valerian, *Matrix III: The Psycho-Social, Chemical, Biological, and Electronic Manipulation of Human Consciousness* (Leading Edge Research, 1992).

65. Valdamar, Valerian, "Orion Technology and Other Secret Projects," YouTube video, 1:47:33, posted by "Tantarum I," May 28, 2013, https://www.youtube.com/watch?v=ybiKIiYW37Q.

66. Richard Morin, "New Facts and Hot Stats from the Social Sciences," *Washington Post*, July 27, 1997.

67. Ibid.

68. Ibid.

69. Karlyn Bowman and Andrew Rubb, "Public Opinion on Conspiracy Theories," American Enterprise Institute for Public Policy Research, November 2013.

70. Ibid.

71. Louise Radnofsky, "Nazi Philip Wanted Diana Dead, Fayed Tells Inquest," *Guardian*, February 18, 2008; Michael Pearson and Atika Shubert, "Newly Revealed Conspiracy Claim in Princess Diana Death Sparks Talk," CNN, August 19. 2013; Tina Brown, "No, Conspiracy Theorists, Princess Diana Was Not Murdered," Daily Beast, August 19, 2013.

72. Thomas Hargrove and Guido Stempel III, "New Poll: A Third of US Public Believes 9/11 Conspiracy Theory," 911Truth.org, August 1, 2006, accessed May 15, 2015, http://www.911truth.org/article_for_printing.php?story=20060802215417462.

73. Ibid.

74. Associated Press-National Constitution Center Poll, 2010.

75. Ibid.; Mark Jaycox, "Update: Polls Continue to Show Majority of Americans against NSA Spying," Electronic Frontier Foundation, January 22, 2014.

76. Steve Ander and Art Swift, "Americans Rate Postal Service Highest of 13 Major Agencies," Gallup Poll, November 21, 2014.

77. Mark Schlosberg and Nicole A. Ozer, "Under the Watchful Eye," ACLU, August 2007.

78. Sarah Lyall, "Britons Weary of Surveillance in Minor Cases," *New York Times*, October 24, 2009; "Council Spied on Woman 21 Times, BBC News, November 5, 2009.

79. "Surveillance: Citizens and the State—Constitution Committee Contents," parliament. uk, accessed May 16, 2015, http://www.publications.parliament.uk/pa/ld200809/ldselect/ldconst/18/1803.htm.

80. Lyall, "Britons Weary of Surveillance in Minor Cases."

81. David Risser, "Snooping Garbage Bins in City of London Ordered to Be Disabled," Bloomberg Business, August 12, 2013.

82. Sheila Marikar, "La Toya Jackson Reveals What Michael Jackson's Kids Saw, Heard, in His Final Days," ABC News, June 22, 2011, accessed May 15, 2015, http://abcnews.go.com/Entertainment/la-toya-jackson-reveals-michael-jacksons-kids-heard/story?id=13896058.

CHAPTER 13: WHAT CAN BE DONE ABOUT THE PARANOIA PROBLEM?

1. Peter Hermann and Ann Marimow, "Navy Yard Shooter Aaron Alexis Driven by Delusions," Washington Post, September 25, 2013.

2. Ibid.

3. Leda Cosmides and John Tooby, "Evolutionary Psychology: A Primer," Center for Evolutionary Psychology, accessed May 18, 2015, http://www.cep.ucsb.edu/primer.html.

BIBLIOGRAPHY

(A complete bibliography of over seven hundred references
used in preparing this book is available upon request from the author)

Aiello, L. C., and R. I. Dunbar. "Neocortex Size, Group Size, and the Evolution of Language." *Current Anthropology* 34, no. 2 (1993): 184–93.

Amerithrax Investigative Summary. Department of Justice. June 2000.

"Amphetamine and Methamphetamine Emergency Department Visits, 1995–2002." *Drug Abuse Warning Network*. July 2004.

Andryszewski, T. *The Militia Movement in America*. Brookfield, CT: Brookfield Press, 1997.

Angrist, B. et al. "Early Pharmacokinetics and Clinical Effects of Oral D-Amphetamine in Normal Subjects." *Biological Psychiatry* 22 (1987): 1357–68.

Arnold, Thomas. *Observations on the Nature, Kinds, Causes, and Prevention of Insanity*, vol. 2. London: G. Ireland, 1786.

Arrigo, Bruce A., and Jennifer L. Bullock. "The Psychological Effects of Solitary Confinement on Prisoners in Supermax Units: Reviewing What We Know and Recommending What Should Change." *International Journal of Offender Therapy and Comparative Criminology* 52 (2008): 622–40.

Bamford, James. *The Shadow Factory*. New York: Anchor, 2009.

Barnett, O. W. et al., "Jealousy and Romantic Attachment in Violent and Nonviolent Men." *Journal of Interpersonal Violence* 10 (1995): 473–86.

Bassiony, M. M., and C. G. Lyketsos. "Delusions and Hallucinations in Alzheimer's Disease." *Psychosomatics* 44 (2003): 388–401.

Begley, Sharon. "Why Do We Rape, Kill and Sleep Around?" *Newsweek*. June 29, 2009.

Berke, J. H. et al., eds. *Even Paranoids Have Enemies*. London: Routledge 1998.

Bett, W. R. "Benzedrine Sulphate in Clinical Medicine: A Survey of the Literature." *Postgraduate Medical Journal* 22 (1946): 205–18.

Bishop, Greg. "Paranoia as Prevalent as Special Teams in American Football." *New York Times*. November 13, 2007.

Block, Melissa. "Anything That Connects: A Conversation with Taylor Swift." National Public Radio. October 31, 2014.

Bonner, H. "The Problem of Diagnosis in Paranoid Disorder." *American Journal of Psychiatry* 107 (1951): 677–83.

Brauser, Deborah. "Cannabis-Related ED Visits Rise in States with Legalized Use." *Medscape*. December 16, 2014. Accessed April 3, 2015. http://www.medscape.com/viewarticle/836663.

Brigham, A. "The Medical Treatment of Insanity." *American Journal of Insanity* 3 (1847): 353–58.

Buchanan, A. "Acting on Delusion: A Review." *Psychological Medicine* 23 (1993): 123–34.

Buchanan, A. et al. "Acting on Delusions II: The Phenomenological Correlates of Acting on Delusions." *British Journal of Psychiatry* 163 (1993): 77–81.

Buss, David M. *The Dangerous Passion*. New York: Free Press, 2000.

————. "Evolutionary Psychology." *Psychological Inquiry* 6 (1995): 1–30.

Buunk, B., and R. B. Hupka. "Cross-Cultural Differences in the Elicitation of Sexual Jealousy." *Journal of Sex Research* (1987): 12–22.

Changeux, J., and J. Chavaillon, eds. *Origins of the Human Brain*. Oxford: Oxford University Press, 1996.

Coid, Jeremy et al. "The Relationship between Delusions and Violence." *Journal of the American Medical Association Psychiatry* 70 (2013): 465–71.

Collip, D. et al. "Does the Concept of 'Sensitization' Provide a Plausible Mechanism for the Putative Link between the Environment and Schizophrenia?" *Schizophrenia Bulletin* 34 (2008): 220–25.

Cooper, A. F. et al. "A Comparison of Deaf and Non-Deaf Patients with Paranoid and Affective Psychoses." *British Journal of Psychiatry* 129 (1976): 532–38.

Corbin, S. L., and M. R. Eastwood. "Sensory Deficits and Mental Disorders of Old Age: Causal or Coincidental Associations?" *Psychological Medicine* 16 (1986): 251–56.

Creese, I., ed. *Stimulants: Neurochemical, Behavioral, and Clinical Perspectives*. New York: Raven Press, 1983.

David, Anthony, and John Cutting, eds. *The Neuropsychology of Schizophrenia*. Hillsdale, NJ: Lawrence Erlbaum Associates, 1994.

Dees, Morris, and J. Corcoran. *Gathering Storm: America's Militia Threat*. New York: HarperCollins, 1996.

Delgado, A. R., and R. A. Bond. "Attenuating the Attribution of Responsibility: The Lay Perception of Jealousy as a Motive for Wife Battery." *Journal of Applied Social Psychology* 23 (1993): 1337–56.

DeSteno, D. A., and P. Salovey. "Evolutionary Origins of Sex Differences in Jealousy?" *Psychological Science* 7 (1996): 367–72.

Eaton, W. et al. "Screening for Psychosis in the General Population with a Self-Report Interview." *Journal of Nervous and Mental Disease*, no. 179 (1991): 689–93.

Eells, Josh. "The Reinvention of Taylor Swift." *Rolling Stone* (September 25, 2014), p. 40.

Ellett, L., B. Lopes, and P. Chadwick. "Paranoia in a Nonclinical Population of College Students." *Journal of Nervous and Mental Diseases* 191 (July 2003): 425–30.

Farrington, D. P., and J. Grunn, eds. *Aggression and Dangerousness*. New York: John Wiley & Sons, 1985.

Fernandez, M., and N. Schweber. "Binghamton Killer Kept His Fury Quiet." *New York Times*. April 12, 2009.

Foster, C. et al. "A Randomized Controlled Trial of Worry Intervention for Individuals with Persistent Persecutory Delusions." *Journal of Behavior Therapy and Experimental Psychiatry* 41 (2010): 45–51.

Freckelton, Ian. "Querulent Paranoia and the Vexatious Complainant." *International Journal of Law and Psychiatry* 11 (1988): 127–43.

Freedman, R., and P. J. Schwab. "Paranoid Symptoms in Patients on a General Hospital Psychiatric Unit." *Archives of General Psychiatry* 35 (1978): 387–90.

Freeman, Daniel et al. *Overcoming Paranoid and Suspicious Thoughts*. New York: Basic Books, 2008.

Freeman, D., and D. Fowler. "Routes to Psychotic Symptoms." *Psychiatry Research* 169 (2009): 107–12.

Freeman, D. et al. "Concomitants of Paranoia in the General Population." *Psychological Medicine* 41 (May 2011): 1–14.

Freeman, D. et al. "How Cannabis Causes Paranoia: Using Intravenous Administration of Δ^9–Tetrahydrocannabinol (THC) to Identify Key Cognitive Mechanisms Leading to Paranoia." *Schizophrenia Bulletin* (July 15, 2014).

Freeman, D. et al. "Psychological Investigation of the Structure of Paranoia in a Non-Clinical Population." *British Journal of Psychiatry* 186 (2005): 427–35.

Fremouw, W. J. et al. "Stalking on Campus: The Prevalence and Strategies for Coping with Stalking." *Journal of Forensic Sciences* 42 (1997): 666–69.

Funder, Anna. *Stasiland: Stories from behind the Berlin Wall*. New York: Harper Perennial, 2011.

Galton, Francis. *Memories of My Life*. London: Methuen, 1908.

Garety, P. A., and D. R. Hemsley. *Delusions: Investigations into the Psychology of Delusional Reasoning*. Oxford: Oxford University Press, 1994.

Grant, B. F. et al. "Prevalence, Correlates, and Disability of Personality Disorders in the United States: Results from the National Epidemiologic Survey on Alcohol and Related Conditions." *Journal of Clinical Psychiatry* 65, no. 7 (2004): 948–58.

Grassian, Stuart. "Psychiatric Effects of Solitary Confinement." *Washington University Journal of Law and Policy* 22 (2006): 327–80.

Hall, John R. *A New Breed: Satellite Terrorism in America*. New York: Strategic Book Publishing, 2009.

Hamdy, R. C. "Paranoid Delusions?" *Southern Medical Journal* 96 (2003): 635–36.

Harris, C. R., and N. Christenfeld. "Jealousy and Rational Responses to Infidelity Across Gender and Culture." *Psychological Science* 7 (1996): 378–79.

Haslam, John. *Illustrations of Madness*. London: Routledge, 1810.

Hitson, H. M., and D. H. Funkenstein. "Family Patterns and Paranoidal Personality Structure in Boston and Burma." *International Journal of Social Psychiatry* 5, no. 3 (1959): 182–90.

Humphreys, M. S. et al. "Dangerous Behavior Preceding First Admissions for Schizophrenia." *British Journal of Psychiatry* 161 (1992): 501–505.

Inouye, S. K. "Delirium in Older Persons." *New England Journal of Medicine* 354 (2006): 1157–165.

Jay, Michael. *The Air Loom Gang*. New York: Four Walls Eight Windows, 2003.

Kaffman, M. "Paranoid Disorders: Family Sources of the Delusional System." *Journal of Family Therapy* 5, no. 2 (1983): 107–16.

Kalayam, B. et al. "Patterns of Hearing Loss and Psychiatric Morbidity in Elderly Patients Attending a Hearing Clinic." *International Journal of Geriatric Psychiatry* 6 (1991): 131–36.

Kessler, R. C. et al. "Lifetime Prevalence and Age-of-Onset Distributions of DSM-IV Disorders in the National Comorbidity Survey Replication." *Archives of General Psychiatry* 62 (2005): 593–602.

Kienlen, K. K. et al. "A Comparative Study of Psychotic and Nonpsychotic Stalking." *Journal of the American Academy of Psychiatry and the Law* 25 (1997): 317–34.

Kosfeld, M. et al. "Oxytocin Increases Trust in Humans." *Nature* 485 (2005): 673–76.

Lanzkron, J. "Murder as a Reaction to Paranoid Delusions in Involutional Psychosis and Its Prevention." *American Journal of Psychiatry* 118 (1961): 426–27.

Laurens, K. R. et al. "Community Screening for Psychotic-Like Experiences and Other Putative Antecedents of Schizophrenia in Children Aged 9–12 Years." *Schizophrenia Research* 90 (2007): 130–46.

Lee, R. B., and I. Devore. *Man the Hunter*. Hawthorne, NY: Aldine de Gruyter, 1968.

Linden, M. et al. "The Psychopathology of Posttraumatic Embitterment Disorder." *Psychopathology* 40 (2007): 159–65.

Linden, M. et al. "Diagnostic Criteria and the Standardized Diagnostic Interview for Posttraumatic Embitterment Disorder." *International Journal of Psychiatry in Clinical Practice* 12, no. 2 (2008): 93–96.

Lyall, Sarah. "Britons Weary of Surveillance in Minor Cases." *New York Times*. October 24, 2009.

Maher, B. A. "Delusions: Contemporary Etiological Hypotheses." *Psychiatric Annals* 22 (1992): 260–68.

March, Dana et al. "Psychosis and Place." *Epidemiologic Reviews* 30 (July 2008): 84–100.

Mathes, E. W., and C. Verstraete. "Jealous Aggression: Who Is the Target, the Beloved or the Rival?" *Psychological Reports* 72 (1993): 1071–74.

Miczek, K. A., ed. *Ethopharmacology: Primate Models of Neuropsychiatric Disorders*. New York: Alan Liss, Inc., 1983.

Migliorelli, R. et al. "Neuropsychiatric and Neuropsychological Correlates of Delusions in Alzheimer's Disease." *Psychological Medicine* 25 (1995): 505–13.

Mithin, S. *After the Ice Age*. Cambridge, MA: Harvard University Press, 2004.

Monahan, J., and H. Steadman, eds. *Violence and Mental Disorder*. Chicago: University of Chicago Press, 1994.

Morin, Richard. "New Facts and Hot Stats from the Social Sciences." *Washington Post*. July 27, 1997.

Mowat, R. R. *Morbid Jealousy and Murder*. London: Tavistock Publications, 1966.

Mullen, Paul E. "Editorial: Jealousy and the Emergence of Violent and Intimidating Behaviours." *Criminal Behaviour and Mental Health* 6, no. 3 (1996): 199–205.

Mullen, Paul E., and J. Martin. "Jealousy: A Community Study." *British Journal of Psychiatry* 164 (1994): 35–43.

Munro, A. *Delusional Disorder*. New York: Cambridge University Press, 1999.

Neugebauer, R. "Treatment of the Mentally Ill in Medieval and Early Modern England." *Journal of the History of the Behavioral Sciences* 14 (1978): 158–69.

Olfson, M. et al. "Psychotic Symptoms in an Urban General Medicine Practice." *American Journal of Psychiatry* 159, no. 8 (August 2002): 1412–19.

Oltmanns, T. F., and B. A. Maher. *Delusional Beliefs*. New York: John Wiley, 1988.

Ordine, B., and R. Vigoda. *Fatal Match*. New York: Avon Books, 1998.

Östling, S., and I. Skoog. "Psychotic Symptoms and Paranoid Ideation in a Nondemented Population-Based Sample of the Very Old." *Archives of General Psychiatry* 59 (2002): 53–59.

Page, S., and T. Fletcher. "Auguste D: One Hundred Years On." *Dementia* 5 (2006): 571–83.

Palermo, G. B. et al. "Murder-Suicide of the Jealous Paranoia Type." *American Journal of Forensic Medicine and Pathology* 18 (1997): 374–83.

Richardson, E. D. et al. "Othello Syndrome Secondary to Right Cerebrovascular Infarction." *Journal of Geriatric Psychiatry and Neurology* 4 (1991): 160–65.

Rössler, W. et al. "Psychotic Experiences in the General Population: A Twenty-Year Prospective Community Study." *Schizophrenia Research* 92 (2007): 1–14.

Sales, Nancy Jo. "Taylor Swift's Telltale Heart." *Vanity Fair*. April 2013.

Satel, S. L., and W. S. Edell. "Cocaine-Induced Paranoia and Psychosis Proneness." *American Journal of Psychiatry* 148 (1991): 1708–711.

Sato, M. et al. "Acute Exacerbation of Paranoid Psychotic State after Long-Term Abstinence in Patients with Previous Methamphetamine Psychosis." *Biological Psychiatry* 18 (1983): 429–40.

Sato, M. et al. "Relapse of Paranoid Psychotic State in Methamphetamine Model of Schizophrenia." *Schizophrenia Bulletin* 18 (1992): 115–22.

Schlesinger, L. B., ed. *Explorations in Criminal Psychopathology*. Springfield, IL: Charles C. Thomas Publisher Ltd., 1996.

Schultz, Mark. *Foxcatcher*. New York: Penguin Group, 2014.

Scott, J. et al. "Psychotic-Like Experiences in the General Community." *Psychological Medicine* 36 (2006): 231–38.

Scull, Andrew. *Madhouse: A Tragic Tale of Megalomania and Modern Medicine*. New Haven, CT: Yale University Press, 2005.

Sedler, M. J. *Psychiatric Clinics of North America*. Philadelphia: W. B. Saunders Company, 1995.

Semple, D. M. et al. "Cannabis as a Risk Factor for Psychosis: Systematic Review." *Journal of Psychopharmacology* 19 (2005): 187–94.

Sengupta, Somini. "A Cheap Spying Tool with a High Creepy Factor." *New York Times*. August 2, 2013.

Shalev, Sharon. "Solitary Confinement and Supermax Prisons: A Human Rights and Ethical Analysis." *Journal of Forensic Psychology Practice* 11, no. 2-3 (2011): 151–83.

Shapiro, David. *Neurotic Styles*. New York: Basic Books, 1965.

Shapiro, Gary. "What Happens When Your Friend's Smartphone Can Tell That You're Lying." *Washington Post*. October 31, 2014.

Shaver, Richard. *Reality of the Inner Earth*. New Brunswick, NJ: Global Communications/Inner Light Publications, 2005.

Shepherd, M. "Morbid Jealousy: Some Clinical and Social Aspects of a Psychiatric Symptom." *Journal of Mental Science* 107 (1961): 687–753.

Shrestha, K. et al. "Sexual Jealousy in Alcoholics." *Acta Psychiatrica Scandinavica* 72 (1995): 283–90.

Slomski, Anita. "A Trip on 'Bath Salts' Is Cheaper Than Meth or Cocaine but Much More Dangerous." *Journal of the American Medical Association* 308 (2012).

Stam, Rianne. "Posttraumatic Stress Disorder and Stress Sensitization." *Neuroscience & Biobehavioral Reviews* 31, no. 4 (2007): 558–84.

Stern, K. S. *A Force upon the Plain.* New York: Simon & Schuster, 1996.

Stickney, B. M. *All-American Monster: The Unauthorized Biography of Timothy McVeigh.* Amherst, NY: Prometheus Books, 1996.

Swanson, J. W. et al. "Violence and Psychiatric Disorder in the Community: Evidence from the Epidemiologic Catchment Area Surveys." *Hospital & Community Psychiatry* 41 (1990): 761–70.

Sweeney, H. M. *The Professional Paranoid.* Venice, CA: Feral House, 1998.

Thier, Dave. "Study: 1 in 20 Americans Have Been Victims of Identity Theft." *Forbes.* February 24, 2012.

Toner, Robin, and Marjorie Connelly. "9/11 Polls Find Lingering Fears in New York." *New York Times.* September 7, 2006.

Torrey, E. Fuller. *The Insanity Offense: How America's Failure to Treat the Seriously Mentally Ill Endangers Its Citizens.* New York: W. W. Norton & Company, 2012. Torrey, E. Fuller, and Judy Miller. *The Invisible Plague.* New Brunswick, NJ: Rutgers University Press, 2001.

Turkington, C. A. *No Holds Barred.* Atlanta: Turner Publishing, 1996.

Valenstein, Elliot S. *Great and Desperate Cures.* New York: Basic Books, 1986.

Valerian, Valdamar. *Matrix III: The Psycho-Social, Chemical, Biological, and Electronic Manipulation of Human Consciousness.* Leading Edge Research, 1992.

Van Os, J. et al. "Do Urbanicity and Familial Liability Coparticipate in Causing Psychosis?" *American Journal of Psychiatry* 160 (2003): 477–82.

Van Os, J. et al. "Prevalence of Psychotic Disorder and Community Level of Psychotic Symptoms." *Archives of General Psychiatry* 58 (2001): 660–68.

Vassos, Evangelos et al. "Meta-Analysis of the Association of Urbanicity with Schizophrenia." *Schizophrenia Bulletin* 38 (2012): 1118–23.

Verdoux, H. et al. "A Survey of Delusional Ideation in Primary-Care Patients." *Psychological Medicine* 28, no. 1 (1998): 127–34.

West, D. J., and A. Walk, eds. *Daniel McNaughton.* Ashford: Gaskell, 1977.

Whitaker, R. *Mad in America.* New York: Basic Books, 2002.

Winchester, Simon. *The Professor and the Madman.* New York: HarperCollins Publishers, 1998.

Young, D., and W. B. Scoville. "Paranoid Psychosis in Narcolepsy and the Possible Danger of Benzedrine Treatment." *Medical Clinics of North America* (1938): 637–46.

Zeller, Tom. "A Sinister Web Entraps Victims of Cyberstalkers." *New York Times.* April 17, 2006.

Zimbardo, P. G. et al. "Induced Hearing Deficit Generates Experimental Paranoia." *Science* 212 (1981): 1529–531.

INDEX